W9-BNW-862

Restructuring Schools

Promising Practices
and Policies

Restructuring Schools
Promising Practices and Policies

Edited by

Maureen T. Hallinan
University of Notre Dame
Notre Dame, Indiana

Plenum Press • New York and London

Library of Congress Cataloging-in-Publication Data

Restructuring schools : promising practices and policies / edited by
   Maureen T. Hallinan.
      p.   cm.
   Edited papers from a conference held Mar. 19, 1994, at the
University of Notre Dame.
   Includes bibliographical references and index.
   ISBN 0-306-45034-8
   1. School management and organization--United States--Case
studies.   2. Educational change--United States--Case studies.
3. Total quality management--United States--Case studies.   4. School
-to-work transition--United States.   5. Educational sociology-
-United States--Case studies.   I. Hallinan, Maureen T.
LB2805.R46   1995
371.2'00973--dc20   95-37412
                                                                     CIP

ISBN 0-306-45034-8

© 1995 Plenum Press, New York
A Division of Plenum Publishing Corporation
233 Spring Street, New York, N. Y. 10013

10 9 8 7 6 5 4 3 2 1

Printed in the United States of America

To Chris and Renee
may your learning be unbounded

Contributors

DAVID P. BAKER, Department of Sociology, The Catholic University of America, Washington, D.C. 20064

ANTHONY S. BRYK, Center for School Improvement and Consortium on Chicago School Research, Department of Education, The University of Chicago, Chicago, Illinois 60637

ELIZABETH G. COHEN, School of Education, Stanford University, Stanford, California 94305

JAMES S. COLEMAN,[†] Department of Sociology, The University of Chicago, Chicago, Illinois 60637

PETER W. COOKSON, JR., Office of the Provost, Adelphi University, Garden City, New York 11530

MIHALY CSIKSZENTMIHALYI, Committee on Human Development, The University of Chicago, Chicago, Illinois 60637

ADAM GAMORAN, Department of Sociology, University of Wisconsin, Madison, Wisconsin 53706

MAUREEN T. HALLINAN, Department of Sociology, University of Notre Dame, Notre Dame, Indiana 46556

BARBARA HEYNS, Department of Sociology, New York University, New York, New York 10003

NICOLE HOLTHUIS, School of Education, Stanford University, Stanford, California 94305

STEPHANIE ALTER JONES, Center for Urban Affairs and Policy Research, Northwestern University, Evanston, Illinois 60208

ALAN C. KERCKHOFF, Department of Sociology, Duke University, Durham, North Carolina 27708

SHAUNTI KNAUTH, Department of Education, The University of Chicago, Chicago, Illinois 60637

RACHEL A. LOTAN, School of Education, Stanford University, Stanford, California 94305

CHARLOTTE S. LUCKS, Hillcrest High School, Queens, New York 11432

JENNIFER S. MANLOVE, Child Trends, Inc., Washington, D.C. 20008

ANNA NEUMANN, College of Education, Michigan State University, East Lansing, Michigan 48824-1034

[†]*Deceased.*

AARON M. PALLAS, College of Education, Michigan State University, East Lansing, Michigan 48824-1034

JAMES E. ROSENBAUM, Center for Urban Affairs and Policy Research, Northwestern University, Evanston, Illinois 60208

BARBARA SCHNEIDER, National Opinion Research Center, The University of Chicago, Chicago, Illinois 60637

Preface

Dissatisfaction with the U.S. public school system seems to be more pervasive today than at any other point in history. Disturbing contemporary trends, such as the rise in crime and violence, drug and alcohol abuse, AIDS, single-parent families, teenage pregnancies, and unemployment, are more common among youth than in other sectors of the population. Schools are often either blamed for these trends or are expected to counter them. Public concern about social pathologies motivates citizens to call for school reform in the hope and expectation that schools will solve or at least reduce these problems. Hence, proposals for school reform are constantly presented to the public for its support. Some of these reforms are far more successful than others and offer hope that schools can be improved. Whether an increased effectiveness of schools actually alleviates societal problems is less an issue than whether schools can attain the ends for which they were established—to facilitate student learning.

Most school reform plans can be characterized as efforts to restructure schools. Restructuring can occur at any level of an institution or organization. The chapters in this book describe models of school reform at several different organizational levels and propose ideas and plans for substantial change at each of these levels. Four sets of models are presented: school organization and governance, the social organization of students, classroom processes, and school-to-work transitions. The chapters specify the mechanisms that link school structure and processes to student outcomes at each of these levels. In so doing, they provide a broad picture of how effective schools work and have immediate implications for school policy and practice.

The origin of this book was the conference "The Social Organization of Schools" held at the University of Notre Dame on March 19, 1994. Papers by Bryk, Coleman, Cookson, Hallinan, Heyns, Kerckhoff, and Pallas were presented at the conference; these were revised (Lucks with Cookson and Neumann with Pallas) for inclusion in this volume. I am grateful to the Institute for Scholarship in the Liberal Arts and to the Paul M. and Barbara Henkels Foundation for providing funding for the conference and to the many sociologists and educators who attended the sessions. The remaining papers by Cohen, Lotan, and Holthuis; Gamoran and Hallinan; Manlove and Baker; Schneider, Csikszentmihalyi, and Knauth; and Rosenbaum and Jones were invited specifically for this volume.

The authors are acknowledged for their responsiveness to my editorial suggestions, for their cooperation with deadlines, for their conscientious adherence to publishing guidelines, and, moreover, for the high quality of their contributions to this book. I also am indebted to Sylvia Phillips for her assistance in preparing the manuscripts for publication and for her gracious humor and encouragement during pressing moments. And I owe my gratitude to that indefatigable New York editor, Eliot Werner of Plenum Publishing Company, whose support and appreciation of research in sociology of education made this volume possible. The many opportunities created by this project to experience Eliot's unique sense of humor prompt me to hope that the future brings a repeat performance. Finally, I thank my family for their loving support and encouragement during this and all my professional projects.

Maureen T. Hallinan

Notre Dame, Indiana

Contents

II.   ORGANIZING STUDENTS FOR INSTRUCTION

III.   CLASSROOM PROCESSES

Introduction

Maureen T. Hallinan

A school is a complex system comprised of interdependent parts that must work together to function efficiently and effectively. One dimension of the system is its organizational structure, including the hierarchical arrangement of personnel, division of labor, rules and regulations, and philosophy and mission. Another dimension of a school system is the social organization of its student body, including the organization of students for instruction, communication patterns, and social networks. A third component of a school is the set of classroom processes that govern a student's cognitive and social learning. A final aspect of a school is its relationship to the community and society it serves and for which it prepares its students to live and work. How well these various dimensions operate, separately and in tandem, determines whether a school achieves its aim of preparing students to live independently and to contribute to adult society.

In the present decade of pervasive interest in school reform, each aspect of a school's functioning has been analyzed and evaluated repeatedly. Numerous reforms have been proposed to alter and improve the formal organization of the school and the practices and policies that govern its operation. Proposals abound for modifying school structure and governance, improving pedagogy, reorganizing students for instruction, updating the curriculum, utilizing peer networks for academic ends, and improving communication patterns among teachers, parents, students, and community members. Many of these proposals were viewed as infeasible by school practitioners or policymakers and were never carried out. Other reform plans were tried, but without measurable improvement in

Maureen T. Hallinan   Department of Sociology, University of Notre Dame, Notre Dame, Indiana 46556.

Restructuring Schools: Promising Practices and Policies, edited by Maureen T. Hallinan. Plenum Press, New York, 1995.

student outcomes. A few reforms have become popular and, on the basis of empirical data, appear to succeed in increasing student learning.

How does one recognize a school practice or policy that has the potential to improve student achievement and other academic and social outcomes? Three characteristics are necessary for a proposed reform to be successful. First, the reform must have broad appeal in order for its advocates to win support in the face of political and ideological opposition. Changes in the governance of a school, as, for example, in the case of charter schools, have been successful when supported by vocal advocates who obtained local support for their proposals.

Second, while promising a positive outcome, a reform must not jeopardize existing successful school practices. Support for detracking schools will not be widespread, for example, if detracking lowers test scores for high-ability pupils. Moreover, teachers will reject detracking, even if it increases students' academic achievement, if at the same time it imposes unreasonable pedagogical burdens on them.

Finally, the likelihood that a reform will succeed depends on whether it promises to benefit all students. Educational changes that violate norms of equity and that create differential access to school resources by students' ascribed or achieved characteristics will fail to obtain wide backing from educators, parents, or other community members.

The chapters in this book focus on a wide array of educational issues that command attention at the end of the 20th century. The authors reflect on various aspects of contemporary schooling and propose models of school organization and functioning that are expected to make schools run more effectively. Their theoretical and empirical contributions fall into four categories, each concerned with one dimension of the school system. These four areas are models of school organization and governance; models of student organization; models of classroom processes; and models of school-to-work transitions. The individual chapters are theoretically based and located in relevant literature. Some provide empirical analyses to support the stated arguments. All of the chapters are just one step removed from practice and have immediate policy implications. Taken together, the volume provides a broad view of the possibilities and options open to educators as they plan educational reforms for the next decade.

The first five chapters propose models of school organization and governance. Until recently, 20th century schools in the United States have functioned like bureaucracies, with centralized decision making. Recent reform efforts have concentrated on restructuring schools by changing the focus of control, by empowering teachers, parents, and even students, by updating the curriculum, by raising graduation standards, by ensuring a more equitable distribution of funding for schools, and by creating alternate types of schools, such as charter and magnet schools. Restructuring efforts have involved major changes in school design, organization, governance, and goals. The five chapters concerned with school organization present models for restructuring and describe contemporary schools that are the result of recent restructuring efforts.

In his chapter on school design, Coleman compares administratively driven and output-driven organizational structures. He demonstrates that contemporary schools manifest characteristics of both types of structures, but argues that neither appropriately focuses on student achievement. He suggests that schools would be more effective if they followed an achievement-oriented design and he outlines the requisite properties of such a school.

In Chapter 2, Pallas and Neumann describe a particular management style, total quality management (TQM), that has been adopted successfully in some industrial organizations. Interest in TQM in the business sector has led educators to consider utilizing its principles in educational organizations. Pallas and Neumann identify the unique characteristics of schools that make an unqualified adoption of TQM principles inappropriate. Basic assumptions of the TQM philosophy about how an organization should be run and for whom are not completely applicable to the complex social system that is a school. Nevertheless, while facile adoption of TQM or any other organizational model could be perilous, aspects of TQM and other management models do provide insights and ideas about how to improve various aspects of school functioning. Pallas and Neumann's chapter provides a valuable reminder that one must be discriminating, yet open, in borrowing successful organizational models from business and industry in efforts to improve schools. Their analysis identifies features of schools that must be taken into account in making organizational changes.

In Chapter 3, Heyns describes the school reform movement in Poland, best characterized by the rapid growth of private or "social" schools. While fiscally dependent on the state, these new schools are run by non-state agencies, such as the Church, or by individuals. The curriculum in these schools is similar to that of the state-run schools, but the governance is different in that it is based on democratic principles that encourage parental participation. Heyns discusses the strengths and weaknesses of this private school movement, as it is being played out in the new political climate and market economy of Poland. She adeptly links the organizational changes in the "social" schools to student achievement, cautioning that the most successful aspects of the new schools are those that directly affect student learning. Heyns's analysis provides salutary lessons for U.S. educators intent on modeling public schools on private ones.

Chapter 4 also concentrates on private schools. Bryk draws on his extensive research on Catholic high schools in the United States to identify characteristics of Catholic schools that account for their success in promoting student achievement. He highlights four distinctive features of Catholic schools: a focused academic program, communal organization, an inspirational ideology, and decentralized governance. He generalizes from this research to suggest ways that public schools can alter their internal organization and governance to create a productive learning climate. Of particular interest is Bryk's analysis of the role of the inner-city school in student socialization and in offsetting negative pressures inner-city children experience out of school. Bryk argues that the successes attained in Catholic schools, especially with underprivileged students, can be replicated in public schools if they create the kind of supportive learning community found in private schools.

In Chapter 5, Cookson and Lucks discuss school choice, which is an educational reform meant to improve schools through the operation of market forces. Allowing parents to send their child to any public school within a school district, across school districts, and possibly to any private school is expected to create competition among the schools. Competition, in turn, should lead to better schools. If parents have school choice, they can demand an achievement-oriented school, as described by Coleman, a school that encourages parental governance, as portrayed by Heyns, or a school with a communal environment, as depicted by Bryk. School personnel then will put resources and energy into these types of schools, hopefully improving the quality of education. However, in their case study of school choice in New York City, Cookson and Lucks outline not only the advantages of school choice, at least as predicted by the theory, but also the disadvantages and pitfalls of implementing the policy of school choice in a large urban school district. Their analysis suggests that while the mechanisms that enable school choice to affect educational improvement are sound, significant political and economic obstacles make its implementation and effectiveness difficult. Their chapter stands as a sobering reminder that theory and practice must work hand in hand to create a workable organizational reform.

Chapters 6 and 7 are concerned with the organization of students for instruction in school. The primary bases for grouping students for instruction are age and ability, although some schools also group by gender and by curricular interests. To the extent that students' background characteristics—such as class and ethnicity—are correlated with ability, these characteristics may be disproportionately distributed across instructional groups in school. The primary objection to ability grouping is that it creates unequal access to the curriculum. Typically, higher-ability students have greater access to the curriculum and are offered higher-quality pedagogy than their lower-ability peers. The consequences of differential and inequitable educational experiences in school for student academic outcomes and social attitudes and behaviors are significant. In reaction, several reform efforts have been directed toward changing the organizational differentiation of students in school.

In Chapter 6, Gamoran and Hallinan discuss the practice of tracking in middle and secondary school and its effect on student achievement. Given that the extensive body of empirical research on tracking identifies several negative results of tracking, Gamoran and Hallinan draw implications from this research for restructuring schools. Some of these recommendations have to do with how schools implement tracking; others address related questions concerning teacher and student incentives within a tracking structure. They, like Cookson and Lucks, stress the importance of taking the political and economic climate into account in designing and implementing structural and organizational changes in schools.

Manlove and Baker present an empirical study in Chapter 7 that demonstrates the gap that can exist between a national plan for educational reform and the local context in which it must be implemented. Concerned with curriculum reform in mathematics, they examine curriculum accessibility within a high school, school-level factors that affect opportunities to learn, and the implications of these factors for educational equity and excellence. Observing considerable variation in the mathematics curriculum across schools and variation in access to the curriculum within schools, they conclude that local contexts and conditions can impede the implementation of national educational reforms. Their results are a further reminder that equality of educational opportunity must remain an explicit goal in every effort to reform schools, and that implementing reform on the local level demands the same kind of commitment to equity that is found at the national level.

The next two chapters in the volume consider classroom processes. Learning in school occurs in a social setting that is characterized by intellectual and social exchanges. Students learn the curriculum primarily through interaction with their teacher and peers. They learn social behavior through peer influences, friendships, and modeling behavior in their social networks. These interactive cognitive and social psychological processes can be utilized by school personnel to promote academic achievement, build social skills, and increase student self-esteem.

Chapter 8 presents an empirical study by Cohen, Lotan, and Holthius that specifies the conditions that promote student learning of complex tasks. Relying on the proposition that participation in group discussion promotes learning, they derive four hypotheses that predict conditions under which students will learn complex material. Their results identify several factors that foster student learning. The study demonstrates that schools can improve learning through the way they structure task-based interactions in the classroom.

In Chapter 9, Schneider, Csikszentmihalyi, and Knauth investigate the daily experiences of high school students in school, arguing that variation in experience accounts in part for differences in academic challenge, student motivation, and self-esteem. Survey data reveal differences by track, with students in the academic track having more challenging experiences and higher self-esteem but lower motivation and enjoyment of tasks than those in the vocational track. Their results, coupled with those of Cohen *et al.*, demonstrate that classroom processes have a powerful impact on student outcomes. Their results suggest that school authorities can structure classroom experiences in such a way as to increase the likelihood of positive academic and social outcomes.

The final two chapters discuss programs and practices that govern the school-to-work transitions of high school students. Recent research has extended existing conceptualizations of stratification and mobility to include educational processes as well as labor market processes. This work has examined the role of the school and of particular school programs in preparing students for the work force and in channeling them to status positions in the labor market. Some of this research is based on cross-national comparisons while other studies examine educational processes that occur primarily in U.S. educational institutions. Variation in school properties including organization, curriculum, pedagogy, and job counseling are seen as causal factors affecting the likelihood of a student's obtaining employment after graduation, the occupational prestige of their first and subsequent jobs, and their career mobility. The studies by Kerckhoff and Rosenbaum and Jones exemplify this area of research and make important contributions to it.

The analysis Kerckhoff presents in Chapter 10 describes how characteristics of U.S. schools affect the career trajectories of students. Kerckhoff identifies several properties of U.S. high schools that distinguish them from schools in other countries and that have a direct influence on the careers of students. In so doing, he points to a broad area for future educational reform that has previously been ignored. Arguing that schools should take a larger role in improving the fit between education and employment, Kerckhoff's proposals for educational reform promise more effective school-to-work linkages.

In the final chapter, Rosenbaum and Jones examine the role of teachers in facilitating and directing the school-to-work transition. Somewhat unique in focusing on teachers, the chapter analyzes how the ambiguity of the teacher role—with respect to vocational guidance and the absence of institutional rewards for teachers' counseling efforts—acts as a barrier to a teacher's inclination and efforts to help students gain entry to the work force. Relying on interview data from teachers, the authors describe vocational counseling as it is practiced in many secondary schools and the institutional factors that limit its usefulness. They also point to the successful efforts of some teachers to match students to jobs despite institutional barriers to effective counseling. A more promising model of vocational guidance is presented, one that makes explicit use of teachers and their networks in the guidance process and provides institutional support for teachers' efforts in counseling.

The effectiveness of the models of school structure and process presented in this volume depends, to a large degree, on whether they satisfy the three conditions for successful school reform stated earlier. On analysis, each of the chapters presents a model or practice that has the potential to win broad support, that improves one component of schooling without decreasing the effectiveness of related practices, and that upholds norms of equity and excellence. Consequently, adoption of the models and implementation of the practices discussed in this volume should make a significant contribution to school reform.

1

School Organization and Governance

Achievement-Oriented School Design

James S. Coleman[†]

Schools are *constructed* organizations, designed for a purpose. In this, they are like manufacturing organizations, business firms generally, and most organizations that are bureaucratic in form. Unlike *primordial* organizations, of which families are the prime example, the success of constructed organizations may be judged by the degree to which they achieve their purpose. In effect, the design of the organization may be evaluated by the organization's efficiency in achieving its purpose.

The classical design of constructed organizations has been a bureaucratic design, with authority residing at the top and delegated down, through an administrative hierarchy. Yet there have been developments in the design of business organizations that call into question some aspects of the bureaucratic form. Some of these developments are based on principles that appear to be directly applicable to the design of schools. As will be apparent, schools and school systems can be found that incorporate one or more of these principles. Yet the design of most U.S. schools does not incorporate these principles, but follows more nearly the classical bureaucratic design. Furthermore, there are developments in U.S. education that, while apparently innocuous or beneficial, can diminish or threaten the current use of the principles. I will describe these principles, indicating how they have been implemented in some organizations. I will

[†]*Deceased.*

James S. Coleman   Department of Sociology, The University of Chicago, Chicago, Illinois 60637.

Restructuring Schools: Promising Practices and Policies, edited by Maureen T. Hallinan. Plenum Press, New York, 1995.

also indicate what the developments are that threaten the current use of these principles, weak though this current use is.

OUTPUT-DRIVEN VERSUS ADMINISTRATIVELY DRIVEN STRUCTURE

As firms have grown to massive size, economies of scale appear sometimes to be counterbalanced by diseconomies of administrative complexity. One of the first developments this spawned was what has been called the multidivisional firm (see Chandler, 1962), in which each division was given more autonomy (principally in purchasing of its factor inputs and in marketing of its products), and was held accountable to constitute a "profit center." This was introduced by General Motors in the 1930s, with—for example—end product divisions having the right to buy parts from outside suppliers rather than in-house parts producers, and parts producers having the right to sell their products to customers outside the firm. This practice continues (e.g., Saginaw Steering Gear, a division of General Motors, sells adjustable steering columns, on which it holds patents, to a number of other automobile manufacturers). However, the principle has been lost, or overwhelmed by the reassertion of central bureaucratic authority, in most aspects of General Motors's functioning, leading to the inefficiencies that became apparent when confronted by low-cost Japanese manufacturers.

One of the most recent organizations to become an aggressively multidivisional firm, with each division standing on its own feet, is IBM. The once-monolithic firm has subdivided itself into a number of semiautonomous firms. A few examples are: Lexmark, which makes and sells printers, Ambra, a low-cost personal computer producer and marketer, and Value Point, a marketing organization that sells not only IBM personal computers, but other brands as well. IBM's decision to break apart in this way may have been brought about by the initial success of its personal computer division, which in Boca Raton, Florida, had been given an unusual amount of autonomy, followed by setbacks as this autonomy was withdrawn.

A second set of devices for replacing a bureaucratic authority structure has been the spin-off or joint venture. In a spin-off, a subgroup that has developed a potentially marketable product is given control and partial ownership of a new enterprise, with the parent firm serving primarily as provider of financial services. 3M, in Minneapolis, was one of the early innovators in this organizational form.

Joint ventures have a similar structure, except that they combine resources from two or more firms, each of which has a particular area of expertise. This form has proliferated in the computer industry particularly in the United States. As an aside, I should say that the two most fertile fields for empirical study of innovations in organizational design are the computer industry (both software and hardware) and the biotechnology industry, primarily in the United States, but spanning national boundaries.

One way of looking at all of these design innovations is in terms of the dichotomy between market and hierarchy, a distinction made well known by Oliver Williamson. These innovations all have the character of introducing some aspect of a market into what had been a hierarchical structure. In effect, some portion of the hierarchy, which as a part of a hierarchical structure is subject only to administrative discipline, which is often malleable, has a boundary drawn around it and becomes subject to market discipline. Its outputs must have greater market value than its inputs. If this fragment of a bureaucracy is to be successful, it must achieve a design which is output-driven rather than administratively driven. This implies an internal organizational structure that replaces, in at least certain respects, administrative authority with the authority of a market. How this may be done will differ depending on the technology of the production process. But there are certain elements that must be common in these designs. One has to do with the length of the feedback loop from the end product to the production workers. Every firm in a market economy is, as a whole, subject to market discipline. If the products are not successful in the market, the firm fails. But the larger the firm, the longer the feedback loop from the customer to those who are directly responsible for the quantity of production and the quality of the product, that is, those directly engaged in the production process. The success of the design of the organization depends on breaking the long feedback loop into much shorter ones, that is, by bringing some form of market discipline into each minute part of the organization.

If we examine actual organizational design, it is apparent that firms have long ago introduced, at the level of the production process, marketlike or output-driven patterns. In manufacturing, this has taken the form of piecework; in sales, it has taken the form of commissions. Piecework has a checkered history, and is much less widely used in manufacturing than the above considerations would lead one to expect. Commissions to salespersons, on the other hand, particularly for outside salespersons, are very widely used. I will not go into detail about the reasons for this difference, but will mention two differences: First, salespersons generally have much more control over their rate of sales than production workers do over their rate of production. Second, production workers work in close relation to other workers, which introduces a social aspect into the response of workers to a method of payment. (A third element plays an important role in economists' principal-agent theory, which essentially asks the question: What method of payment to the agent is optimal for the principal, flat rate with supervision or piece rate? This element is the cost of supervision, which is obviously greater for outside salespersons than for production workers in a plant.)

The fact that flat (hourly) rates have survived in many production settings suggests that establishing output-driven principles at the level of individual workers is not so simple as was anticipated when piece rates were introduced. It is not true, however, that piece rates or other means of incentive payments at the level of production workers has vanished. Rather, there are now numerous forms, including group piece rates, group target rates, bonuses, and others (see Petersen, 1992, for research results on the use of these incentive systems).

There is one example of an apparently quite successful introduction of output-driven structure in a mature industry, the automobile industry. This innovation, which began with Japanese firms and is being imitated in some U.S. firms, can be described as a reallocation of rights.

The rights that are involved are those having to do with rejecting parts and stopping the production line. In the classical manufacturing organization, the supervisor or foreman in an assembly line may have the right to reject input parts that are out of specification, or may only have the right to request from a higher supervisor in the plant that the parts be rejected. The decision may depend on whether it is possible to work around the defect without shutting down the assembly line. If it is a defect that can be repaired, a tag is put on the car, and at the end of the line, all cars with tags on them are shunted to a repair facility. Whatever the decision, the right to make that decision is never in the hands of the assembly line worker. It is in the hands of either the line foreman, or a superior of the line foreman.

In the Japanese auto assembly line, the rights are allocated somewhat differently. First, many of the rights and responsibilities that would ordinarily be held by the line foreman are held instead by a collectivity consisting of the members of the line [called a Quality Control Circle or a Quality Circle (QC)]. The foreman is in most cases altogether missing, the position being absent from the firm's organization. One specific right, the right to reject out-of-specification inputs, is held by the individual worker on the line who must use these parts in accomplishing the task. The right includes the right to shut down the line. Execution of the right, that is, rejecting out-of-specification parts, is made more likely by the fact that the workers in the next group that handles that component of the automobile have the right to reject the component for any out-of-specification parts. Thus, the right to reject input parts is accompanied by the responsibility for the output being *in* specification. The worker thus has an incentive not to accept input parts that are out of specification as well as to ensure that labor input does not result in an out-of-specification output.

The general character of the incentives that are introduced by this structure of rights is fairly obvious. It is an incentive on the part of the worker to carefully inspect input parts and to be careful about possible errors introduced during processing. The set of rights that are involved in a production process like that involved in building automobiles is a string of rights that mirrors the production process itself. The workers who receive worker A's output have the right to reject worker A's production, and thus to affect A's pay, which is partly based on bonuses (and depending on other aspects of the organization of work, possibly also to affect the pay of others in the same worker group as A). The holder of the ultimate right is outside the organization altogether, that is, the shipper, the dealer, and finally, the customer, each of whom can reject the finished product.

An additional right that accompanies these rights of workers is the right to extra pay (paid as a bonus) depending on quality and quantity of output by the work group. As much as a third of a worker's pay may be in the form of a bonus.

The allocation of rights that I have just described produces a policing of the quality of the product that reverberates backwards step by step through the production process of the organization. The feedback process from the production of a defect to the discovery of the defect and then back to the producer of the defect is an extremely short loop. This contrasts with the long loop of the feedback process that is characteristic of the classical hierarchical structure of rights. Figure 1 shows diagrammatically the two structures.

There is one important aspect of the allocation of rights that I have just described. The Quality Circle, constituting the members of an assembly or subassembly line, has rights as a group that give it collective authority over its members, replacing the authority of the line foreman or supervisor. This, together with the fact that members' bonuses are dependent on the group's quality–quantity productivity, means that norms develop in the group that are consistent with and reinforce the organization's goals. For this to occur, it is important that the group not be too large, and the Quality Circles typically have 8–12 members.

The organizational innovation I have just described does more than transform the structure from one that is administratively driven to one that is output-driven. It introduces as well a second principle, to which I now turn.

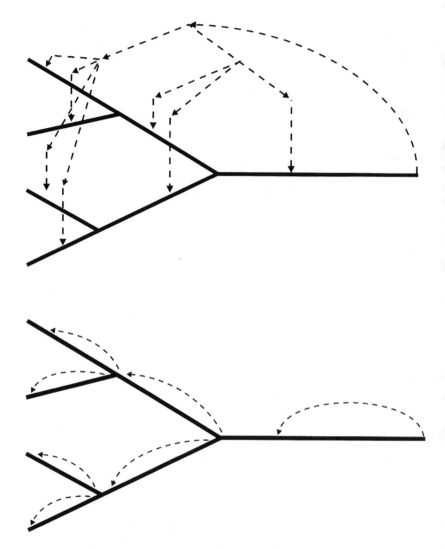

Figure 1. Structures of two feedback processes.

SOCIAL CAPITAL GENERATED BY
ORGANIZATIONAL STRUCTURE

In the reallocation of rights on Japanese automobile assembly lines, it is not accidental that a portion of the rights are reallocated not to individual workers, but to the work group. Its authority replaces that of the line foreman or supervisor, whose position no longer exists. And bonuses are paid not on the basis of individual performance, but on the basis of the quality–quantity productivity of the work group, that is, the Quality Circle.

Ever since the Western Electric studies of the 1930s, research has shown that work-group norms develop, and can greatly affect production (Roethlisberger and Dickson, 1939). As the researchers discovered, the norms that develop can oppose organizational goals and severely limit production, but under other conditions, norms develop that further organizational goals and enhance the quality and quantity of production.

As various organizational innovators have found, and as is apparent in the case of Quality Circles in auto assembly plans, the formal organizational structure can affect the direction these norms take. In the case of Quality Circles, the work group as a group was allocated three kinds of rights: first, the right to reject any unit it received from the preceding line if it did not meet specifications; second, the rights ordinarily held by the line foreman to exercise authority over members of the work group in performance of their jobs; and third, the right to bonuses based on quality and quantity of production. It is, I suggest, this allocation of rights to the group that generates norms furthering organizational goals. When this occurs, we can say that the organizational design has created *social capital* which augments organizational performance.

Many instances of organizational design have employed this principle in one way or another. For example, Mackie (1991) describes a workers' cooperative planting trees under contract to the U.S. Forest Service, which was organized into groups of about 12 members each. Each member of the work group monitored the quality and quantity of work of the adjacent workers; and the work group was paid a lump sum with the right to determine how it was divided among members. With this size work group, this work task, and this allocation of rights, the work groups developed strong norms, acting as social capital augmenting the organization's performance.

There are undoubtedly other principles in recent organizational innovations that are useful for the design of achievement-oriented schools, but I will focus only on two: output-driven structure and organizational structure that generates social capital for the organization's goals. What becomes problematic is just how these principles may be applied to schools.

APPLICATION TO THE DESIGN OF SCHOOLS

Schools are obviously not manufacturing organizations. They are, however, constructed to be productive organizations, producing cognitive skills as well as other capabilities in children and youth. There are, of course, a number of questions that must be answered before attempting to apply principles such as those described above to schools. One is the question of just who is analogous to the workers in the production process: teachers or students? If teachers, then clearly the youthful material they are working with is not passive, but has purposes of its own. If students, what is the role of teachers?

In any application to schools, it is clear that the principles must be applied to both students and teachers. But since the product of the school's activity is the development of capabilities among the students, it must be this output that is used to drive the actions of both teachers and students. With respect to the social capital principle, norms develop in all schools both among students and among teachers. As in other formal organizations, these norms may turn against organizational goals or may provide social capital for augmenting those goals.

Because changes in children and youth constitute the productive output of schools, the children and youth as they enter school must be considered the primary inputs to the organization. As such, there is one central way in which these inputs differ from those involved in most organizational production. The inputs, in the form of children and youth, are not homogeneous, but are quite heterogeneous, leading to extensive disparities in performance.

The disparities in performance give rise in schools to strong egalitarian anticompetitive sentiments—from teachers, from students, from parents, and from educational policymakers. This in turn has produced, given the way schools are currently organized, continual reductions in standards as schools have become more and more inclusive.

This need not be. There are ways other than the use of internal "population-adjusted" standards that are found in U.S. schools. The method of coping with heterogeneous inputs that I will describe later on is again taken from industry. It is use of the idea of value added, or performance gain rather than level of performance. I will return to this later.

Recognizing these differences between schools and many other productive organizations, it remains possible to apply the two principles discussed earlier to schools. It is useful first, however, to take note of the low levels of performance of U.S. schools compared to that in schools of most developed countries.

At the lower levels, the ineffectiveness of inner-city schools is well known, and the weak performance of the children who attend them is extensively documented. What is not recognized, however, is that the weak performance is found throughout the distribution. As one investigator writes, "the gap between American high school seniors in middle class suburbs and their counterparts in many northern European countries and Japan is *larger* than the two to three grade level equivalent gap between whites and blacks in the U.S." (Bishop, 1991, pp. 1–2, using data from NAEP, 1988b, and IAEEA, 1987).

These low levels of performance of U.S. students at the high end of the achievement distribution are ordinarily forgotten. But the well-known SAT test score decline of the 1970s and 1980s shows the greatest loss at the top end of the distribution, (Murray and Herrnstein, 1992).

This low level of performance in U.S. schools is reinforced by another aspect of most schools: in middle schools and high schools, across the socioeconomic spectrum and among all racial and ethnic groups, the informal norms that develop among students are *not* norms that extol achievement, but are norms that scorn effort, and reward scholastic achievement only when it appears to be done without effort.

This need not be true, of course, and in fact there are some high schools in which it is not true. There are even more schools in other countries where it is not true. It is a mark of incorrect organizational design that such norms exist in schools.

The sources of the low effort put into high achievement are several, but one is important: the lack of well-publicized external criteria of performance from which meaningful consequences flow. In the absence of such criteria, there can come to be an implicit compact to reduce the strain imposed by high standards (including extensive homework), and parents unable to enforce extensive homework. The implicit compact can result in quite low levels of performance.

Theodore Sizer reports the implicit compact in describing one teacher's class; a teacher whom he calls Brady:

> He signaled to the students what the minima, the few questions for
> a test, were; all tenth and eleventh-graders could master these with
> absurdly little difficulty. The youngsters picked up the signal and
> kept their part of the bargain by being friendly and orderly. They did

not push Brady, and he did not push them. . . . Brady's room was quiet, and his students liked him. No wonder he had the esteem of the principal who valued orderliness and good rapport between students and staff. Brady and his class had agreement all right, agreement that reduced the efforts of both student and teacher to an irreducible and pathetic minimum. [Sizer, 1984, p. 156]

How can a teacher gain the friendly and orderly classroom climate that Brady has and at the same time the kind of effort and involvement that generates high achievement? The teacher seems caught in a bind: Either impose high standards and sacrifice the good climate and risk a rebellion or reduce the standards and sacrifice achievement. One of the few ways out, in the absence of strong parental demands that hold a rebellion in check, is for the teacher to be freed from the task of setting the standards. Then the teacher and the class can be engaged in a common task, that of beating the externally established standards. The standards may be those of an external test, or those imposed by a contest with students in another school, or perhaps in a different way. But so long as the standards are out of the teacher's control, the teacher and students have a common interest that generates both the effort needed for achievement and a positive climate.

Young people have a time-and-attention budget, just as adults do. In that budget, the time spent on homework has declined to about $3^{1}/_{2}$ hours per week, half of what it was in the 1960s before the SAT test score decline. Time spent in sports, in part-time jobs, in TV viewing, in consumption of popular culture with friends all compete with homework for the teenager's time. While the time on homework has declined, the time spent in part-time jobs (about 10 hours on average for high school seniors) and in television watching has increased. Television, at 20 hours per week, is two to three times that in other OECD countries. It is clear that since the 1960s, other activities, such as watching television and earning money at part-time jobs, have come to occupy a more important place in the average teenager's life, and schoolwork has come to occupy a less important place. Parents, meanwhile, appear unable to prevent this.

SCHOOLS AS ADMINISTRATIVELY DRIVEN AND SCHOOLS AS OUTPUT-DRIVEN

The organizational innovations that were described earlier constitute a change from an administratively driven organization to one that is output-driven. Schools as they exist are not pure forms of either of these.

Most schools, as any teacher knows, are hierarchical authority systems, with the building principal the immediate authority. Principals in turn are under the school district superintendent as the central authority, often with little discretionary authority over resources, over hiring of teachers, and other decisions. The structure of schools follows that of the bureaucratic administratively driven organization quite well.

At the same time, there are various examples, some the result of intentional design but others not, which show the power of output demands in education. One of these is the importance of college entrance requirements for high school courses taken. College entrance requirements in the United States have traditionally specified 16 "Carnegie units" of high school courses, including specific requirements, such as two years of a foreign language. These entrance requirements have dictated the "college prep" curriculum in high schools. In the 1960s and 1970s, with the onslaught of the youth revolt and the civil rights movement, colleges liberalized their entrance requirements. Most elite colleges dropped the foreign language entrance requirement. A consequence of this was that foreign language course-taking in high school dropped precipitously. Only in the late 1980s, as colleges reinstated entrance requirements, has course-taking in foreign languages revived. Note an additional point: This is an external demand, which imposes requirements *not* on output but on actions. By "passing courses," the student meets the demand, and the teacher is free to determine the criteria for passing. Even though the Carnegie-unit demand has this crucial flaw, the example of foreign languages illustrates how relaxation of a demand has its effects.

As the example illustrates, educational systems are in part output-driven, despite their hierarchical authority structure. In fact, containing these two conflicting modes of organization, schools create an untenable situation for teachers. They are under the constraint to meet certain output demands, yet are subject to authority which eliminates their autonomy in meeting these demands. However, as I will suggest, the character of the output demands is defective, which means that the system reverts to an administratively driven system, and the teachers set flexible internal standards—as in Mr. Brady's class—to make the situation tolerable.

The absence of external standards for actual performance has several negative consequences. It puts teachers in the position of establishing the requirements, by deciding what levels of performance will be necessary in order to receive a given grade. By placing this task on the teacher, the school puts the teacher in two roles with conflicting interests: as the person who sets the standards, and as the person who tries to get students to meet the standards. This creates an ambivalent relation between teacher and students, quite different from that between coach and performers.

The coach can devote undivided efforts to improving the performance of the team members; the teacher's efforts must be on two fronts: to improving students' performance, and to struggling with students over the level of performance required for a given grade. This can poison the student–teacher relation, voiding the effort on the first front. It is also an important element in generating the norms among students to restrict output. Students would have no reason to develop such antiachievement norms if the standards used to measure performance were not under the teacher's control.

Another defect of internally established standards is that they introduce noise into the information the receiving institution (further education or employer) gets from the school about the student's performance. Employers seldom use the information at all, and colleges augment rank in class by scores on the SAT or ACT test, and sometimes by a ranking of the high school itself. None of this would be necessary if standards were externally set rather than set internally.

A major reason for schools' use of internal standards of achievement rather than externally established ones is the great disparities between performance of students from different backgrounds and with different preparation. The use of internal standards is clearly a defective way of addressing this problem; I shall show later another method of doing so that has none of these defects.

WORKING BACKWARD

In the design of an output-driven system, it is necessary to begin at the end and work backwards. The necessity arises from the fact that it is the standards at the final output that, properly employed, provide the motive force that reverberates back through each of the earlier stages to energize and focus actions. What is necessary, then, is a reward for performance at the end of the process of elementary and secondary education. It cannot, however, be a reward that comes only to teachers, or only to students, or only to parents. It is clear that there are three parties whose actions are directly relevant to achievement: the child, the parent, and the teacher. High achievement requires that each of these three parties be motivated to bring it about.

There are several requirements that must be met by the evaluation system on the basis of which teachers, students, and parents are rewarded.

1. *The standards must be externally designed, by those parties that will be the institutions receiving the "graduates" of the school.*

Comment: For the high school, there is such a test for college admission, the SAT test and the ACT test. There are no such tests for high school graduates who will enter other institutions. However, for sports played in high school that are also collegiate sports there are good evaluation systems. These result from the extensive interscholastic competition that allows high school students to exhibit their competence. In areas where interscholastic debate is widespread, the same is true to a lesser extent for debaters. In those states that have statewide interscholastic competition in music, drama, and other areas, there is the basis for such an evaluation system in these areas as well. Advanced Placement tests provide a starting point for such evaluation in particular academic areas.

There are international "olympics" at the high school level in some specialized technical areas, in which students from some countries (not the United States) participate. There is also an academic olympics at least in fields of mathematics, in which some countries (Hungary and Poland, for example) participate. Thus, in many specialized areas, there already exists the basis for externally designed performance tests.

There exists little basis for externally designed standards for the end of middle school and the end of elementary school. Following the logic of output-driven organization, and more specifically backward policing, the design should come from, or at least be extensively informed by, teachers at the next level: high school teachers for the tests at the end of middle school, and middle school teachers for the tests at the end of elementary school. These tests, however, can hardly be designed without knowledge of what the criteria at the end of high school will be.

2. *The system must evaluate not "basic abilities," but achievement.*

Comment: The SAT and ACT tests, currently used in the United States for college admission, fail this criterion. From the outset, the SAT test was designed to be "curriculum-free," and students were told that it is not possible to study for the SAT. It is, in fact, possible to increase one's performance on the SAT test; there are commercial organizations providing courses that do just that. But the fiction was strongly maintained by the SAT test-makers at Educational Testing Service (which constructs the SAT) until it lost a court case in which one such organization proved its claim to be able to improve performance substantially.

One original aim of the SAT was to give students from weaker high schools the same chance to score a good grade as students from stronger high schools. The effect, however (in contrast to English O- and A- levels, French Baccalauréat, German Abitur), was to deprive the SAT of any motivating power toward achievement. Note that the SAT and ACT tests, in transmitting the notion that what is tested is aptitude or ability, are *less* egalitarian than a test that is explicitly tied to curriculum, because it creates the belief that the score measures one's self, fixed and immutable, relative to others.

3. *The system must evaluate not only the performance* **level**, *but also the performance* **gains** *over the period between test administrations (a year for a 4-year school). The performance gains may be thought of as* **value added** *by the school.*

Comment: This point follows directly from the heterogeneity of students as inputs to the system. If an evaluation provides rewards only for level of achievement, there are at least two negative consequences. First, it leads only to interpersonal comparison (rather than to comparison with the students' own prior performance), which tends to differentially motivate persons who are at different points in the distribution of achievement. Only those at the high end of the distribution are highly motivated. Second, it can be seen as unfair to teachers, parents, and students. If we accept that different children have different abilities, then to measure all against a single standard of performance is not to have a level playing field: Different abilities give, in effect, differentially efficient equipment to students, parents, and teachers, to reach the same goal. Nor does it measure the benefits, or value added, brought about by efforts of students, parents, and teachers.

But if an evaluation provides rewards only for gains in achievement, then there are at least two negative consequences. One is that this creates a moral hazard: gains in achievement can be brought about not only by high final levels of achievement, but also by low initial levels of achievement. Thus, this creates a motivation to have low initial performance as well as a motivation to have high final performance. Second, a system of evaluation with rewards only for gains in achievement lacks the authenticity that one having rewards for level of achievement automatically carries. Thus, it would lack the legitimacy necessary for a stable evaluation system.

Note that not only do the evaluations used in the United States, SAT and ACT, fail this criterion, but also the Baccalauréat, Abitur, and A levels fail it as well. Each measures level of performance, and thus serves its motivating function only for high performers; there is no measure of gain in performance or value added.

4. *The evaluation must provide rewards that motivate teachers, parents, and students.*

Comment: Certain evaluation systems, such as those in the Japanese and Hungarian systems and, to a lesser extent, those in various European countries, meet this criterion, despite failing others. The Hungarian system does this through contests, local, regional, national, and international. Teachers in certain subjects gain prestige and the opportunity to move to a more prestigious school by having high-performing students, just as coaches do in the United States. Students and parents are motivated to win the prize. The defect, of course, is that the effectiveness of this reward differs greatly at different points in the distribution of performance. It is most effective for high achievers, and for teachers and parents of high achievers.

Teachers can be motivated by pay, by career opportunities, and by autonomy in their jobs. Students and parents can be motivated by various benefits, and also by recognition for doing well; but recognition for doing well academically is not automatic.

Yet recognition depends on conditions under the control of educational policy. For example, schools now have informal rankings in parents' and teachers' minds in terms of the *level* of performance of students. This is reinforced by the reporting of standardized test scores in local newspapers. But if the year-to-year *gains* in performance (e.g., gains in percentile position or standard score) were reported, there would be a shift in the rankings, as a consequence of publication of the gain scores. Further, because these gain scores represent value added in the school, the rankings would be closer to a true measure of the benefits provided by the school.

SOCIAL CAPITAL AMONG TEACHERS AND STUDENTS

The example of Quality Circles in Japanese auto firms contains an element central to the generation of social capital; rights and responsibilities are allocated not only to individuals, but to the group itself. Such principles can be, and in some settings, have been, implemented in schools. For example, teaching methods known as cooperative learning have been introduced in a number of schools, and these methods give some rights and responsibilities to groups of students. Also, some teachers use group projects in teaching. Both of these approaches take steps toward the creation of social norms that mobilize efforts toward the group task. Yet these approaches constitute a small fraction of the total teaching-and-learning methods used in U.S. schools. For students, efforts, rewards, and responsibilities in school remain highly individualistic, losing the potential that appropriately allocated rights and responsibilities to groups of students (classes, groups within a class, or teams otherwise organized) have for the creation of social capital and mobilization of energies.

For teachers as well, schools are highly individualistic. In a high school, disciplinary departments have collective responsibilities, but these are partitioned individually. There are few or no group rights or rewards.

The existence of external criteria for value added, as described earlier, makes quite feasible the provision of rewards to departments based on the value they have added over the school year to their students' performance. This could be in the form of a bonus to the department to be divided among the members, or money for additional equipment, or other rewards. As in the case of students, such group rewards can be expected to create norms for high efforts, as well as collaborative work and closer coordination among the teachers.

CONCLUSION

I will not discuss specific designs of schools that incorporate the principles I have described. Rather, I will list three properties that an achievement-oriented school design should have, together with implications of each for aspects of the design.

1. The school should be output-driven rather than administratively driven. *Implications:*
   a. Externally established criteria and externally administered performance tests.
   b. Criteria for performance at the end of a stage of school are set by recipients of children at the next stage.
   c. Performance-based rewards to teachers, students, and parents.
2. The formal structure should generate social capital toward organizational goals. *Implications:*
   Rights and rewards should go to social groups as well as individuals, to bring within-group cooperation
   a. To a group of teachers responsible for a set of students
   b. To groups of students in the same class or same school
3. Rewards recognize heterogeneity of inputs. *Implications:*
   a. Rewards should be given not only for level of performance, but also for value added.
   b. Teacher rewards should be primarily for value added.
   c. Curriculum and rewards must cover a wide range of types of performance: academic, technical, performing arts, athletic.
   d. Heterogeneity of inputs limits efficiency of division of labor. *Implication:*
   Apart from responsibility for subject-matter performance, one teacher must have responsibility for overall functioning of a given child.

Finally, I want to add a note about threats to achievement-oriented schools.

THREATS TO ACHIEVEMENT-ORIENTED SCHOOLS

Standardized tests, largely of the multiple-choice variety, have been the principal externally designed and externally administered tests of school achievement. These tests, both used internally by schools to track their students' performance, and used at the end of high school in college admission, have been widely criticized for both good and bad reasons. The good reason is that such tests are poorer measures of achievement than are other measures that make fewer compromises with time of the test-taker and the test-scorer. The bad reason is that the tests, by giving each student a numerical score, introduce competition and invidious distinction.

Both of these reasons have given rise to a movement in U.S. education described as authentic assessment. Authentic assessment ordinarily involves some kind of performance, and may result in a "portfolio" of materials produced by the student. Authentic assessment has much in common with the kinds of performances in music or drama auditions, or artists' portfolios, or athletic contests, all of which have long provided the basis for decisions on admission or scholarships to postsecondary institutions which provide further training for these skills. There is much to recommend these methods of assessment. There are, of course, practical problems in implementing these methods broadly, and in attempting to replace current grading systems or current standardized testing with these methods. It is these practical problems, principally the time required to obtain an assessment, that have prevented them from being more widely used at present. Were these practical problems to be overcome, the performances, demonstrations, and portfolios of authentic assessment could replace current standardized testing.

However, there are certain aspects of authentic assessment that constitute a threat to high achievement in U.S. schools. The threat they pose is not inherent in authentic assessment, but lies in the ease with which authentic assessment can be made compatible with reduced performance levels by those who would eliminate competition in schools. Some elements of authentic assessment that make it easily shaped to fit these interests are:

1.   Assessments are in many disciplines not objective but subjective, depending on judges' evaluations.

2.   Most current prescriptions for authentic assessment in schools do not make use of external evaluations, but depend on the teachers themselves. Thus, the principle of an output-driven organization is missing. In some forms of authentic assessment, there is no comparative evaluation of students' performances at all; the merit is in the eye of the beholder. In this, current proposals for authentic assessment are unlike their forebears, in which external judges determine the awarding of admission or scholarships on the basis of performance or portfolios.

3.   The creation of a portfolio, while purportedly the work of the student, may well include significant contributions by the teacher, who has an incentive to make her or his students' performance appear impressive to parents. Such contributions by the teacher may be easier than developing the skill in the student.

4.   The ambiguity of evaluations of performances can reduce or remove altogether the incentive of student, parent, and teacher toward improved performance.

As I indicated earlier, the threat to achievement-oriented schools is not inherent in authentic assessment. There is much that can be taken from performance-oriented approaches that can greatly improve current standardized testing. However, it seems quite possible that the strongest drive toward authentic assessment comes from the aim of eliminating comparative evaluation in schools. As I have indicated earlier, the egalitarian impulse has already led U.S. schools down an unfruitful path. Rather than to eliminate or reduce standards, the fruitful direction is to redirect comparison of the student's performance with his or her own earlier performance. This provides a measure of the value added for that student by the school, which is what the school is there for in the first place.

REFERENCES

Bishop, J. (1995). Incentives to study and the organization of secondary instruction. In William Becker and William Baumol (Eds.), *Assessing educational practices: The contribution of economics.* Cambridge, MA: MIT Press, pp. 99–160.

Chandler, A. D. (1962). *Strategy and structure: Chapters in the history of the industrial enterprise.* Cambridge, MA: Harvard University Press.

IAEEA (1987). *The underachieving curriculum: Assessing U.S. school mathematics from an international perspective.* Curtis C. McKnight, J. Crosswhite, J. Dossey, E.

Kifer, J. Swafford, K. Travers, and T. Cooney (Eds.) Champaign, IL: Stipes Publishing Company.

Mackie, G. (1991). The rise and fall of the forest workers' cooperative of the Pacific Northwest. M.S. thesis, Department of Political Science, University of Oregon.

Murray, C., & Herrnstein, R. J. (1992). The education impasse. *The Public Interest, 106* (Winter), 32–56.

NAEP (1988). *The NAEP mathematics report card.* Princeton, NJ: Educational Testing Service.

Petersen, T. (1992). Individual, collective, and systems rationality in work groups: Dilemmas and market-type solutions. *American Journal of Sociology, 98*(3), 469–510.

Roethlisberger, F., & Dickson, W. (1939). *Management and the worker.* Cambridge, MA: Harvard University Press.

Sizer, T. (1984). *Horace's compromise: The dilemma of the American high school.* Boston: Houghton Mifflin.

2

Lost in Translation
Applying Total Quality Management to Schools, Colleges, and Universities

Aaron M. Pallas and Anna Neumann

As the institutional legitimacy of educational organizations has grown increasingly fragile in recent years, educational leaders and policymakers have sought to model school policies and practices on the apparent successes of the private sector. Management fads such as management by objectives and strategic planning surfaced in education only a brief time after their prominence in the management of industrial organizations. It comes as no surprise, then, that Total Quality Management (TQM), a management philosophy developed and popularized in the manufacturing sector by consultants such as W. Edwards Deming, Joseph Juran, and Philip Crosby, is being considered for adoption in hundreds, possibly thousands, of schools, colleges, and universities across the United States.

Will TQM have a salutary effect on U.S. education? Although current data are inconclusive, this chapter responds to this question by analyzing the theory and practice of TQM as applied to educational settings. The chapter begins by briefly summarizing the principles of TQM. It then considers how TQM has been translated for K–12 schools and colleges and universities, drawing on the "how-to" literature aimed at education practitioners and on empirical accounts of the implementation of TQM in educational organizations. The chapter next analyzes these educational applications of TQM in light of organizational theory, and concludes by

Aaron M. Pallas and Anna Neumann   College of Education, Michigan State University, East Lansing, Michigan 48824-1034.

Restructuring Schools: Promising Practices and Policies, edited by Maureen T. Hallinan. Plenum Press, New York, 1995.

questioning the fit between TQM and the human problems it is intended to address.

As shown below, TQM refers to a generic management philosophy that is largely independent of a particular organizational context. However, because schools, colleges, and universities are distinctive organizations, TQM must be translated so as to be applicable to them. In part, this analysis considers what may, in essence, be lost in translation—for TQM, but also for education—when TQM is applied to educational organizations.

FUNDAMENTAL ASSUMPTIONS OF TQM

Many discussions of TQM begin with a set of propositions codified by W. Edwards Deming as the "14 Points." These points are listed here, although they are not explicated fully because of space considerations. More complete explanations are available in Deming's (1986) major exposition on his philosophy of management, as well as in the writings of his proponents in business and education, including Aguayo (1990), Chaffee and Sherr (1992), and Gitlow and Gitlow (1987).

1. Create constancy of purpose for improvement of product and service.
2. Adopt the new philosophy.
3. Cease dependence on mass inspection.
4. End the practice of awarding business on the basis of price tag alone.
5. Improve constantly and forever the system of production and service.
6. Institute training.
7. Adopt and institute leadership.
8. Drive out fear.
9. Break down barriers between staff areas.
10. Eliminate slogans, exhortations, and targets for the work force.
11. Eliminate numerical quotas for the work force; eliminate numerical quotas for people in management.
12. Remove barriers that rob people of pride of workmanship.
13. Encourage education and self-improvement for everyone.
14. Take action to accomplish the transformation by marshalling the organization's resources so as to transform both the production process and the philosophy that underlies it.

According to Deming and his interpreters, these 14 points, along with additional commentary, represent a holistic philosophy of organizational management. Many of the points draw on existing schools of management, such as the scientific management and human relations schools, as well as systems theory, strategic planning, and organic models of organization (Dill, 1992; Spencer, 1994; Stampen, 1987). This point will be discussed later, when TQM is examined from diverse theoretical vantage points. The current discussion emphasizes those features of the TQM philosophy that differentiate it from these preceding schools of thought: the notion of a customer, the definition of quality, the nature of variation, and the reliance on statistical process control.

THE NOTION OF A CUSTOMER

A basic premise in the TQM philosophy, expounded by virtually every text on TQM, is that an organization must be responsive to its "customers." Although this may appear to be a simple corollary to open systems theory emphasizing organizations' dependence on and responsiveness to their external environments (Katz & Kahn, 1978), TQM casts organizations as responding to customers who are both external and internal to the organization. External customers are the beneficiaries (Chaffee & Sherr, 1992) or recipients of the products or services produced by the organization, and internal customers are the people within the organization who work together to generate those products and services. For example, the primary "product" of a K–12 schooling system is a graduate, and the beneficiaries of this product include the children who are educated, their parents and family members, the community, local employers seeking skilled labor, regional and national colleges and universities seeking able incoming students, and society at large (which benefits from an educated citizenry), to name the most obvious customers.

Conversely, there are many internal customers as well, including the clerical and technical staff who process attendance reports, payroll checks, and financial statements, teachers and other instructional support staff, and perhaps students themselves. The TQM philosophy encourages viewing organizations as systems within which people serve each other the products of their handiwork in a service-provider and service-consumer (customer) configuration. For example, in an elementary school, third-grade teachers are the customers of the second-grade teachers, as the "products" of the second-grade teachers, graduates of second grade, are the raw inputs that the third-grade teachers use to produce graduates of third grade.

TQM views educational organizations as consisting of academic subsystems and administrative subsystems, with customer–supplier linkages embedded within individual subsystems, but also spanning them. Individuals may simultaneously be customers and suppliers, depending on the particular work process involved. A geometry teacher is both a supplier of students to a calculus teacher, and a customer or beneficiary of an algebra teacher. In some cases, as when a school curriculum is hierarchical and tightly sequenced, these connections will be obvious; in other cases, they will be more ambiguous.

QUALITY AS BOUNDED UNIFORMITY

Consistent with its emphasis on the customer, TQM defines quality in terms of customer needs and desires. Quality consists of providing a product or service that meets the needs and expectations of the customer. It follows that a quality production process can consistently and reliably produce a product or service according to customer desires. The issue of consistency and reliability is an especially important aspect of the way that the TQM philosophy operationalizes quality. An inconsistent or unreliable product or service is unlikely to meet the needs or expectations of a customer (see Crosby, 1979; Juran, 1989).

Thus, quality is defined in terms of the amount of variability both in the production process and in the output of that process (Aguayo, 1990). The TQM philosophy argues that it is imperative to understand and control the amount of variation in the production process, so as to minimize the variation in the outputs (Gitlow & Gitlow, 1987). But the elimination of variation is an ideal that can never be achieved, so "bounded uniformity," the attempt to restrict variation in process and/ or outcome to a specified range, may be a more useful characterization of quality.

THE NATURE OF VARIATION IN THE PRODUCTION PROCESS AND STATISTICAL PROCESS CONTROL

The TQM philosophy asserts that there are different kinds and causes of variation in production processes, and that diverse forms of variation should be addressed in diverse ways (Deming, 1986). Some kinds of variation are related to unpredictable events, distinct from the production process but impinging on it, and hence are not amenable to systemic correction; others are outgrowths of the production system itself, and can only be reduced by "fixing" or otherwise altering the production process itself (Aguayo, 1990; Deming, 1986, 1993). These two kinds of variation are referred to as variation related to unique (or special) causes, and variation related to common causes (see Aguayo, 1990; Deming, 1986).

If, for example, an elementary school's library is flooded, and its students precluded from access to the books comprising its elementary reading program, it may happen that in the year of the flood, the school's second-grade students did not improve their reading skills as much as students in preceding or subsequent second-grade classes. In this case, there is a specific, unpredictable cause of the variability in student performance, the flood, and it is reasonable to assume that when the books dry out and the library is cleaned up, students will once again make use of the facility in the usual way. This kind of variation is related to a special or unique cause, the flood, and is not amenable to intervention (except, perhaps, taking greater precautions against natural disasters).

In contrast, perhaps all of the second-grade teachers in that elementary school are using a method of teaching reading that emphasizes parts of speech while neglecting vocabulary skills. There will be some variation in the vocabulary skills of the second graders, as some children are likely to be building their vocabulary through out-of-school activities, whereas others lacking the relevant educational resources at home will not. Thus, the third-grade teachers will routinely be receiving students with widely varying vocabulary skills at the beginning of third grade.

This kind of variation, stemming from the nature of what TQM refers to as the production process, is called common variation in that it is rooted in common causes. In TQM, common variation is reduced by altering the production process itself, since common variation reflects the nature of that process (e.g., the nature of the way in which reading is taught) rather than something existing apart from the process though influencing it (e.g., the flood). In this example, the introduction of a new reading curriculum in second grade would amount to a process change that could reduce the variation in children's vocabulary skills as they exit second grade and enter third grade.

Of course, one would only recognize this variation if one looked for it. An important feature of the TQM philosophy is the analysis of data representing the intermediate and final outputs of a production process. Through the use of statistical process control, it is possible to determine whether the variation in outputs around some desired target value is related to a common cause or a special cause of variation (see Aguayo, 1990).[1] When the major source of variation in outputs is common, the only way to increase quality is to improve the production process, by redesigning either the components (e.g., the second-grade reading curriculum) or their interrelationships.

TRANSLATIONS OF TQM FOR EDUCATIONAL ORGANIZATIONS

Whereas the discussion above treats TQM as a generic management philosophy that is applicable to all types of organizations, the discourse around TQM in educational settings emphasizes some features of the philosophy and ignores or downplays others. This section considers how TQM has been translated for the educational community in its practice-based literature. Amid the rhetoric justifying the consideration of TQM in educational settings, cast largely in business-oriented language such as "meeting customers' needs" or "benchmarking," a series of themes has emerged, based loosely on Deming's 14 points. Of course, some authors diverge from a literal translation of Deming to schools and colleges, in some cases questioning its educational applicability (Keller, 1992; Kohn, 1993), whereas others adhere more closely to Deming's ideas. Those elements that are common to most educational translations of TQM are noted here.

Focusing on Shared Purpose and Continuous Improvement

Drawing on Deming's Point 1 (constancy of purpose) and Point 5 (improve constantly and forever the system of production and service), most writers call for an organizationwide consensus on the purpose and mission of schools, colleges, and universities. Some go further to emphasize that the formulation of purpose must be anchored in commit-

---

[1]If a production process is stable, the variation in the outputs of that process will be stable or predictable, and there will be no trends or cycles in the data. If a process is in statistical control, then statistical rules can help determine whether a given batch of sampled data fall inside or outside of the range of what should be expected. Roughly speaking, if a process is in statistical control, all data points should fall within three standard deviations of the target value. In such a case, a data point outside the control limits (i.e., either above the upper limit or below the lower limit) is probably the result of a special cause of variation, rather than a common cause (Aguayo, 1990).

ments to identify and meet customer needs. Coupled with this shared mission is a shared norm for continuous improvement in both teaching and administrative processes, on the one hand, and student outcomes, on the other.

Centering on "Others"

Unlike the human relations school of management, which focuses on the psychological and other needs of organizational workers, translations of TQM to education emphasize the needs of external customers, such as students, parents, and other individuals and corporate entities, both now and in the anticipated future. Although TQM articulates support for the growth and development of individual workers (Points 6 and 13), this is cast instrumentally, as a means for improving workers' abilities to be of service to students and other customers. There is some disagreement in the literature, however, over the extent to which customer (i.e., student) needs ought to be defined by students themselves or by other stakeholders (Seymour, 1992), as opposed to being mediated by the professional judgment of educators (Chaffee & Sherr, 1992).

Reconceptualizing Educational Organizations

Contemporary theories of educational organization envision schools, colleges, and universities as bureaucratic structures, human communities, political systems, interpretive systems, and cultures, to cite some of the dominant images (Morgan, 1986). Although TQM incorporates some aspects of bureaucratic and rational management as well as human relations approaches on organization, those writing on TQM in education have emphasized a view of schools and colleges as a series of technical processes by which raw inputs (students) are transformed into "products" such as graduates. Many contemporary images of organization, particularly those repudiating mechanistic metaphors or critiquing traditional human relations perspectives aimed at making workers more compliant (e.g., Foster, 1986; Frost, Moore, Louis, Lundberg, & Martin, 1991), are not reflected well in writing on TQM.

Managing by Data

Writers translating TQM for educational organizations typically retain the strong emphasis on data analysis evident in Deming's writings.

Organizational change is enacted through the controlled experimentation of the PDCA cycle (plan, do, check, act) developed by Walter Shewhart and popularized by Deming. In this view, plans for innovation are formed in light of empirical knowledge about organizational functioning, and the implementation of such plans and their effects on the production process and products are monitored through empirical observation. In most cases, the data analyzed in the PDCA cycle are quantified, and thus the production process and its components must be conceived of in quantitative terms. Many educational processes, however, are not easily amenable to quantification.

Reconceptualizing Work as a Collective Endeavor

Most of the writings on TQM in education view the work of educators, particularly teachers, as a collective and interdependent activity (Chaffee & Sherr, 1992), rather than as an independent effort or as a simple sum of individual efforts. Consistent with Deming, most authors advocate the development of cross-cutting work teams that span the various subsystems of educational organizations, differentiated by function (e.g., academic, support, and administrative), subject matter (e.g., departments and colleges), and age/grade configuration (e.g., grade level or year).

This view does, of course, stand in opposition to the traditional conception of teachers and teaching as isolated and individualistic. The writings on TQM in education further promote a collectivist orientation through school- or college-wide socialization experiences that are intended both to teach faculty, administrators, and other staff members about the principles of TQM and to encourage them to use such principles in their daily work.

Requiring Adoption of TQM in Entirety

Although the literature on TQM in education frequently exhorts educators to adopt TQM in entirety, the meaning of "entirety" is ambiguous. For example, writers on TQM in education vary as to whether "adoption in entirety" refers to (1) all faculty, staff, and administrators being required to embrace TQM's foundational principles (Marchese, 1989), (2) all work processes being subjected to quality management (Chaffee & Sherr, 1992), (3) all customers (students) being touched by it (Seymour, 1993), or (4) all aspects of Deming's philosophy being adopted (by people or by organizational units or processes), based on the idea that piecemeal adoption of TQM will dilute the overall impact of the organizational transformation (Chaffee & Sherr, 1992).

Conceptualizing Leadership

Although current reforms in education frequently emphasize shared leadership between administrators, on the one hand, and teaching faculty and staff, on the other, writings translating TQM for education often reify the distinction between management and workers. According to this literature, the responsibility for instituting TQM—including the development of constancy of purpose and provision of education and training—is in the hands of management. Administrators are portrayed as working *on* the system, whereas teachers and other staff are seen as working *in* the system (Crawford, Bodine, & Hoglund, 1993). With few exceptions, then, the literature on TQM in schools casts administrators and teaching faculty in a hierarchical relationship that is only partly offset by joint participation in crosscutting teams.

Reconceptualizing Teaching

Although there is relatively little empirical evidence of the implementation of TQM in classrooms, the emerging literature on TQM in education does encourage teachers at all levels of the education system to adopt TQM principles in their classrooms. Consistent with the service orientation of TQM in schools, cast broadly, classroom teaching is conceptualized as the delivery of a service or a product to student-customers. Thus, teachers are exhorted to study and respond to students' learning needs and preferences, with most attention directed to the technology of instruction—i.e., ensuring that students can see a blackboard or overhead transparency clearly, or relying more heavily on experiential classroom activities than lectures. This emphasis on logistics and instrumentality obscures the possibility of more fundamental reforms in the teaching of subject matter at all levels of the system.

REVIEWING ACCOUNTS OF THE IMPLEMENTATION OF TQM IN SCHOOLS AND COLLEGES

This section presents an overview of the kinds of process changes in schools and colleges that have been attributed to the implementation of

TQM principles. This presentation is of necessity partial, and should not be construed as a research review. First, much of what is reported here comes from descriptive accounts appearing in practitioner-oriented educational publications such as *Educational Leadership* and *AAHE Bulletin*. Second, these summaries are not derived from careful evaluations of the effects of TQM, but rather represent the attributions of the authors of these works. There is not yet a literature on the effects of TQM in educational organizations that conforms to conventional standards of scientific inquiry. Third, although the presentation in this section is representative of the available writings on the implementation of TQM in educational organizations, it may not be representative of the range of actual TQM implementation strategies and results, including cases in which TQM is being implemented purposefully but without being named as such.

Despite the substantive and analytic weaknesses of this literature it is important to review critically, because it is this literature that is constructing TQM as a social phenomenon and drawing practitioners to it. Thus, although the real effects of TQM cannot yet be assessed, its espoused content can be examined in light of established knowledge about organizations in general, and schools and colleges in particular.

An extensive review of more than 100 articles, book chapters, books, and technical reports describing various aspects of the implementation of TQM in schools and colleges yielded several accounts of the kinds of process changes in organizational functioning that would likely accompany this implementation. The literature on the implementation of TQM in K–12 schools is much sparser than the writings on TQM in higher education, perhaps because of the greater institutionalization of an institutional research function in higher education than in the K–12 sector. Table 1 reports process changes that have been cited in five K–12 schools and school districts, whereas Table 2 provides examples of process changes reported in 11 colleges or universities. Analysis of the examples reported in Tables 1 and 2, as well as other examples not cited in those tables, leads to the following tentative conclusions:

1. *TQM is much more frequently directed at administrative processes than at academic processes.* There are many more examples listed in Tables 1 and 2 of streamlining or modifying administrative processes than there are of changes to academic processes concerned directly with teaching and learning. Although the improvement of administrative processes is valuable, such processes are not directly related to the "technical core" educational activities of teaching and learning.

2. *Changes in academic processes frequently amount to tinkering around the edges rather than fundamental changes in teaching and learning processes.*

**Table 1.   Examples of Process Changes in K–12 Schools Attributed
to the Implementation of TQM**

Crawford Central School District, PA	• Reduced time on processing of purchase orders • Minimized amount of downtime on students' computers • Sped up time of repairs
Rappahannock County Schools, VA	• Parent–teacher–staff team designed report cards • Resolved disciplinary problems on "bus runs"
Mt. Edgecumbe H.S., Sitka, AK	• Restructuring of class day from seven 50-minute periods to four 90-minute periods • Reorganization of classroom schedule allows for an additional 3 hours of staff development and preparation time per week • Students receive 90 minutes per week of quality improvement training and schoolwide problem solving • Students initiated a study sampling how others did their homework. As a result, they became more attuned to their own work habits, and grades improved
Wilde Lake H.S., Columbia, MD	• Eliminated failing grades. Students perfect their work until they deserve at least a C grade
George Westinghouse Vocational and Technical H.S., New York City, NY	• Persuaded parents to sign contracts to check on student homework, resulting in a lower rate of students failing classes • Reduced the number of students wearing hats and "Walkmen" around the school building

Sources: Bonstingl (1992a,b), Kelly (1991).

For example, among the academic process changes reported in Tables 1 and 2 are obtaining a sufficient number of left-handed desks for students, provision of chalk and erasers to classrooms, and changing the dates of tests and assignments to provide for better feedback to students. None of these changes can be claimed as outcomes of a fundamental rethinking of teaching and learning processes. This is not to say that such changes will not have desirable effects, because they certainly have the potential to be helpful to teaching and learning. Rather, such changes may be viewed as logistical adjustments to, rather than as substantive epistemological shifts in, teaching and learning. That is, the changes noted pertain more to the "nuts and bolts" of teaching and learning, and the manipulation of time and resources, than to what is sometimes referred to as constructivist approaches to teaching and learning, including "teaching for understanding" (Cohen, McLaughlin and Talbert, 1993; Prawat, 1989).

Table 2.   Examples of Process Changes in Colleges and Universities
Attributed to the Implementation of TQM

University of Pennsylvania	• Improved recovery of research funds from external sources • Improved trash collection • Supplied chalk and erasers to classrooms
Oregon State University	• Physical plant team reduced average duration of remodeling jobs by 27% • Budgets and planning team improved the budget-at-a-glance report to meet "customer" needs and cut report's preparation time from 10 days to 5 days • Human resource staff benefits team increased number of phone calls getting an initial human response
Maricopa	• Districtwide groups conducted occupational course-by-course analyses to ensure that students are learning the competencies most required by potential employers
St. John Fisher College	• Reduced the time it took to mail catalogs to prospective students from 6 weeks to 2 days • Scholarship team recommended guidelines for gift acceptance, named chairs, professorships, and buildings • Admissions office team developed a comprehensive manual that allows a new admissions counselor to plan and execute a complex program from start to finish
University of Central Florida	• A team looked at causes and effects of student retention in introductory algebra classes
Georgia Tech	• Reorganized Office of Minority Education Development, CHALLENGE program for entering minority students
Samford University/Belmont University	• A team of students designed a survey to determine which testing styles their classmates prefer and which type of test helps them learn best • Obtained enough left-handed desks for students • Changed dates of tests/assignments to provide for better feedback to students • Helped the computer center to provide training to lab assistants on all programs used by students within particular labs • Developed "buddy" assignments to improve class preparation and participation
Pennsylvania State University	• Teams focused on teaching physics to engineering undergraduates; chemical management; client satisfaction in the registrar's office; procurement of scientific equipment; students' transition to University Park; Upward Bound; reducing inventories in General Stores

Table 2.   (Continued)

University of Wisconsin–Madison	• Revised graduate admissions processes • In response to a student survey, a statistics professor reduced the amount of computer homework and downgraded a required textbook to a reference book
Fox Valley Technical College	• Faculty and staff met to define quality elements and competencies for the successful teacher at the college • Relocated the offices of several student services to provide students with a centralized service area • Improved ventilation of large lab area • Developed a comprehensive in-service program for new adjunct faculty • Improved course scheduling • Improved responsiveness of students' emergency phone calls • Changed frequency and format of management meetings
University of Chicago Graduate School of Business	• Faculty members worked with lab course students or student teams to improve ongoing courses • Team of students worked with the behavioral science group as a unit to design a new required course in behavioral science • Used fast-feedback questionnaires to identify problems with hearing or understanding the instructor, reading the writing on the board, or seeing the visuals; lack of sufficient examples or applications to illustrate concepts; and the pace of the class

Sources: Assar (1993), Bemowski (1991), Keller (1992), Marchese (1992), Nagy *et al.* (1993), Seymour (1993), Spanbauer (1992), and various issues of *TQM in Higher Education*.

Moreover, most of these changes are self-contained in a unit like a class-room or a department, rather than systemic and crosscutting.

A further example of these points is provided in Spanbauer's (1992) account of the quality teaching model at Fox Valley Technical College. The quality elements for curriculum and instruction that Spanbauer (1992, pp. 74–75) cites include: mastery learning with competency-based approaches in curriculum design, adequate course planning for learning following a set standard, written course prerequisites, preassessment processes that identify learning styles, criterion-based student measurement systems, credit for past learning and other experiences of students, multiple-entry/exit delivery systems with opportunities for accelerated learning, emphasis on the learning environment itself with a focus on creating enjoyable experiences which are linked to the objectives, advisory committee involvement in reviewing the teaching/learning processes, evaluation/audits of instruction and programs, articulation with other levels of education, class and laboratory management standards, techniques for retraining students, customized training systems, and use of current technology by both faculty and students.

What appears to be lost in this generic set of requirements is a concern for how teachers continuously construct the content of what they teach [what Shulman (1986) and Grossman (1990) have called pedagogical content knowledge], and similarly how students continuously construct their learning of school subjects (Peterson, in press; Schoenfeld, 1992). Though Fox Valley Technical College ought not be singled out, most academic process changes attributed to TQM appear similarly indifferent to current thinking about teaching and learning as constructivist endeavors.

3. *The closer TQM is to the classroom, the more likely that the changes that do result will involve core teaching and learning processes.* TQM-related changes in academic processes seem most likely to occur at the classroom level, and are successively less likely to occur the farther one moves away from the classroom (e.g., at the level of curricular reform or graduation requirements). Thus, changes in teaching and learning are more likely to emanate from individual faculty at the classroom level than from the building or campus level, and much more so than from the district or system level. This observation is, of course, consistent with much of the expository writing on TQM, which holds that workers close to the production process are the ones who know the process best and are in the best position to recommend improvements.

4. *TQM is more likely to take hold in educational settings where TQM is part of the subject matter being taught.* Many of the examples of changes in academic processes attributed to TQM are drawn from the fields of engineering, business, and statistics. This observation parallels Entin's (1993) survey, in which he found no examples of liberal arts faculty implementing TQM.

It is not surprising that teachers and administrators of academic subjects concerned with quality management and production processes should seek to integrate TQM principles into their own teaching and administrative activities. There is, moreover, a great deal of anecdotal evidence regarding the resistance of faculty to TQM, which may account for why most implementations of TQM principles in educational organizations begin with administrative processes. Nevertheless, it is worth entertaining the possibility that some academic subjects are more amenable to TQM than others, regardless of the predilections of the teachers involved.

Teachers may find it easier to apply TQM principles in the classroom when teaching subjects that organize their content in a structured linear sequence (such as engineering or statistics) than when teaching subjects that are more diffuse and less hierarchical (such as the humanities or social sciences). Of course, much depends on the extent to which TQM balances what is characterized here as logistical as opposed to epistemological perspectives on teaching and learning.

5. *Although the changes noted in Tables 1 and 2 are attributed by various authors to TQM, there is rarely enough evidence presented in their accounts to know whether this attribution is reasonable.* In most cases, schools and colleges are undergoing multiple changes at once, only some of which may be attributable to the TQM philosophy described earlier. For example, decisions to streamline processes of various kinds may emanate from routine administrative reviews as much as from TQM-based consideration of customers or analysis of production processes.

One widely reported example of a change attributed to TQM is the smoked salmon export business developed by students in an entrepreneurship class at Mt. Edgecumbe High School in Sitka, Alaska. Tribus (1991) and others have noted the economic success of this business, and its capacity for teaching students about TQM principles such as focusing on the customer and analyzing the production process. Although the value of this innovation is not in dispute, there is little evidence that it was TQM, as opposed to something else (perhaps the imagination of teacher David Langford), that led to the development of this smoked salmon export business.

6. *Many of the kinds of process changes cited also take place in other educational settings that are not explicitly pursuing a TQM philosophy.* The process changes themselves, though perhaps identified through a TQM process, appear to be quite similar to changes that are undertaken routinely through the work of administrators and faculty, working singly or in combination, in schools and colleges throughout the country. This is true especially of reforms such as site-based management, outcomes-based education, and a variety of school restructuring proposals.

In sum, the practitioner literature on TQM in education appears to construct TQM primarily as a matter of logistics. Hence, the time and attention that teachers devote to TQM compete for and perhaps displace the time and attention that teachers might devote to noninstrumental concerns, such as teachers' and learners' construction of knowledge. Moreover, the success often associated with TQM, especially in early phases of implementation, may be attributed improperly when several changes are occurring in educational organizations simultaneously.

ASSESSING EDUCATIONAL TRANSLATIONS OF TQM: UNSETTLED POSSIBILITIES

One of the distinguishing features of the practice-based TQM literature in education is its lack of intersection with established academic knowledge, particularly organizational theory in education. With some exceptions (e.g., Betts, 1992; Dill, 1992), writers favoring adoption of TQM in schools and colleges make but passing reference to established or evolving ideas in discipline-based, theoretically grounded studies of school and college life (e.g., Cohen & March, 1986; Meyer & Rowan, 1978; Weick, 1976). Most writings favoring the adoption of TQM in schools and colleges treat the 14 Points of W. Edwards Deming as a theoretical base, although these points lack the coherence of a theory, and are themselves unconnected to organizational theory. Only a few treatments that raise critical questions about TQM, or that in other ways consider TQM's limitations in addition to its strengths (see, e.g., Capper & Jamison, 1993; Dill, 1992; Sitkin, Sutcliffe, and Schroeder, 1994), connect their argument to theory.

Despite this weak association of theory and practice in the education-based TQM literature, several theoretical lenses may illuminate TQM's viability as a management innovation in education and guide research on its implementation and possible effects. In this section, TQM is first examined from the standpoint of established and emerging ideas about the structure of educational organizations, including open systems theory, the organization of work, and loose coupling. Then TQM is examined in relation to organizational learning and to political perspectives on school and college life. The analysis is posed as a set of unsettled possibilities, since sweeping inferences as to TQM's likely good or harm are inappropriate, in view of the weak empirical base of evidence.

Open Systems Theory

The application of TQM to schools, colleges, and universities holds the possibility of blurring the distinction between these organizations and their external environments. Educational organizations have traditionally been viewed as open systems that interact with external environments that supply them with "raw materials," including students and fiscal and human resources, and that are influential in defining the purposes, goals, and processes of such organizations. Open systems theory thus emphasizes how schools depend on their environments (Katz & Kahn, 1978), placing the locus of control outside the school rather than within. TQM, though retaining the general conceptualization of the open system, may reposition this locus of control within the school or college, for example, by enabling administrators, teachers, and other staff to decide what their outputs will be and to design production processes and identify "appropriate" inputs for them (Chaffee & Sherr, 1992). Thus, TQM may enable educational organizations to become more self-directed and self-controlled (Marchese, 1989).

Although this image of the empowered school or college is appealing, it obscures the extent to which internal decisions about inputs, processes, and outputs continue to rely on the external environment, since TQM specifies that such decisions must be framed in terms of customer needs, preferences, and desires (i.e., external factors). Whether such customer preferences are taken as given (i.e., defined directly by the customer) or are influenced by the organization (as through marketing and public relations efforts), TQM's foundational commitment to customer needs may hamper attempts by organizational members to think about personal and organizational commitments and agendas in any other way. By institutionalizing the reliance of schools and colleges on their environments (expressed as customer needs) for the framing of their agendas, TQM blurs distinctions between internal and external, and between that which is school and that which is not school.

Thus, although TQM promises to improve on traditional open-systems views of education, the emerging view is one that must be considered with extreme caution, since it threatens the existence of schools, colleges, and universities as bounded organizations that interact with the larger world of which they are a part though existing as distinct within it. The issue is important because it raises the question of what school is and what education is, as distinct from that which is not school and is not a desirable form of education.

Designing Organic Schools and Colleges

By creating work teams that purposefully span compartmentalized and specialized units (e.g., academic departments, admissions office) in schools and colleges, TQM attempts to supplant mechanistic bureaucratic structures with more organic structures that simultaneously enlarge organizational members' conceptions of their work and enlarge the expertise and perspectives applied to organizational problems. Rather than delegating the solution of a problem in the admissions process to the admissions office, for example, the TQM philosophy advocates the development of a crosscutting team that might include admissions specialists, selected

faculty, students, parents, academic administrators, public relations officials, financial aid officers, and others, all of whom may have something
valuable to say about the admissions problem.

Such teams are not, however, immune from issues of organizational
politics and power, two topics on which the TQM philosophy is virtually
silent. For example, the composition, assembly, and formally stated purposes of crosscutting work teams cannot be taken for granted, and are
likely to be negotiated within the power dynamics of the organization.
Moreover, there are a number of substantive challenges in the formation
of crosscutting work teams. Since some organizational members are more
capable of contributing meaningfully to a particular problem than others,
some team configurations will be relatively effective, and others less so.
Yet it is not clear how to identify individuals who can move the team
forward in a productive way.

Nor is it clear how a team should develop a statement of purpose.
A managerially driven charge to a crosscutting work team might restrict
the scope of the team's endeavors to a previously defined arena of thinking
and action, and may reinstate some of the hierarchy that the TQM philosophy professes to weaken. Conversely, a team that goes to work without
a clear purpose or problem in mind may squander valuable time, energy,
and other resources. Although the development of crosscutting work
teams in schools and colleges presents these and other challenges that
still need to be resolved, this feature of TQM bears promise for improving
the management of educational organizations.

Loose and Tight Coupling in Educational Organizations

Although Weick (1976) and others have argued that the loose coupling often evident in educational organizations may enhance organizational functioning, many of the educational reforms of the last two decades
have attempted to create tighter couplings among organizational subunits
and processes and between intentions and actions (e.g., Edmonds, 1979).
The application of the TQM philosophy to schools and colleges appears
to call for tighter coupling in virtually all phases of organizational life,
even though schools, colleges, and universities are internally diverse, with
some areas exhibiting clear and timely connections among organizational
elements and others exhibiting sporadic or diffuse connections (Orton &
Weick, 1990). What effect might the admonition that TQM be adopted in
entirety have on this possible "mixed" pattern of internal connections,
often referred to as "loose coupling" in educational organization?

Although analytic sensitivity to loose coupling in schools and colleges
is occasionally interpreted as a justification for maintaining the status

quo, the promises and problems of a more tightly configured organization may be understood from the perspective of contingency theory (Galbraith, 1973). The tighter coupling implied by TQM may be desirable in some aspects of school and college functioning, and undesirable in others. In particular, the process controls of TQM may lead to improvement in work processes that are relatively certain, definable, and predictable (Sitkin *et al.*, 1994), but have minimal or even counterproductive impacts on work processes that are less certain and routinized.

For example, physical plant maintenance, budget processes, and admissions processes are relatively certain and routine, whereas teaching and research generally are not. Viewed through the lens of TQM, teaching may be at risk of routinization, through the "constant improvement" of syllabi, or class procedures that rarely undergo fundamental change. Similarly, scholarly research that is encased within a TQM framework might tend more toward extension of previous conceptualization than to fundamental rethinking of problem, method, or perspective. Uncertainty and certainty are, however, never fully separable in educational organizations: Some seemingly definable and predictable processes encounter surprising uncertainties (as in the case of a physical plant maintenance crew dealing with a natural disaster). And some seemingly uncertain tasks (teaching and learning) require predictable frameworks, standards, and technologies for their enactment (syllabi, grades, enrollment sheets, readable transparencies).

Therefore, this analysis suggests that TQM should not be adopted in entirety—if entirety means all aspects of a school or college adopting all aspects of TQM. Rather subparts of the organization might selectively choose to implement TQM—in whole, in part, or not at all. Moreover, it may be important to have all members of a school, college, or university understand that TQM's adoption may be good in some areas of organizational functioning, and unnecessary, even detrimental, in others.

TQM and Organizational Learning

TQM organizations may be seen as highly goal-directed. In TQM, as in other management systems, goals serve, in part, as "guiding lights," defining the general boundaries around areas of desired action for members who seek direction in their work. But by virtue of providing such boundaries—however general—goals inadvertently serve as constraints (Scott, 1992), discouraging members and activities from deviating beyond desired bounds.

An organization's use of goals to channel worker activity in prespecified (officially sanctioned) directions, thereby discouraging deviations from what has been prespecified, results in a vision of bounded coherence for organization. But in their qualities of boundedness, goals may effectively lessen the possibility of learning and change *beyond* the boundaries that have been prespecified, and even of change in the nature of the boundaries (and thereby, the goals) themselves. Taken literally, the plan–do–check–act cycle of TQM (Deming's Point 5) would limit teachers' and principals', and professors' and administrators', activities to that which has been thoughtfully worked out beforehand, providing little room for learning from unplanned and surprise activity or simply reflection-in-action (Schon, 1983).

This analysis suggests, therefore, that "constancy of purpose" may provide direction to teachers, administrators, and other staff members in schools and colleges, but that there are risks incurred if the purpose becomes "too constant." Overarching goals might be developed in ways that do not rob individuals and organizational subunits of the discretionary thought and action that contribute to organizational growth and learning.

Organizational Politics

In many ways, TQM paints a picture of an organization where rationality has won over politics. In the TQM perspective, organizations are cast as responding clearly to customer needs and wants. Within the organization, rational processes of choice, closely tied to a customer perspective, guide the conceptualization and analysis of problems, usually in the context of teams composed of members representing diverse expertise. Moreover, in TQM-run organizations, individual workers' preferences and decisions are generally subservient to the preferences and decisions of the group to which the individual is presumed to belong (Chaffee & Sherr, 1992). In a rational webbing such as this, politics would seem, virtually, to disappear as rational and collectivist controls outweigh individual and coalitional preferences.

The image of organization portrayed by the TQM philosophy, however, overlooks the assertion of political power extended in more subtle ways. First, it is not obvious how to adjudicate the often conflicting needs, wants, and desires of multiple customers. Hence, the process whereby organizational members, living in a world of finite resources, choose among conflicting customer preferences may become politicized, as customers with clout get more attention than those without. Moreover, TQM seems to overlook the possibility that some customers may—by virtue of privilege, power, or simply chance—be better positioned to articulate their wants than others. How, for example, does TQM enable a public school to mediate between a broad societal obligation to educate all of the children in its catchment area and the interests of a highly vocal group of well-to-do parents?

Second, TQM is largely oblivious to the idea that even the most objective of conceptualizations and research designs are likely to be highly subjective—that is, reflective of the conceptualizer's values and preferences of thought, and thereby inattentive to the values, interests, and conceptualizations of those without power to articulate them (e.g., in scientific terms when science is cast as a "privileged" language and culture). Whereas TQM's emphasis on scientific rationality and collective controls may, therefore, appear to minimize aspects of political activity, traditionally construed, it does so in a very political way, and thus may amplify the political character of organizational life overall.

Educational organizations undertaking TQM may wish, therefore, to maintain a high level of self-consciousness about identifying the interests of all their clients, members, and stakeholders, and about the goal-setting process. Although this is no guarantee that politics and power will not dominate organizational life, the self-reflective organization can at least design its work processes in light of its admitted biases.

CONCLUSION: IF TQM IS THE SOLUTION, WHAT'S THE PROBLEM?

Why should schools, colleges, and universities adopt TQM? It is reasonable to speculate that many proponents of TQM in education are striving to construct educational organizations capable of resolving difficult, culturally embedded problems that primordial social institutions (like the family) have, seemingly, been unable to resolve, at least in the United States.

For example, one of the ideas that surfaces, though implicitly, in the TQM literature is a desire to transform individual human beings, i.e., individual workers in organization, into more responsible people—more responsible for their work, for their customers, for meeting legally and other formally agreed-upon organizational goals. A related idea that surfaces in the educational literature on TQM is a desire to transform educational organizations into more responsible social agencies committed to addressing the problems of society and advancing its developmental agendas. One of the ways in which TQM apparently seeks to accomplish such aims is by enhancing the responsiveness of both educational workers and educational organizations to those existing outside them, i.e., in a client-based (or customer-based) relationship with them.

This theme of responsiveness resonates strongly with what might be termed TQM's overarching "other-orientation." TQM envisions virtually all professional actions as circumscribed by an aim to provide satisfying service (the desired response) to customers, and in this way, TQM-based education, analyzed from the perspective of service providers, emerges as virtually selfless. Although TQM contains provision for worker development (see Points 6 and 13), such individual development mainly is oriented to TQM's efforts to meet customer-defined needs.

If enhanced personal and organizational responsiveness, linked to desires for enhanced social responsibility on the part of educational organizations, is, indeed, a driving concern behind TQM, then several cautions may be in order. Responsibility and responsiveness are closely related but different concepts: Although responsiveness may indicate a sense of responsibility to the "other" to whom one responds, this does not hold true in all cases; moreover, responsibility may show itself in ways other than responsiveness. What seems to be missing at this point is a conversation among educators, citizens, and public officials about the meaning and manifestation of education-based social responsibility, its possibilities, but also its natural limits. What also seems to be missing is a conversation about the possibilities and necessary limitations of responsiveness as applied to professional workers and organizations in education. It is doubtful that any system, TQM included, will make people and organizations more responsible.

In the meantime, efforts to translate TQM from business to education may result in meaningful aspects of schools and schooling being lost or disfigured in translation. In its potential to cloud important differences between educational organizations and other social institutions, TQM may diffuse certain aspects of schools and schooling that are worth keeping. The long-range consequences of such a transformation for students and society at large are unknown.

ACKNOWLEDGMENTS.   An earlier version of this chapter was presented at the 1993 Annual Meeting of the American Educational Research Association in Atlanta, Georgia. We are grateful to Ellen Earle Chaffee, James S. Coleman, Brian DeLany, David D. Dill, William Firestone, Phyllis Grummon, Maureen Hallinan, Iwao Ishino, Penelope Peterson, Richard Prawat, Brian Rowan, Charles Thompson, and members of the Detroit Area Deming Study Group for their helpful comments on an earlier draft of this chapter. We alone are responsible for its contents, however. We also thank Phyllis Grummon for sharing with us her collection of resources on TQM in education, and Porntip Chaichanapanich for her able research assistance.

REFERENCES

Aguayo, R. (1990). *Dr. Deming, the American who taught the Japanese about quality.* New York: Fireside/Simon & Schuster.

Assar, K. E. (1993, May/June). Case study number two: Phoenix, quantum quality at Maricopa. *Change, 25*(3), 32–35.

Bemowski, K. (1991). Restoring the pillars of higher education. *Quality Progress,* (October), 37–42.

Betts, F. (1992). How Systems Thinking Applies to Education. *Educational Leadership, 49* (November), 38–41.

Bonstingl, J. J. (1992a). The quality revolution in education. *Educational Leadership, 49* (November), 4–9.

Bonstingl, J. J. (1992b). *Schools of quality: An introduction to total quality management in education.* Alexandria, VA: Association for Supervision and Curriculum Development.

Capper, C. A., & Jamison, M. T. (1993). Let the buyer beware: Total quality management and educational research and practice. *Educational Researcher, 22*(8), 15–30.

Chaffee, E. E., & Sherr, L. A. (1992). *Quality: Transforming postsecondary education. ASHE–ERIC Higher Education Report 3.* Washington, DC: George Washington University.

Cohen, D. K., McLaughlin, M. W., & Talbert, J. E. (Eds.). (1993). *Teaching for understanding: Challenges for policy and practice.* San Francisco: Jossey–Bass.

Cohen, M. D., & March, J. G. (1986). *Leadership and ambiguity: The American college president* (2nd ed.). Boston: Harvard Business School Press.

Crawford, D. K., Bodine, R. J., & Hoglund, R. G. (1993). *The school for quality learning: Managing the school and classroom the Deming way.* Champaign, IL: Research Press.

Crosby, P. B. (1979). *Quality is free: The art of making quality certain.* New York: McGraw–Hill.

Deming, W. E. (1986). *Out of the crisis.* Cambridge, MA: MIT Press.

Deming, W. E. (1993). *The new economics for industry, government, education.* Cambridge, MA: MIT Press.

Dill, D. D. (1992). Quality by design: Toward a framework for academic quality and management. In J. C. Smart (Ed.), *Higher education: Handbook of theory and research* (Vol. VIII, pp. 37–83). Bronx, NY: Agathon Press.

Edmonds, R. (1979). Effective schools for the urban poor. *Educational Leadership, 37*(1), 15–24.

Entin, D. H. (1993, May/June). Case study number one: Boston, less than meets the eye. *Change, 25*(3), 28–31.

Foster, W. (1986). *Paradigms and promises: New approaches to educational administration.* Buffalo, NY: Prometheus Books.

Frost, P. J., Moore, L. F., Louis, M. R., Lundberg, C. C., & Martin, J. (1991). *Reframing organizational culture.* Beverly Hills, CA: Sage.

Galbraith, J. (1973). *Organizational design.* Reading, MA: Addison–Wesley.

Gitlow, H. S., & Gitlow, S. J. (1987). *The Deming guide to quality and competitive position.* Englewood Cliffs, NJ: Prentice–Hall.

Grossman, P. (1990). *The making of a teacher.* New York: Teachers College Press.

Juran, J. M. (1989). *Juran on leadership for quality: An executive handbook.* New York: Free Press.

Katz, D., & Kahn, R. L. (1978). *The social psychology of organizations.* New York: Wiley.

Keller, G. (1992, May/June). Increasing quality on campus: What should colleges do about the TQM mania? *Change, 24*(3), 48–51.

Kelly, T. (1991, October). Elementary quality. *Quality Progress,* 51–56.

Kohn, A. (1993, September). Turning learning into a business: Concerns about total quality. *Educational Leadership,* 58–61.

Marchese, T. (1989). Managing quality in higher education: An interview with Daniel Seymour. *AAHE Bulletin, 41*(8), 3–7.

Marchese, T. (1992). TQM at Penn: A report on first experiences. *AAHE Bulletin, 45*(3), 3–5, 14.

Meyer, J. W., & Rowan, B. (1978). The structure of educational organizations. In M. W. Meyer (Ed.), *Environments and organizations* (pp. 78–109). Beverly Hills, CA: Sage.

Morgan, G. (1986). *Images of organization.* Beverly Hills, CA: Sage.

Nagy, J., Cotter, M., Erdman, P., Koch, B., Ramer, S., Roberts, N., & Wiley, J. (1993, May/June). Case study number three: Madison, how TQM helped change an admissions process. *Change, 25*(3), 36–41.

Orton, J. D., & Weick, K. E. (1990). Loosely coupled systems: A reconceptualization. *Academy of Management Review, 15*(2), 203–223.

Peterson, P. L. (in press). Learning and teaching mathematical sciences: Implications for inservice programs. In S. Fitzsimmons (Ed.), *Pre-college teacher enhancement in science and mathematics: Status, issues and problems.* Washington, DC: National Science Foundation.

Prawat, R. S. (1989). Teaching for understanding: Three key attributes. *Teaching & Teacher Education, 5,* 315–328.

Schoenfeld, A. (1992). Learning to think mathematically: Problem solving, metacognition, and sense making in mathematics. In D. A. Grouws (Ed.), *Handbook of research on mathematics teaching and learning* (pp. 334–370). New York: Macmillan Co.

Schon, D. A. (1983). *The reflective practitioner: How professionals think in action.* New York: Basic Books.

Scott, W. R. (1992). *Organizations: Rational, natural, and open systems* (3rd ed.). Englewood Cliffs, NJ: Prentice–Hall.

Seymour, D. (1993, May/June). Quality on campus: Three institutions, three beginnings. *Change 25*(3), 14–27.

Seymour, D. T. (1992). *On Q: Causing quality in higher education.* New York: American Council on Education and Macmillan Co.

Shulman, L. (1986). Those who understand: Knowledge growth in teaching. *Educational Researcher, 15*(2), 4–14.

Sitkin, S. B., Sutcliffe, K. M., & Schroeder, R. G. (1994). Distinguishing control from learning in total quality management: A contingency perspective. *Academy of Management Review, 19*(3), 537–564.

Spanbauer, S. J. (1992). *A quality system for education: Using quality and productivity techniques to save our schools.* Milwaukee: ASQC Quality Press.

Spencer, B. A. (1994). Models of organization and total quality management: A comparison and critical evaluation. *Academy of Management Review, 19*(3), 446–471.

Stampen, J. O. (1987). Improving the quality of education: W. Edwards Deming and effective schools. *Contemporary Education Review, 3*(3), 423–433.

Tribus, M. (1991). The application of quality management principles in education, at Mt. Edgecumbe High School, Sitka, Alaska. In American Association of School Administrators, *An introduction to total quality for schools.* Arlington, VA: AASA.

Weick, K. E. (1976). Educational organizations as loosely coupled systems. *Administrative Science Quarterly, 21*, 1–19.

3

Markets for Organizational Reform
Private Education in Post-Communist Poland[1]

Barbara Heyns

While educational reform is scarcely a new hat, market reforms have become prominent feathers in the policy cap. Arguments in favor of educational markets in this country are based partly on economic theories, and partly on comparisons between private and public schools; invariably, however, the deficiencies of U.S. public education are rehearsed. John Chubb and Terry Moe (1990), for example, argue that efforts to create effective schools have failed, and that democratically controlled public education should be abandoned in favor of an open market in schooling. Effective schools are characterized by a cluster of common traits: strong leadership, responsible teachers, clear goals, high standards, and strong parental support. These characteristics are instrumental for fostering and sustaining high achievement; moreover, they tend to be associated with institutional autonomy, such as that found in the private sector. The agenda for public education should be set by parents, teachers, and students, rather than external groups such as state and local bureaucracies, teachers unions, civic authorities, taxpayers, and even business leaders. Market mechanisms are the best way to return educational control to consumers. Schools should be legally autonomous institutions, allowed

---

[1]Information regarding the independent schools movement is based on numerous interviews with STO activists and members of the Ministry of National Education in Warsaw. The philosophy of the movement, and the views of prominent members, are reprinted in various issues of the STO journal, *Edukacja i Dialog*, published since 1989.

Barbara Heyns   Department of Sociology, New York University, New York, New York 10003.

Restructuring Schools: Promising Practices and Policies, edited by Maureen T. Hallinan. Plenum Press, New York, 1995.

to structure their own curriculum, governance, and personnel relations, and "to operate as they see fit."

Institutions, Chubb and Moe argue, whether based on markets or direct political control, "create the basic structures that more or less determine how everything else works," including school performance. Market-based choice would promote effective schools because school autonomy would be one consequence of vesting authority for education in parents, teachers, and students. Autonomy, combined perhaps with competition, would encourage the development of schools that reflected and incorporated values into the curriculum, lending moral authority to the educational project and enhancing student motivation to learn. When bureaucratic authorities control education, moral convictions tend to be either ignored or substantially diluted; values and controversial positions, whether religious or political, tend to be omitted from the curriculum. The problem, however, is that such omissions, while reducing dissension, may also lessen and weaken both student interest and parental support. Controversy can enliven the curriculum; parents would have a bigger stake in schools and educational programs that reinforced their own moral values. A school system without an explicit set of values is, therefore, lacking strong community support and involvement. Giving communities ownership rights in their schools would improve achievement because particular communities could create and support schools reflecting their shared values; strengthening the moral bases of education would enhance student interest and engagement. Schooling would become a "moral endeavor," as it is argued to be in so many Catholic schools in this country (Bryk, Lee, & Holland, 1993). Markets, by increasing diversity and choice, would improve educational outcomes by permitting schools to focus on moral values and by eliciting support from communities of parents that share these values.

The question of values has traditionally been a serious stumbling block for market reforms (Levy, 1986). Arguments in support of diversity implicitly assume either that public schools have no values, or that the values represented are weak, inadequate, or irrelevant to achievement. Moreover, the question of how school organization is related to values, in order to produce achievement, is often unclear. In the work of James Coleman (1990), in contrast, the argument in support of market-based reforms is structural. Public schools do endeavor to involve communities and to live up to pluralist ideals; however, traditional public school values dictated an organizational form that no longer supports these ideals. He describes four educational values once deemed essential for U.S. schools, and then indicates the reasons why these values no longer further either achievement or equality of opportunity. Moreover, he suggests why and how the organizational structures that embodied these values must be changed if we aim to improve educational outcomes.

The four ideals discussed by Coleman are (1) the common school, (2) local control of education, (3) local funding of schools, and (4) *in loco parentis*. These ideals have been decimated, or at least seriously compromised in the United States, by patterns of social change. The common school ideal assumed that all American children—or, more accurately, all children in the United States—must learn and come to share the values on which the Republic was founded, including respect for the democratic process and for individual and property rights; a belief in the fundamental equality of all men (women came later, of course); and a commitment to the responsibilities of citizenship. Education was central to these ideals because, as Thomas Jefferson noted long ago, democracy without an educated citizenry is either a tragedy or a farce.

Local control and local funding were, to some extent, policies of expedience as much as expressions of fundamental ideals. In a dispersed and largely agrarian society, with a federal structure that guaranteed extensive rights to localities rather than the national government, centralized funding and control made little sense either practically or theoretically. Moreover, local control and local funding facilitated the exercise of parental duties and obligations; these values and the schools that embodied them, enabled families to develop trust in the institutions that schooled their children. And this trust was, of course, the basis for *in loco parentis*, the fourth member of the quartet.

For all of the familiar reasons, these values have, over the course of the last century, been challenged or violated, and have gradually eroded. Urbanization and extensive geographic mobility have changed residence patterns, creating more homogeneous neighborhoods, and effectively segregating communities by class, race, and ethnicity. Although schools are larger and more differentiated as well, they tend to serve relatively homogeneous groups. Values—especially, but not exclusively, those dealing with religion—have been effectively eliminated from the public school curriculum. As school systems grew larger, bureaucratic hierarchies lengthened, increasing the stretch between parents as citizens and taxpayers and their children's classrooms. For better or worse, professionals now control education, rather than families; local school boards are subordinated to state departments of education, in terms of both policy and financing. Most important of all, the relations of authority between adults and the young have gradually disintegrated, including the expectations and demands that made education possible.

The problem for Coleman is not with universalism, pluralism, or large meritocratic institutions, at least not directly. Nor does he envision turning clocks back to another historical era. The problem is that individual values have been divorced from modern institutions. The values sought by the common school—quality and equality of educational outcomes—are still considered paramount ideals for U.S. education. But the strong communities, integrated by shared values rather than residence that are basic to this ideal, are missing. And without community support, educational institutions confront insurmountable obstacles to achieving either educational quality or equality.

For Coleman, the elements of a successful reorganization of education would include abandoning obsolete assumptions such as assigning students according to residence and the myth of local control. Restructuring education involves both new ideals and new organizations, and "a pluralistic conception of education, based on communities defined by interests, values, and educational preferences rather than residence; a commitment of parent and student that can provide the school a lever for extracting from students their best efforts; and the educational choice for all that is now available only to those with money" (Coleman, 1990, p. 249). Moreover, with community support, it is possible to "design" achievement-oriented schools by adapting market-based organizational principles as discussed in this volume.

Debates on how market mechanisms would operate in U.S. education are, by necessity, based on the theories of how markets work, and on comparisons between existing public and private schools. Market reforms, however, would represent a staggering institutional transformation, with systemic consequences that are difficult to anticipate. Many European countries support private schools, both financially and politically, but sudden, radical transformations in the logic of funding and educational control are rare. Moreover, private schools are not usually advocated as an essential component of democratic education. For these reasons, comparative data on the experience of countries aiming to democratize and privatize their schools at the same time are relevant to the debates in the United States, perhaps to an even greater extent than contrasts between existing public and private schools.

The empirical portion of this chapter consists of an account of the emergence and development of private education in Poland, a formerly socialist country. Establishing and expanding private education represents an even more radical departure for formerly Communist countries than it would be for the United States. There are, however, clear parallels. Private schools in Eastern Europe emerged as a popular cause and a progressive movement, in opposition to monolithic state structures that, it was argued, could not be reformed otherwise. Parents and community groups, with values strongly opposed to those of mainstream educational bureaucrats, organized a private school movement with broad grass-roots support. These new schools retain democratic values and ideals that bear a striking resemblance to the ethos of the U.S. common school; private schools are argued to enhance democratic education in Eastern Europe because they elicit parental participation and because they embody and promote diverse community values. Private schools are needed because the state has failed to provide either equality or quality (Heyns, 1991, 1992; Kozakiewicz, 1992; Kopp, 1992; Białecki & Heyns, 1993; Heyns & Białecki, 1993; Sadlak, 1994). Unlike market-oriented reforms launched in Europe and Australia, the primary goals have not been to reduce state expenditures or to control the expansion of higher education (Chitty, 1989; Psacharopoulos, 1992; Marginson, 1993; Walford, 1989). The private school movement has without doubt contributed to diversity and educational choice during the last five years. Although the evidence is not conclusive, the new private schools claim with some justification to have improved both quality and equality in schooling. They have surely fostered diverse philosophies of education, new pedagogic methods, and innovative organizational forms that promise to become models for the state schools. Market reforms in Eastern European schools seem to have accomplished many of the goals U.S. reformers endorse. Hence, the experience of the newest market economies may offer perspectives on private schooling and educational reform that are relevant to U.S. policy debates.

RHETORIC AND PHILOSOPHY:
PRIVATE EDUCATION AS REFORM

Since the collapse of communism, private schools and reform movements have emerged at every level of schooling. The goals and the philosophy of these movements resonate with the liberal, market-oriented ideologies that are prevalent in the region. The dominant themes include diversity and pluralism, individual choice and community empowerment, combined with a pronounced hostility to state control. Institutions must be democratized and decentralized; the state monopoly over the provision of goods and services must be broken. Rigid educational hierarchies must be replaced with schools and teachers who are responsive to the needs of individual parents and children. The curriculum needs to be completely overhauled, and all traces of ideological indoctrination must be expunged. Schools must be liberated not only from communist dogma but from the state as a whole; the organization and control of schools should be lodged in democratically organized community groups; families are uniquely competent to monitor the education their children receive. A free market for schooling can replace, or at least supplement, state control. These themes lead directly to the assumption that the only workable strategy for eradicating state control of education is to establish new, independent private schools under the control of autonomous parents' groups.

Społeczne Towarzystwo Oświatowe (STO), which literally means the Social Education Association, is the best example of the school reform movement in Poland. It has had phenomenal success in a very short time in challenging the monopoly of state schools and in creating viable educational alternatives. In 1989, the first year of the organization, 35 nonstate or semistate schools were in operation; in September, 1993, more than 130 "social" schools opened their doors, along with some 400 other independent schools organized by some 36 different local associations and 160 educational foundations. STO currently claims over 10,000 members, as well as many sympathizers (*Edukacja i Dialog*, selected issues, 1989–1994; Skorzynska, 1991; Więckowski, 1994; Zahorska & Sawinski, 1991).

The term "social schools" means private schools, and it is used in contrast to "state." It includes virtually all independent or nonstate education, whether religious or nondenominational. Social is sometimes translated as "civic" or even "public" education. Only a handful of the new private schools are wholly supported by private funds, however, but all proclaim the right to establish autonomous educational institutions, subject to democratically elected governing bodies. Private schools can, under the new Polish laws, be run by "nonstate self-governments, legal or natural persons," but virtually all of the new schools are still fiscally dependent on the state.[2] In practice, social schools are run by foundations, private companies, the Church or one of the various convents, and individuals.

The style and the rhetoric of STO owe a great deal to the political opposition in Poland. Virtually all of the founders of the organization had been activists in Solidarity. As an organization, STO was the result of the decisions made in 1987, to try to register an association of parents explicitly claiming the right to control the education of their children and to establish private schools. These rights were, in theory, guaranteed by Polish law, under a statute passed in 1961; but official permission was needed in order to exercise such rights, and such permission had never been granted before. Neither the Ministry of National Education nor the 23 persons who signed the petition requesting approval believed, in 1987, that an organization like STO would be allowed to exist.

---

[2]In January, 1991, the Minister of National Education agreed that the state should subsidize social schools, "up to" half the current costs per child in the state schools in the region; schools sponsored by foundations or business concerns do not qualify for state subsidy, although denominational schools do. Tuition in STO schools, like costs, has escalated more quickly than inflation.

When the Ministry turned down the petition for registration, however, the fledgling organization appealed the decision through the courts. After a brief legal battle, STO, and two affiliated groups in Wrocław and the Malopolska region, won their suit; in December, 1988, they were formally registered with the intent of establishing private schools. The stage was set for the first nonstate alternative schools.

A petition requesting official permission to open a private school was submitted to the Ministry of National Education in June, 1988. The Ministry responded quickly and predictably, rejecting the petition and arguing that it would be against the Polish Constitution to collect fees for education. Anna Jeziorna, the Krakow parent who had submitted the petition, then appealed the decision to the High Administrative Court. This case attracted considerable attention; it was the first time in which a group of concerned parents had challenged the right of the Ministry to determine where and how their children would be educated. The timing was, of course, fortuitous. Plans for the round table talks were under way, and Solidarity was about to be reinstated as a key actor in negotiations between the state and civil society. The impending political changes were not lost on the legal system. On February 23, 1989, at almost the same moment that the round table talks were beginning, the High Court handed down its decision: the administration had been wrong to deny the petition. Parents did have the legal right to open private schools in the People's Republic of Poland. As it turned out, the right to establish private schools would outlive the People's Republic of Poland.

The "social" or civic schools take democratization to be both their fundamental purpose and their principal grievance with state education. The dominant impetus behind STO, and a central motif in the new STO schools, is democratic education. Although STO does not endorse any particular educational philosophy, except democratic pluralism, STO schools share many basic assumptions with progressive education in the West. Schools should be open institutions, fostering community participation and parental involvement. Parents should be actively involved in the education of their children at every stage; teachers should attend to individual differences among children and address the needs of particular students individually. Education should preclude all forms of dogma and ideology. The surest way to change the passive attitudes and conformist behavior associated with 40 years of socialism is to establish new and altogether different kinds of institutions. The curriculum must be modernized and upgraded, although this does not mean that standards should be lowered or that the curriculum should be watered down intellectually. The parents who have so ardently supported these new schools do not want their children to be at a competitive disadvantage with the graduates of state schools.

CURRICULUM, COMMUNITY, AND EDUCATION CONTROL

The predominant objectives of STO are democratic schools with extensive parental participation. Teaching methods, therefore, tend to be more important issues than content; while the schools are diverse and often quite innovative, the academic substance of what is taught and learned has not changed a great deal. Local educational authorities, or the *Curatoreum*, still have responsibility for reviewing and monitoring educational programs; all Polish schools must offer the minimum core curriculum set by the Ministry of National Education. Curricular modifications most often consist of reorganizing and integrating course work, rather than altering the subject matter. New courses are added, but traditional subjects are not abandoned. Entirely new courses, particularly in civics or the social and political sciences, are common, but the basic curriculum in STO schools is dominated by classical, university-oriented preparation, with more emphasis on the humanities than on math or science.

Courses in STO schools are similar to those offered in the best Polish academies, although often with a more practical twist. Modern languages are emphasized, and students are expected to learn at least two in depth. English, German, and French are, not surprisingly, more popular than Russian. Courses in democratic procedure are a common curricular addition, although many schools aim to instill democratic participation and ideals directly. In one school, students organized and ran a mock parliamentary government for the school, complete with elections and legislative initiatives. On balance, however, and despite liberated practices, STO secondary schools are most like the traditional elite *lyceum.* STO parents do not anticipate much change in the rigorous examination system for admission to higher education in Poland, and the vast majority expect their children to attend the University.

In addition to a broad university preparation, civic schools often incorporate forms of education that were simply unavailable under state socialism, even in the best *lyceum.* In sports, for example, several schools offer tennis and swimming.[3] The best socialist schools, in contrast, gave students soccer and gymnastics. Soccer, like most team sports, requires minimal individual coaching and much less expensive equipment for each student. Gymnastics can be taught in an empty room furnished with a few mats; when the weather is inclement, these courses provided good indoor exercise, but at relatively low cost. The civic schools prefer to offer

[3]One Civic High School in Warsaw supplements the sports curriculum by offering "swimming, skiing, skating, horseback riding and the rudiments of self-defense" (*Edukacja i Dialog,* 26/27, March/April 1991, p. 31).

individual athletic activities, and especially those that would have been considered lavish "frills" under socialism. Parents have high aspirations for their children, even when they lack elite backgrounds themselves, and there is considerable pressure to provide expensive courses and equipment, even when they do not necessarily enhance achievement or democratic process. Concerns with status enter both the formal and the informal curriculum in this way; civic schools aspire to offer their students both everything state schools have, as well as everything that was unavailable previously (Nowakowska, 1993).

The most essential difference in teaching methods is the change in the relationships between teachers and students, and the strong emphasis on individual attention in virtually all of the didactic materials. Peer relations are also encouraged, and informal discussion groups are common. Teachers are encouraged, indeed required, to give attention and empathy to each and every child. Classes are smaller, and teachers much more supportive than those in the state schools; even the best state schools are viewed as excessively punishing and authoritarian. The STO schools have apparently been particularly successful with hyperactive or rebellious children, for whom the regular state system would have spelled doom.

The STO schools make uncommon demands on parents, both financially and in terms of social support. Some of the STO schools made parental participation a requirement for admission; others simply could not exist without it. The Statutes of the First Community School in Warsaw, for example, make the issue plain:

> Parents should participate actively in school life. Through their delegates to the School Advisory Committee, parents will influence the process of teaching and education and the welfare of their children. The school treats parents as the advocates of the family, it respects parental power and the right of parents to supervise school activities.[4]

The social schools—and the "Koła," or "circles" that organize them—have managed to create and support idealistic private schools that embody both democratic decision-making and high levels of achievement. Funding, however, is another matter. Private school expenses have risen much faster than inflation, and many parents are hard-pressed to pay tuition. For the moment, the STO schools seem to have succeeded in maintaining the fragile balance between partial state funding and parental control, but this may not be a stable formula in the long run. Participation is high, and both parents and students are much more satisfied with private

---

[4]This passage is taken from Article Nine.

education than their peers in public schools (Nowakowska, 1993; Białecki & Heyns, 1993; Skorzynska, 1991; Zahorska & Sawinski, 1991). STO schools have, moreover, become a model for democratic education and egalitatrian participation. The question remains, however, whether private schools can survive the market transition in Poland.

CONTEMPORARY PROBLEMS: FINANCING THE MOVEMENT, STAFFING THE SCHOOLS

Tuition in the new private sector varies enormously. Although education under socialism was "free," in point of fact student subsidies had been inadequate for some years; parents were regularly charged for meals, books, and all special courses or outings. The estimated costs of education rose 36.3% between 1989 and 1993 in Poland, higher than in any other country in the region (UNICEF, 1993). These costs are over and above the estimated 20% of all educational expenses that Polish parents paid in 1989. Moreover, between 1989 and 1993, real incomes fell to less than 70% of their 1989 value.

Polish private schools have managed to find various sources of funding, but it is fair to say that all of them are beleaguered by rising costs and limited revenues. The first Solidarity governments passed legislation in 1991 that gave state funding to accredited private schools—at the rate of half of the costs of education within their respective educational districts, or *gmina*. Since STO schools tend to be located in urban areas, subsidies tend to be in excess of the national average. At the same time, the real costs of education have risen much faster than inflation. STO schools often began in someone's home; they then renovated space, rented parish buildings, or in some cases offered classes in the state schools. At the outset, many schools could rely on legal, accounting, and administrative help from volunteers; schools also received in-kind contributions from parents or community groups when they started, such as desks and school furniture, books, and even microcomputers; such donations do not pay rent or teachers' salaries, however. Teachers in the STO schools make slightly higher salaries and have smaller classes than in state schools; if the school is to be successful, however, teachers must be willing to spend enormous quantities of time and energy working with individual students and meeting parents. Hence, their hours tend to be longer, and their interpersonal contacts more intense. Private schools do not provide teachers with either "Teacher's Rights" or with salaries and promotion schedules specified in the "Teacher's Chart" pertaining to state schools. Despite donations, state resources, and the enthusiasm of volunteers, post-Communist private schools have trouble keeping the costs of education within the reach of many families; moreover, both parents and administrators were at times naive about how much money education costs.

As the market transition wears on, many more parents are financially pinched and many teachers become aware of alternative employment possibilities. The staff was willing to make sacrifices for the pleasure of teaching in and belonging to an STO *koła*; at present, the turnover rate among teachers is higher than in state schools. State schools do not expect teaching to be a full-time activity; fewer contact hours are required and there are many opportunities to moonlight. The skills that STO schools want to offer—foreign languages or knowledge of computers, for example—can be sold in the marketplace for much more per hour than any school could pay. It is hard to fault teachers who earn less than $300 a month from accepting fees for private, informal teaching; at the same time, a school that aspires to provide individual attention to all pupils, that has several meetings a month with parents, and that organizes a large number of extracurricular events and outings, cannot compete with the state schools in terms of pedagogic autonomy or limited work hours.

A second and related problem is the excessive demands of parents and students in the schools. STO teachers must make a large commitment to the school and the community, or *koła*; they must also negotiate the perilous border between responding to parents who believe they "own" the schools that they pay for, and are thus the employers of the teachers they hire, and reaching out to include parents who would prefer to delegate educational business entirely to the school. STO schools face spiraling costs, and teachers are stretched to the limit, even if they manage to provide competitive salaries.

Recent issues of *Edukacja i Dialog*, the STO journal, discussed the limitations of "dialogue," and the lack of understanding many parents have regarding educational programs. The schools are caught between the need to provide the "core curriculum" common to all accredited schools, and the need to offer something special, something exceptional, to parents who are being asked to pay ever-increasing costs. STO schools each contribute 1% of their base budget to the central organization, but this organization is under pressure to develop new curricula, provide outreach to international organizations and foundations, and to arrange exchanges, motivational seminars, and conferences for teachers and parents. Some schools have formed alliances with other organizations, nationally and internationally, but most rely on the central organization for their contacts. STO is also asked to arbitrate conflicts between parents and teachers, the most common concerning questions of educational control. Schools typically resolve such conflicts by separating questions of administrative responsibility, which parents share with teachers, from didactic responsibilities, which belong exclusively to teachers. These problems are perhaps inevitable in any school that aims to involve parents directly in the education of their children; STO schools solve them better than most, but at the cost of some enthusiasm and spontaneity. In 1993, Wojciech Starzynski, the president of STO, described the evolution of STO as involving "less enthusiasm and more professionalism."

Private education, despite the problems, is still a growth industry in Poland, particularly in secondary schools. Elementary schools are only a small part of the educational market share, with less than 0.3% of all primary students in private schools. Primary education has, in fact, been massively decentralized since 1991; many local governments have taken over the responsibility for managing elementary schools, and now absorb and distribute educational resources from the central government. Secondary schools are more expensive, yet the private sector accounts for a much larger share of the age cohort, enrolling nearly 4% of all secondary students in 1992–1993. STO schools are among the most selective, although they no longer dominate the market for private education. Table 1 provides the most recent published data on enrollments by level and type of control. As these data indicate, private secondary schools now constitute about 14.4% of all schools; including the schools that are locally controlled, 16% of Polish secondary institutions are not controlled by the central Ministry of National Education.

The success of STO has meant not only imitation, but increased competition. To this issue we now turn.

Table 1. Enrollments in Private and Nonstate Schooling by Control and Level, Poland 1992–1993[a]

	Primary		Secondary	
	Schools	Students	Schools	Students
Total	16,841	5,213,173	1,511	555,379
State schools	14,309	4,338,544	1,276	532,615
Nonstate	2,532	874,629	235	22,784
Local	2,302	857,098	17	4,747
Civic	156	12,806	131	10,830
Church	10	1,032	32	4,407
Other	64	3,693	55	2,800

[a]Source: *Olwiata i Wychowanie w Roku szkolnym* 1992/93. Selected Tables. Warsaw: Główny Urzad Statystyczny, 1993.

ACHIEVEMENT AND VALUES: THE PERILS OF DIVERSITY

The growth of STO since 1989 has been phenomenal, an "avalanche" of new private schools and intense educational activity. At present, some 600 private schools are estimated to exist, and STO is only one of several different networks supporting private education. Alternatives to the STO model of education have sprung up, and informal ranking schemes for the new schools proliferate. The most visible schools advertise their staff and curricula, as well as their fees; each new school seems keen to outdo those that came before. The range of both fees and educational opportunities is enormous. In Warsaw, one school with the unlikely name of *Enigma* is alleged to have only two students and to charge $1000 a month in tuition, in addition to registration fees of $1500. "In snobbish circles," commented one astute Warsaw observer, "education has become a status symbol as important as the make of car one drives" (Nowakowska, 1993).

Although there are as yet no definitive studies of private school achievement, there is evidence that the STO schools surpass both public sector schools as well as other private competitors. The first cohort of STO graduates are scheduled to enter university programs this fall, which could provide a crucial test of their effectiveness. In Poland, there are still a number of regional and citywide contests for students that can and often are used to judge schools. Social Lyceum No. 14, for example, is reported to have scored remarkably high on a Polish language and literature test conducted in 19 Warsaw schools last year. In the spring of 1993, for the first time, an STO graduate won the contest for the best maturation exam paper, rather than a graduate of one of the renowned public lyceum (Nowakowska, 1993).

The equality of educational outcomes is also problematic with respect to Polish private schools. On the one hand, classroom participation and the relationships between teachers and students and between the school and the community are undoubtedly much more egalitarian than in state schools. On the other hand, the majority of STO schools were founded with the idea of attending to and even increasing individual differences. It would not be too surprising to observe unequal educational outcomes as a result. The schools claim, and a great many Polish educators concede, that private schools have improved the achievement of their students dramatically, and have done so by creating vital, egalitarian learning environments without sacrificing high standards.

STO schools have maintained their commitment to pluralistic and democratic education; however, questions of values and choice are somewhat more problematic. STO schools endorse liberal, humanistic values;

open discussion of ethical and political issues are essential to the curricula. Religious values, however, were generally neglected. The STO schools aimed to be ecumenical and enlightened, and to reserve judgment on questions of faith. When the Polish parliament voted to mandate religious classes in all state schools, the private schools were in something of a quandary. Instead of being an ally against the state, the Church was suddenly teaching in every public school. In the early years, STO schools could count on the support of the Catholic Church, and many schools depended on space in church buildings and other contributions from the local parish. Now, the Church has become an alternative educational provider. In many STO schools, the issue of religion in schools became enormously divisive. Although STO schools and the organization as a whole have retained a secular orientation, conflicts over religious education have often been intense. Although formally religion classes are voluntary, the majority of Polish students in both the public and private sector attend.

STO parents, who naturally place a high value on educational diversity and choice, complain that religious training in the schools substantially reduces their options, despite the fact that families are overwhelmingly Catholic and few disagree openly with the teachings of the Church. Traditionally, parents paid for religious classes outside of school, and they actively sought a priest who shared their moral values. Now, a priest or lay instructor is assigned to every school, and parents have little say over what will be taught. The Polish clergy varies quite a lot in their social and political attitudes, and for many STO parents, these values are as important as high educational standards. A conservative priest, for example, with intolerant views on birth control, divorce, or abortion, can seriously undermine family values, at least those held by many STO parents. These issues have yet to be resolved, although at present, the question of family values seems to have encouraged STO schools to avoid many questions about values, and to have become even less religious than before. Ironically, the shared values that buttress private education in Poland are secular, rather than religious. Education in the public sector, in contrast, offers an explicit moral agenda.

Advocates of private education in the United States point to the lack of values as one of the major deficiencies. Moreover, values are argued to be one source of higher achievement levels observed in Catholic private schools. Yet compulsory religious classes are inherently divisive, even in Catholic communities. Strong moral values may serve to enhance achievement among students, or they can lead to dogmatic thinking that restricts free inquiry and creativity. The critical question would seem to be how moral issues are addressed within a particular normative order.

Both Polish private schools and U.S. Catholic schools are alleged to be successful at educating their pupils because they create strong communities based on shared values, and it seems clear that in both cases, distinctive core values define the school context and delimit the boundary between private and state schools. However, the particular values described and the manner in which they influence achievement are quite different. Bryk *et al.* (1993) have argued that Catholic schools are effective because schooling is viewed as a moral endeavor; values are an explicit part of the curriculum, and there is "equal concern for what students know and for whether they develop the disposition to use their intellectual capacities to effect a greater measure of social justice" (p. 302). The Polish private schools cannot be characterized as amoral or as unconcerned about issues of social justice; at the same time, in Poland these values are represented as quite separate from the teachings of the Catholic Church. The moral climate in STO schools is based on a democratic philosophy that is antiauthoritarian in the extreme; respect for individual differences and for the secular traditions of the enlightenment are central, rather than the disciplinary regime that is enforced in the public schools. The Polish private schools tolerate disorder and encourage intellectual contention; they view the state system as producing docile and passive citizens, conforming rather than questioning or reforming the public order. The sources of achievement are argued to be individual creativity, and not compliance with a rigorous, structured curriculum. Discipline and order are much less important in these schools than intellectual and artistic freedom; the schools would rather foster disorder than rely on an external moral code to regulate student behavior. Ethics and morality are subjects for discussion, debate, and controversy; but the conception of an external moral code that keeps order and dictates student behavior within the school is anathema to the STO philosophy. Values, however, animate and inspire the STO schools, and they are perceived in stark contrast to those embodied in state education; moreover, shared values are considered the cement that binds STO communities together. However, STO schools separate religious beliefs from educational values, rather than equate them.

In Poland, school discipline is not yet considered a problem; in contrast, convincing students to speak out, to take intellectual risks, and make choices about their future are far more problematic. Polish private schools have undoubtedly expanded educational choice for both students and their families, by removing rigid strictures on thought and behavior. Achievement, however, is equated with freedom, and not discipline and order. The Catholic sector is U.S. private education is thought to be more effective because discipline is enforced, drugs and deviance are sanctioned, absenteeism is low, and homework is required. But even granting that these rules are advantageous for achievement, and that they distinguish Catholic schools in the United States, it does not follow that private education means increased discipline, or that discipline is necessary or sufficient for high achievement. Markets are generally thought to increase choice, but by most accounts, U.S. schools have institutionalized excessive choice, at least for students. It is simply fallacious to equate market mechanisms—which imply expanded choice, more diversity, and increased competition—with greater demands placed on students, unless we also assume that private schools are more likely to enforce discipline and restrict student options. While this might be the case, it is far from automatic.

Polish private schools have many appealing characteristics. But they also can serve to remind us that the links between values and achievement in education are very complex. Moral issues divide communities as often as they unite them; effective parental involvement requires time and effort, even in the private sector where consumers are presumed sovereign; diversity and choice can mean either freedom or coercion, for either students or their parents; private schools can be distinguished, and seek to distinguish themselves, from the public sector on many dimensions other than achievement.

COMMUNITY, ORGANIZATIONS, AND THE MARKETPLACE

Educational reform in Eastern Europe presents a curious paradox. On the one hand, many of the changes in progress resemble those advocated as a means to improve education in the United States and other Western countries. On the other, the organizational goals are precisely reversed. In Eastern Europe as elsewhere, reform efforts are no doubt "highly interrelated with concurrent events in the cultural, social, economic and political realms" (Merritt & Coombs, 1977, p. 249). The themes that dominate the discourse echo those that are heard in other European capitals: educational management should be decentralized and localized; curricula should be streamlined; and costs must be controlled.[5] These terms acquire a radical new meaning, however, when applied to Eastern Europe, where reformers tend to reject any and all blueprints offered by state planners.

Private education has become an integral component of reform in both Poland and the United States; in the two countries, private schools

---

[5]See Limage (1989) and the special issue on *Education in a Changing Europe, Comparative Education Review* 36, 1 (February, 1992).

offer alternative models of what public schools should be like. In Poland and the United States, the private sector appears to outperform the public sector in both the quality and equality of outcomes, and to engender greater effort and higher levels of satisfaction among students, parents, and faculty. Enhanced student achievement is an objective of reform in both systems, and in both countries private education is proposed as the last-ditch remedy for a failed public sector; but arguments in support of private schools are premised on very different conceptions of how public schools have failed. Moreover, pedagogic strategies differ and the theories linking school organization to student performance are quite distinct.

It is worthwhile to examine explicitly the structural and pedagogic theories of student achievement put forth by advocates of private schools in Poland and the United States. The contribution of Jim Coleman in this collection and elsewhere provides a reasonable beginning for such a contrast.

STO schools originated in and serve to perpetuate distinctive communities, like many U.S. private schools. Polish private schools stem from the politics of opposition, however, rather than a threatened religious community; and, like U.S. Catholic schools, they serve to maintain cohesive, communal supports even though that community is less endangered than before. Structurally, private schools constitute "functional communities," in the sense implied by Coleman and others, in both countries (Coleman & Hoffer, 1987; Coleman, Hoffer, & Kilgore, 1982). However, in Poland, the function of the bonds that link parents to their children's school is not to replace deteriorating family relations or to create "intergenerational closure." In Poland, most parents still assert and sustain strong affect and authority relations with their children, quite apart from schooling. The schools may reinforce familial relations, but they do not replace them; schools are an expression of community, rather than the primary source or a substitute. STO schools aspired to create an alternative form of community, one that the Poles refer to as "civil society." This community certainly does encourage "teachers to work hard at their uncertain profession and for students to commit energy to learning subject matter whose immediate utility may be far from obvious" (Bryk et al., 1993, p. 276); but the values shared by community members stress democratic political virtues, rather than communal or spiritual ones. Moreover, these values foster an altogether different philosophy of education, and very different organizational forms. It is paradoxical that market ideologies can lead to such disparate organizational forms and pedagogies.

Educational reform in Poland has led to a radical restructuring of school organization in the private sector. While the schools do not dismiss the importance of student achievement, in certain respects, the process has aimed to dismantle both the traditional incentives for effort and the traditional bases of authority. The rhetoric of free market institutions is a fundamental component of the private school ideology in Poland, but in many respects, the actual organization of the schools belies the rhetoric. The schools describe their pedagogy as liberal, but the meaning of this term is found in the expression of individual differences rather than in increased competition or greater efficiency. The organization of educational incentives and rewards described by Coleman in this volume would, in Poland, be taken as a description of the socialist system of education, in dramatic contrast to the various forms of private education that flourish. In Poland, private education means "free" schools, in spirit if not cost; as the examples given above indicate, STO schools resemble U.S. alternative schools much more than either the public or Catholic sectors.

Post-Communist schools in Poland are fiercely opposed to autocratic education, whether it is "administratively driven" or "outcome-oriented." Both approaches to schooling are viewed as impinging on choice and individual freedom. In higher education, the thrust of reforms has been to increase electives and student choice, to liberalize requirements, and to reduce penalties for changing fields of concentration or hours of course work, even at the cost of standardized curricula. The concept described by Coleman as "backward policing," in which receiving institutions set the standards for graduates of preparatory institutions, finds little favor among Polish academic reformers. The organizational structure of an "autocratic model of education" is described in one well-publicized report, *Academic Economic Education in Change,* as something "between a factory and a bureaucratic office, with a hierarchical system of authority subordinating students to teachers, teachers to Deans, and faculty to central committees" (Beksiak, Chmielecka, Grzelońska, 1992, p. 8). The goal of education in autocratic systems, according to the authors, is the production of certified degree-holders; the stress is "exclusively laid on the product, not on the intellectual development of a human being" (Beksiak *et al.,* 1992, p. 8). In an autocratic school system, students who discontinue their studies for awhile, or who drop out altogether, are viewed as "wasted raw material." Formal requirements, the assignment of particular tasks, and a host of "assessment systems [that] evaluate student progress and knowledge, by reducing examination marks to a common measure via appropriate coefficients" are condemned as well (Beksiak *et al.,* 1992, p. 8). In an autocratic system, given levels of education are subordinated to higher grades, and schools are obligated to educate a given number of students for fixed positions, whatever their interests or abilities. Teaching hours are imposed by central authorities, mapping out the sequence of courses and educational requirements for both faculty and students.

Despite superficial similarities to the "achievement by design" school constructed by Coleman, the autocratic model so detested by these reformers depicts socialist schools under the communist regime. Reforming education consists, therefore, in dismantling the structure of external regulation. The "major, albeit negative, task [for reformers] is to remove—or at least undermine—the whole aggregate of the above mentioned rules," according to these authors (Beksiak *et al.*, 1992, p. 9).

In Poland, curiously, free market ideologies are seen as dictating an organizational form quite unlike that of either a business or a factory. The preferred organizational form is that of a "voluntary contract between student and faculty" for the purpose of pursuing common interests through joint action. Higher education should "be open to everyone who has appropriate preparation, is willing to study and is able to pay for services" (Beksiak *et al.*, 1992, p. 41). Universities are and should remain a "public utility," however, which implies that state funding is required. Universities should not, however, allow their mission or their organization to be controlled by any particular state agency. Higher education should, however, be "generally available and not profit-oriented"; support for schools should therefore be support for students, through vouchers or scholarships. As the authors note,

> If one agrees that making higher schools available to all citizens is a socially desirable goal, which seems natural, the question arises how to reconcile the paid schools with the fact that incomes of numerous citizens make the schools inaccessible to them? . . . The solution of the problem consists in directing state help right to the individuals without making higher schools a kind of social welfare agency [p. 78]

In a separate chapter, the authors also reject an accountability structure that would determine their fees according to the achievement of their graduates. Education should be based on individual choice, and not on fixed criteria for either access or outcomes. State-determined prerequisites or goals are viewed as unacceptable for higher education, even when the state pays the fees. Students, and the institutions themselves, should be allowed to choose their instructors, to pursue independent interests, and to develop their capacities quite apart from price or market demand, and quite independently of either social need or levels of achievement.

These proposals are put forth as desirable organizational characteristics, and quite compatible with free markets. The responsibility for both setting and maintaining educational standards is reserved to educational institutions. These obligations, combined with the duty to conduct their financial affairs responsibly, "according to market principles," constitute the only restraints on educational autonomy. The schools should be allowed to decide for themselves whether to invest in their own improvement or to reduce their fees. So long as the schools and professors maintain high professional standards, they should be allowed to profit from the market for their services. Educational achievement is neither a criteria for funding nor a standard for evaluating outcomes. For students, schooling seems to be governed by *caveat emptor*. Concerns with appropriate mechanisms for allocating rewards and incentives, as discussed by Jim Coleman in this volume, are never mentioned. The assumption is that intellectual effort is its own reward, for both the faculty and students; achievement is not an outcome that requires a special motivational structure. The faculty is not expected to exercise power over students, except for the authority resulting from their competency and knowledge; and neither the government nor the consumer is allowed to influence the institutions. Although the authors acknowledge that primary schools and students may need more direction, this organizational model for free market education is considered adequate for secondary schools as well.

One could argue that educational reformers in Poland are simply naive, and lack sufficient knowledge of the social organization of achievement. Polish educational institutions have not had much experience with the "corrupt bargain" that can be struck between faculty and students with respect to academic work. Alternatively, this organizational form provides many advantages for educational institutions. The free market model advocated surely maximizes professional autonomy and control; if followed, educational institutions, and the faculty who run them, would enjoy considerable freedom from regulation and supervision. In education as in other services, markets are quite compatible with a system that is controlled by and for professionals.

Professional self-interest, however, is only part of an explanation. The organizational model deemed appropriate for the emerging market economy puts a very high premium on knowledge and achievement, quite apart from mechanisms of control. If achievement is not its own reward for both faculty and students, the system will not work. Moreover, the overarching assumption is that any system, whether based on economic incentives and rewards or on bureaucratic dictate and accountability, will work only when achievement is valued for its own sake, as an end and not merely the means to some other goal. Polish educational reformers assume that achievement has intrinsic rewards, and that reforms will be implemented within a cultural context that values achievement highly. Within such a context, it seems likely that virtually any organizational form supported by the community will work. Without such a context, both students and their teachers will resist incentives and controls, and the educational system will be inadequate and dysfunctional.

Thus, the logic of Polish reforms brings us full circle; achievement as a value drives the system, and not markets or the organizational structure. Polish reforms may or may not live up to the hopes of reformers; comparative data serve, however, to remind us that markets and bureaucratic hierarchies are embedded in a system of cultural values. Educational reforms, whether structural or pedagogic, and the outcomes that they produce, are a reflection of these values.

CONCLUSIONS AND IMPLICATIONS

Educational reform is a complicated and paradoxical phenomenon in even one society, much less in two. I doubt that it is possible to deduce lessons for U.S. educational reform based on the Polish experience; however, the comparative data do suggest that some cautionary observations are in order, and perhaps some speculation on market reforms. First, private education in both societies serves to mediate and permit expression for values that are lacking in the public sector; in both societies private schools create diversity and allow choice, much as the market model implies. However, the organizational arrangements, the methods for financing, and the content of the curriculum do not "cause" student achievement. High achievement can be found in schools with either rigorous or permissive disciplinary structures, with demanding or lenient faculty, and governed by diverse moral and ethical codes. The common causal link, and the necessary connection between values and achievement, would seem to derive from the fact that private schools in both countries create and depend on communities with shared values, whether religious or secular. The configuration of values found in U.S. Catholic schools produces disciplined and orderly schools with a record of high achievement, but there is every reason to suppose that progressive schools, with more disorderly classrooms and a less structured curriculum, also produce achievement, provided the schools are supported by a community that values it. Private schools express diverse values, and they can provide the opportunity to link achievement values to diverse pedagogic and organizational forms; but the forms of social capital that support enhanced achievement are a function of the community, rather than the specifics of pedagogy or organization that are created.

The moral that I draw from the literature on values and education is similar to that often drawn from the null findings of studies contrasting diverse curricular programs, or experiments with diverse work groups such as the Hawthorne studies (Jones, 1990). The factors that improve performance are not found in the content of particular programmatic interventions; instead, productivity in school and the workplace depends on the quality of attention devoted to the subjects and the value placed on their tasks. Apathy or indifference reduces student motivation to learn much more than incentives or the imposition of demands can increase it. Social psychologists have shown that self-esteem predicts high achievement and that, among adolescents, self-esteem can be stifled or suppressed by parental indifference; in fact, indifference is argued to be more corrosive than harsh criticism or overt punishment (Rosenberg, 1965). A community with shared values and a shared commitment to education motivates students, thereby extracting greater effort and enhanced achievement, irrespective of the organizational context or the material taught.

It follows that communities that do not value achievement, whatever their social organization, and however they structure incentives and rewards for learning and teaching, will not encourage students to realize their full potential. Such a conclusion implies some pessimism about U.S. educational reform, whether based on market mechanisms or bureaucratic control. Perhaps in the last analysis, societies get the kinds of schools they want or deserve. Certainly contemporary communities in the United States have not mobilized to improve their schools successfully, despite ominous international comparisons and the plethora of dire warnings that have been issued. Americans may have come to prefer the "shopping mall high school," offering such an excess of choice to the consumer. Or perhaps we have moved "beyond credentials." As Martin Trow (1973) observed years ago, mass education at the secondary level fundamentally changed the primary school curriculum, from one emphasizing academic preparation and competitive achievement to one stressing social promotion and the social adjustment of students. By analogy, this argument would imply that as higher education becomes nearly universal, the selective function of secondary schools is lost, and the high school takes on a different role. Perhaps a wealthy society, like the United States, can afford a prolonged "liberal" education, an education that is, fundamentally, *laissez-faire*. Perhaps students are not ill-served by undemanding schools; many do seek the knowledge and the credentials they need when the need is perceived. I am skeptical, however, that either "moral values" or "market discipline" will provide the incentives necessary for more community involvement in schools. And without community interest and support, restructuring incentives for teachers and students, much less rediscovering traditional values, are unlikely to succeed in increasing achievement.

REFERENCES

Beksiak, J., Chmielecka, E., & Grzelońska, U. (1992). *Academic economic education in change.* Warsaw, Poland: Stefan Batory Foundation.

Białecki, I., & Heyns, B. (1993). Educational attainment, the status of women, and the private school movement in Poland. In V. M. Moghadam (Ed.), *Democratic reform and the position of women in transitional economies* (pp. 110–134). London: Oxford University Press (Clarendon).

Bryk, A. S., Lee, V. E., & Holland, P. B. (1993). *Catholic schools and the common good.* Cambridge, MA: Harvard University Press.

Chitty, C. (1989). *Towards a new education system: The victory of the new right?* London: Falmer Press.

Chubb, J., & Moe, T. (1990). *Politics, markets, and America's schools.* Washington, DC: Brookings Institution.

Coleman, J. S. (1990. *Equality and achievement in education.* Boulder, CO: Westview Press.

Coleman, J. S., & Hoffer, T. (1987). *Public and private high schools: The impact of communities.* New York: Basic Books.

Coleman, J. S., Hoffer, T., & Kilgore, S. (1982). *High school achievement.* New York: Basic Books.

Heyns, B. (1991). *Church and/or state: Educational policy in post-Communist Poland.* Paper presented at the Hungarian Sociological Association meetings, June 24–28, Budapest.

Heyns, B. (1992). School reform in Poland. *Wisconsin State Journal,* Sunday edition, Education and Culture Section, January 26, pp. 1–3.

Heyns, B., & Białecki, I. (1993). Educational inequalities in postwar Poland. In Y. Shavit & H.-P. Blossfeld (Eds.), *Persistent inequality: Changing educational attainment in thirteen countries* (pp. 303–335). Boulder, CO: Westview Press.

Jones, S. R. G. (1990). Worker interdependence and output: The Hawthorne studies reevaluated. *American Sociological Review, 55,* 2 (April), 176–190.

Kopp, B. von. (1992). The Eastern European revolution and education in Czechoslovakia. *Comparative Education Review, 36,* 1 (February), 101–122.

Kozakiewicz, M. (1992). Educational transformation initiated by the Polish *Perestroika. Comparative Education Review, 36,* 1 (February), 91–100.

Levy, D. C. (Ed.). (1986). *Private education: Studies in choice and public policy.* London: Oxford University Press.

Limage, L. J. (1989). Survey of events: 1988—Western Europe. *Comparative Education Review, 33,* 2 (May), 278–280.

Marginson, S. (1993). *Education and public policy in Australia.* London: Cambridge University Press.

Merritt, R. L., & Coombs, F. S. (1977). Politics and educational reform. *Comparative Education Review, 21* (June/October).

Nowakowska, E. (1993). Z ulicy na bruk. *Polityka, 12,* 1872 (March 20), 1940–41.

Psacharopoulos, G. (1992). The privatization of education in Europe, essay review. *Comparative Education Review, 36,* 1 (February), 114–124.

Rosenberg, M. (1965). *Society and the adolescent self-image.* Princeton, NJ: Princeton University Press. [Also published by Wesleyan Press, Middletown, CT, 1989].

Sadlak, J. (1994). The Emergence of a Diversified System: The State/Private Predicament in Transforming Higher Education in Romania, *European Journal of Education, 29*(1), 13–23.

Skorzynska, K. (1991, June). *Report on the situation of non-state schools in Poland.* Independent Department of Innovation and Non-State Schools, Ministry of National Education.

Trow, M. (1973). *Problems in the transition from elite to mass higher education.* Berkeley: Carnegie Commission on Higher Education.

UNICEF, United Nations Children's Fund. (1993). *Public policy and social conditions: Central and Eastern Europe in transition.* Florence, Italy: International Child Development Centre.

Walford, G. (Ed.). (1989). *Private schools in ten countries: Policy and practice.* London: Routledge.

Więckowski, S. (1994). Mniej Entuzjazmu—Więcej Profesjonalizmu: Rozmowa z Wojciechem Starzynskim, prezesem STO [Less enthusiasm–more professionalism: An interview with Wojciech Starzynski, president of STO]. *Edukacja i Dialog, 3* (56), March.

Zahorska, M., & Sawinski, Z. (1991). *Szkoły Społeczne na tle szkolpanstwowych: Raport z badania ankietowego* [Social schools for everyone: Report of survey results]. Study conducted by Demoskop for the Ministry of National Education, Independent Department of Innovation and Non-State Schools, Warsaw, 1990.

4

Lessons from Catholic High Schools on Renewing Our Educational Institutions[1]

Anthony S. Bryk

During the 1980s, a spate of research studies and newspaper stories chronicled the unusual effectiveness of Catholic high schools. These accounts claimed that Catholic schools do a better job of engaging students in schooling, have lower dropout rates, and show higher levels of academic achievement, especially for disadvantaged students.[2] Moreover, Catholic schools use only very modest fiscal resources to produce these desired outcomes. Although these reports have been subject to rigorous critique and considerable reanalysis, the basic pattern of results has been sustained.

Promoting greater equality of educational opportunity has been a major theme in educational policy over the past several decades. Catholic high schools appear to be "doing something right" in this regard. Curiously, however, there has been little rigorous examination of the internal operations of Catholic high schools and how their organization might actually produce these desired outcomes. *Catholic Schools and the Common*

[1]This article is drawn from my recent book with coauthors Valerie Lee and Peter Holland, *Catholic Schools and the Common Good,* published by Harvard University Press, 1993. The interested reader is referred to that book for further elaboration of the arguments presented here and for more details about the research evidence and methods.

[2]In terms of the major research studies, see, for example, Coleman, Hoffer, and Kilgore (1982), Greeley (1982), and Coleman and Hoffer (1987).

Anthony S. Bryk   Center for School Improvement and Consortium on Chicago School Research, Department of Education, The University of Chicago, Chicago, Illinois 60637.

Restructuring Schools: Promising Practices and Policies, edited by Maureen T. Hallinan. Plenum Press, New York, 1995.

Good (Bryk, Lee, & Holland, 1993) represents the culmination of almost 10 years of inquiry on this topic. Our findings are based on intensive field work in seven purposefully selected school sites, analyses of extant national data bases on U.S. high schools (both Catholic and public), and an exploration of the history and tradition that form the distinctive character of these institutions.

The first part of this chapter summarizes what we have learned from our investigations about how Catholic schools manage simultaneously to achieve relatively high levels of student learning, have this learning more equitably distributed with regard to race and class than in the public sector, and sustain high levels of teacher commitment and student engagement. The second part highlights some of the implications that we have drawn from these findings for renewing U.S. educational institutions.

WHAT WE HAVE LEARNED ABOUT THE FUNCTIONING OF EFFECTIVE CATHOLIC HIGH SCHOOLS

Our initial reason for undertaking a study of the internal organization of Catholic high schools was to better understand the factors contributing to what Coleman, Hoffer, and Kilgore (1982) reported as the "common school effect." Stated simply, these researchers had concluded that the personal background of students and their families (e.g., ethnicity and social class) had less influence on subsequent academic achievement in Catholic than in public schools. Formally, we describe this phenomenon as Catholic schools having a "more equitable social distribution of achievement." The first phase of our research sought to try to understand better the factors that might contribute to this desirable outcome. We eventually learned that the curricular organization of school played a key role in this regard.

A Focused Academic Program

The central tenet of the academic organization of the Catholic high school is a core curriculum for all students, regardless of their personal background or future educational plans. This curriculum is predicated on a proactive view among faculty and administrators about what all students can and should learn. Required courses predominate students' study plans, with electives limited in their content and number. Some students may begin the curriculum at a more advanced level and proceed in more depth, but the same basic academic goals apply for everyone. Although some tracking occurs, potential negative effects are moderated by school policies that allocate limited fiscal and human resources so that all students make satisfactory progress. At base, integrating these structures and policies, is an active institutional purpose: to advance a common education of mind and spirit for all.

The constrained academic organization of Catholic high schools has important consequences.[3] Analyses of the *High School and Beyond*[4] data, including the *Administrator and Teacher Supplement*[5] (and hereafter referred to as *HS&B*), indicated greater academic course-taking among students in Catholic schools as compared to counterparts in public schools. These differences were especially large when comparing students from nonacademic tracks in these two sectors. Although part of these differences result from the different types of students educated in public and Catholic schools, our analyses also point to strong Catholic school policy effects.

Simple examination of course enrollments can be misleading, however, as students have very different experiences in courses with similar titles in the same school. While Catholic schools make some accommodation in curriculum offerings for both the less well prepared and more talented students, the amount of differentiation among students' academic experiences remains modest in comparison to public high schools. In the field sites that we studied, students shared a broad core of intellectual experiences. For example, different sections of mathematics often used the same textbook, and students read the same literature in English classes, whether honors or regular sections. While honors students might tackle more advanced mathematics problems, read more literature, and write longer and more elaborated essays, the basic intellectual tasks remained the same for all.

We found in parallel *HS&B* analyses of the public and Catholic sectors that public schools respond much more to differences in students' academic background at entry into high school than is the case for Catholic schools. In public schools these differences play a larger role than in Catholic schools in assignment to remedial courses and track placement; track placement in public schools is also a stronger predictor of subsequent achievement and advanced course-taking. Since social class and race/ethnicity are related to achievement differences among students at entry into high school, the overall effect of this allocation system in public

---

[3]In addition to some new analyses presented in Chapters 4 and 10 of Bryk *et al.* (1993), much of the empirical evidence on this point has been previously published by Bryk, Carriedo, Holland, and Lee (1984) and Lee and Bryk (1988, 1989).

[4]See National Center for Education Statistics (1982).

[5]See Moles (1988).

schools is to create greater stratification along race and class lines in students' exposure to academic subject matter.

In general, how schools should properly respond to differences in student background is a central organizational problem in education. In principle, initial differences among students can either be amplified or ameliorated as a result of subsequent school experiences. The constrained academic structure in Catholic high schools acts to minimize the subsequent effects on student learning of these initial differences. In contrast, the modern comprehensive public high school has a highly differentiated academic structure in which students exercise considerable discretion over course-taking. Our statistical results clearly indicate that such school structures amplify initial social differences among students and culminate in a less equitable distribution of achievement. In contrast, a distribution of achievement that maintains a high average level of attainment as well as being socially more equitable (i.e., where student background effects are weak) is more likely to arise when the average level of academic course-taking is high, and the differences among students' programs of study are small.

The effects of a larger school size also bear particular note. In general, Catholic high schools are relatively small. Very few Catholic high schools enroll more than 1500 students, with the average around 500 to 600. Although we found no effect of school size on average achievement levels, size did have a strong impact on the degree of instructional differentiation that occurs within schools. Quite simply, it is easier to create a more varied academic program in a larger school. The limited fiscal and human resources generally found in small schools tend to preclude this. Although instructional differentiation is not a necessary consequence of a larger school size, size does act as a facilitating factor. When accompanied by a dominant public educational philosophy that views individual differences in ability and interest as the organizing principle for determining the subject matter to which students are exposed, the observed results are not surprising.

The first piece of our investigation, about the nature of the academic organization of schools and the consequences that flow from this, now seemed clear to us. The obvious policy implications of this work— increased academic standards for all—caused us to worry a bit. Dropout rates, particularly in urban schools, were already very high; would raising academic standards just exacerbate these problems? Evidence from Coleman and Hoffer (1987), however, suggested that this was not the case in Catholic schools. In fact, these schools had much lower dropout rates than expected given the nature of their enrollments, and again these schools seemed especially effective with disadvantaged students.

Our own fieldwork also raised several related puzzles. We had observed very high levels of teacher commitment in the schools we visited. Discussions about merit pay proposals to stimulate greater teacher productivity were quite commonplace at that time. The underlying microeconomic assumptions here, however, could not explain what we had observed. On average, Catholic high school teachers in our field sites were paid about 75% of prevailing local public school wages. It was very clear from our field observations that economic incentives were not driving teacher behavior.

Similarly, we had observed relatively high levels of student engagement in classroom instruction that we judged as rather ordinary. Many professional educators argue that a more relevant curriculum and stimulating instruction are needed to enhance student engagement in learning. While such developments may be highly desirable, the basic premises here—an appeal for more immediate rewards from learning—was certainly not producing the student engagement that we had observed in Catholic high school classrooms.

Perhaps most significant in all of our fieldwork was the pervasive talk among teachers, principals, and students about their school being a community. Accompanying this language were some distinctive organizational practices, not commonplace in public high schools. Gradually, we came to conclude that our observations about student engagement and teacher commitment were inextricably intertwined with this distinctive organization of the Catholic school as a community. In order to better understand the overall effectiveness of these schools, we needed to probe further what this meant.

Communal Organization

Our field investigations indicated that a communal school structure is formed around three core features. First is an extensive array of school activities that provide numerous opportunities for face-to-face interactions and shared experiences among adults and students. The common academic program described above is a major contributor in this regard. There are also numerous school events—athletics, drama, liturgy, and retreat programs—that engender high levels of participation and provide more informal occasions for interactions among students and adults. These activities afford opportunities to deepen attachments among current school members and to create connections with those who came before, and those who may come after. School rituals can be especially powerful in helping to connect the current social group to a larger tradition.

Second are a set of formal organizational features that enable the community. Chief among these is an extended role for teachers. Teachers are not just subject-matter specialists whose job definition is delimited by the classroom walls. Rather, they are mature persons whom students also encounter in the hallways, playing fields, in the school neighborhood, and sometimes even in their homes. In the numerous personal interactions that occur among adults and students outside of classrooms, many opportunities are afforded for expressions of individual concern and interest.

Collegiality among teachers is also important in this regard. Catholic school faculty spend time with one another both inside and outside of school. These social interactions serve as a resource for school problem-solving and contribute to adult solidarity around the school's mission. In such contexts, school decision-making tends to be less conflictual and more often characterized by mutual trust and respect.

The relatively small size of Catholic high schools provides a significant advantage here, too. The coordination of work in larger organizations typically imposes demands for more formal modes of communication and encourages increased work specialization and more extensive bureaucratization. In contrast, a smaller school size facilitates personalism and social intimacy, both of which are much harder to achieve in larger contexts.

Third and crucial for communal school organization are a set of shared beliefs about what students should learn, about proper norms of instruction, and about how people should relate to one another. Underpinning this educational philosophy in Catholic high schools are a set of general moral beliefs about the person and society and the role of schools to advance a more just society. This set of shared beliefs establishes a common ground that orders and gives meaning to much of daily life for both faculty and students.

Building on our field observations, we used analyses of *HS&B* data to bring empirical specificity to these ideas and to test hypotheses about the effects of communal organization on those who work and learn in such schools. More specifically, we created from the *HS&B* data 23 indicators of the basic elements of communal organization described above, which we then combined into a global measure. Even after controlling for a range of student and teacher background characteristics and school composition measures, our statistical analyses indicated powerful effects of communal organization on both students and teachers. In schools with a strong communal organization, fewer problems with classroom disruptions, class cutting, absenteeism, and dropping out were reported. Teachers were more likely to express a greater sense of efficacy and satisfaction with their work, and staff morale was higher. Moreover, these effects exist in both the public and Catholic sectors. That is, public schools with a strong communal organization have levels of student engagement and teacher commitment similar to those found in the Catholic sector.

Thus, a second strong theme had now emerged from our research. The basic social organization of the high school as a community has substantial social and personal consequences for both teachers and students. Thinking about these results led us toward two more questions: How did Catholic schools come to be organized in this way, and what helps to maintain this distinctiveness? Up to this point, our research had focused primarily on the practices and structures that organize life inside Catholic high schools. These new questions broadened our attention toward concerns about external control. More specifically, they focused subsequent inquiry on the role of an inspirational ideology and decentralized governance. We came to conclude that two major organizational control mechanisms, ideology and markets, interact in complex ways to both guide and anchor the work in Catholic high schools.

An Inspirational Ideology

At the crest of Catholic school enrollment in 1965, serious questions were raised about continuing a separate Catholic school system. Many Catholics had successfully entered mainstream American life, and the need for a separate school system was no longer apparent. Vatican II, in proclaiming a new role for the Church in the modern world, however, created such a purpose. The charter for Catholic schools shifted from protecting the faithful from a hostile Protestant majority to pursuing peace and social justice within an ecumenical and multicultural world. Each school would seek to enact the image of a prophetic Church. While thoroughly engaged in American culture, the aims, organization, methods, and daily life of Catholic schools sought to offer a strong countervailing image—a distinctive vision of democratic education for a postmodern world.

Two important ideas—*personalism* and *subsidiarity*—shape life in Catholic schools. Personalism calls for humaneness in the hundreds of mundane social interactions that comprise daily life. Key to advancing personalism is an extended role for teachers that encourages staff to care about both the kind of people students become as well as the facts, skills, and knowledge they acquire. Moreover, personalism is a communal norm for the school—the kind of behavior modeled by teachers and held out as an ideal for students. As such, personalism is valued not only because it is an effective device to engage students in academic work, but also because it signifies a moral conception of social behavior in a just community.

Similarly, subsidiarity means that the school rejects a purely bureaucratic conception of an organization. Clearly, there are advantages to workplace specialization, and it is hard to imagine the conduct of complex work without established organizational procedures. Subsidiarity, however, claims that instrumental considerations about work efficiency and specialization must be mediated by a concern for human dignity. Likewise, decentralization of school governance is not chosen purely because it is more efficient, although it does appear to have such consequences. Nor is it primarily favored because it creates organizations that are more client-sensitive, although this also appears true. Rather, decentralization is predicated on a view about how personal dignity and human respect are advanced when work is organized around small communities where dialogue and collegiality may flourish. At root is a belief that the full potential of persons is realized in the social solidarity that can form around these small group associations.

Embedded in these ideas of personalism and subsidiarity is a quite different language for discussions about education. It is an evocative language that encourages students to engage questions about the kind of persons they should become and the kind of society we should want. It is a language that also makes important demands on schools—fostering such moral reflections requires that schools themselves must be moral communities.

Decentralized Governance

A fourth distinctive feature of Catholic high schools is decentralized governance. The specific arrangements vary from school to school, depending on the nature of school ownership (parish, diocesan, or private). In reality, the "Catholic school system" is a very loose federation. Virtually all important decisions are made at individual school sites. To the best of our knowledge, no current efforts to promote decentralization in the public sector approach this level of school-site autonomy.

Externally, Catholic high schools, like all private schools, are subject to market forces. These market effects were quite apparent in the 1970s, when parents spurned Catholic schools that adopted such then-popular innovations as an expanded personal development curriculum. As a result, these reforms never took deep root in Catholic schools. Market influences can also be seen in Catholic school history. For example, many immigrant Catholic parents aspired that their children should become something more than just "hewers of wood." These collective aspirations are part of the reason why vocationalism was never taken up strongly in the Catholic sector. Today, market forces contribute to the relatively low dropout and expulsion rates in Catholic high schools. Since most schools are not overenrolled, they have an institutional interest in holding students in order to balance their budgets.

Nevertheless, the control of Catholic school operations involves considerably more than market responsiveness to clients. Many important observations about these schools cannot be reconciled in these terms. Market forces, for example, cannot explain the broadly shared institutional purpose of advancing social equity. Nor can they account for the efforts of Catholic educators to maintain inner-city schools (with large non-Catholic enrollments) while facing mounting fiscal woes. Likewise, market forces cannot easily explain why resources are allocated within schools in a compensatory fashion in order to provide an academic education for every student. Nor can they explain the norms of community that infuse daily life in these schools.

In sum, four key features combine to create a distinctive Catholic school life. A focused academic life is embedded within a larger communal organization. Taken together, these two features create an engaging social institution for both adults and students that produces a more equitable social distribution of achievement. Undergirding this institutional life is a combination of an inspirational ideology that nicely coexists with a decentralized governance and market influences.

SOME LARGER LESSONS FROM CATHOLIC HIGH SCHOOLS

Educational Markets as a Basis for Improvement

After a century and a half of strong public support for a publicly controlled and managed educational system, advocacy for greater parental choice within an expanded educational market has become widespread. We have already noted that some aspects of Catholic school operations are influenced by market concerns. We have also described how the spirit of Vatican II has catalyzed dramatic changes in Catholic schools over the past 20 years. Taken together, these two control mechanisms—ideology and markets—jointly shape the operations of Catholic schools. Vatican II ideals inspire human action, and the market acts as an empirical lever. Absent either one, the contemporary Catholic school would surely be a very different institution.

Consequently, it would be inappropriate to assume that a new system of education, just because it was market-driven, would produce effects similar to those found in Catholic schools. In this regard, there is a ruse to be dispatched. Popular arguments for a system of market controls in education commonly employ a microeconomic explanation that bears little relation to the ideas about schools-as-communities that we have discussed. Under this microeconomic view, stimulating teachers' entrepreneurial motives would make schools more efficient service providers. This conception of teacher thinking and behavior is quite antithetical, however, to the social foundations of a communal school organization. Although individual entrepreneurship may fuel economic development, it rings less true as a basic motivation for processes of human betterment. There is simply no evidence that such motives currently play a role in motivating teachers in Catholic schools. More generally, it is difficult to envision how unleashing self-interest becomes a compelling force toward human caring.

These observations are important because so much of the current rhetoric about privatization and choice can be traced to the recent studies on public and private schools. A clear understanding of these findings is very important. Specifically, many of the positive effects found in Catholic schools are not characteristic of non-Catholic private schools. For example, the more equitable social distribution of achievement, or "common school" effect, that occurs in Catholic schools does not typify all other private schools. Similarly, the reduced dropout rates and unusual effectiveness of Catholic high schools for at-risk youth are not characteristic of private schools in general (Coleman & Hoffer, 1987). The special effectiveness of Catholic girls' schools also does not appear to generalize across the private sector as a whole.[6]

Advocates of choice have argued that "effective organizational practices" are more likely under a market system, because these practices are currently more prevalent in private schools, which benefit from a higher degree of school autonomy. While this is a valid public–private comparison, it is also important to recognize that within the private sector, some of the so-called "effective organizational practices" are actually more prevalent among non-Catholic than Catholic private schools. However,

---

[6]In addition to the research reported in Chapter 9 of Bryk *et al.* (1993), Riordan (1985), using NLS72 data, also found positive effects on achievement for Catholic girls' schools. However, a report on recent field research in progress (Lee & Marks, 1991) suggests that this pattern may not be generally characteristic of other non-Catholic schools. Should these findings be sustained by further analyses, they would confirm other evidence about private schools as a set being a very diverse enterprise with few generalizations appropriate for the entire set.

the positive student outcomes described above do not uniformly occur in non-Catholic private schools.[7]

In short, extant research clearly indicates differences among private schools in both their internal organization and their outcomes. These findings raise doubts about any blanket claim that a move toward greater privatization will ensure better consequences for students. In our view, much more attention is required to the actual content of the values operative in schools and to the consequences that derive from these values.

Fundamental to the operations of Catholic schools are beliefs about the dignity of each person and a shared responsibility for advancing a just and caring society. These aims are formally joined in an educational philosophy that seeks to develop each student as a "person-in-community." Not surprisingly, this educational philosophy aligns well with social equity aims. Moreover, when such understandings meld to a coherent organizational structure with adequate fiscal and human resources, desirable academic and social consequences can result. Absent this particular value system, however, a very different pattern of effects seems likely.

The School as a Voluntary Community

As an alternative to describing a school "as a market-responsive firm" we offer the idea of a school "as a voluntary community." The notion of a school as a voluntary community synthesizes three important features of Catholic high schools.

First, a communal organization, as described earlier, structures daily life within the school. Second, each school possesses a relatively high degree of autonomy in managing its affairs. This autonomy is important because much of the rationale for activity within a communal organization relies on traditions and local judgments. Such schools simply do not meet the criteria and operating principles of centralized bureaucracies, where standardization is seen as an organizational imperative and particularisms as imperfections needing redress.

Third, the voluntary association of both students and teachers with the school marks individual membership. Implicit here is the idea that participation in a particular school is not an inalienable right. While Catholic school faculty go a long way toward helping students and working with parents, reciprocity is also expected. Students who seriously or chronically violate community's norms must leave. Similarly, faculty who don't share the school's beliefs and commitments usually move on as

---

[7]We are referring here to arguments offered by Chubb and Moe (1990).

well, mostly by their own choice. Because membership involves an ongoing exercise of free will, individuals are less likely to interpret school life
as coercive and are more likely to express the personal sentiment, "This
is *my* school."

This notion of membership in a school community in turn licenses
a different form of social relations among parents and professionals.
Rather than "the contract" that formalizes marketplace interactions or
"the client and interest politics" of the public bureaucracy, a set of fiducial
commitments are at the core of the voluntary community. The importance
of these trust relationships is readily manifest in school life. Effective
teaching makes personal demands that leave teachers vulnerable—literally, "I put *myself* on the line each day." To maintain such commitments,
teachers need support both from their colleagues and from parents. That
is, a considerable measure of trust is required among all participants to
sustain engaging teaching.[8]

Thus, the internal life of Catholic schools benefits from a network of
supportive social relations, characterized by trust, that constitutes a form
of "social capital."[9] In this regard, voluntary association functions as
a facilitating condition. Trust accrues because school participants, both
students and faculty, choose to be there. To be sure, voluntary association
does not automatically create social capital, but it is surely harder to
develop such capital in its absence.

Our investigation of Catholic schools suggests that schools formed
as voluntary communities induce important institutional and personal
consequences. On the organizational side, a voluntary community enjoys
a base of moral authority. The commitment from both teachers and students to a particular school makes moral authority possible, since such
authority depends on the consent of those influenced by it. The presence
of moral authority is important because, as noted earlier, much of what
happens in schools involves discretionary action. Great effort may be
required within public bureaucracies to secure basic agreements on issues
that are intrinsically judgmental. In contrast, much of the effort expended
on such matters can be redirected toward the actual work of schooling
in a voluntary community. Moreover, many potentially contentious issues
never develop into conflicts, since communal norms define a broader
realm of "what is appropriate here." Further, because these communities

---

[8]This theme is extensively developed in an essay by Cohen (1988).

[9]Coleman (1987) introduced the idea of social capital in the context of describing Catholic
high schools as functional communities. His explanation, however, was located external
to the school in the structure of relationships among parents and their children. We agree
with Coleman that Catholic high schools benefit from a form of social capital but we locate
that capital in the relations among school professionals and with their parent communities.

value social interactions that are respectful and civil, when disagreements do occur, participants assume good intentions all around. This is quite different from the suspicion, fear, and distrust that often afflict the interest politics surrounding public education.

A base of moral authority also helps to guide the work of individual adults. The latter is particularly important because autonomous action characterizes much of teaching. A major policy lesson of the 1960s and 1970s is that the behavior of teachers is relatively impervious to direct regulation. In part, this reflects the relatively private nature of teaching— typically an individual adult working with a group of students behind a closed door. Also significant is that the craft of teaching involves complex and spontaneous judgments. Because such decisions draw substantially on personal experiences, beliefs, and values, the normative standards of a voluntary community helps to naturally order these judgments.[10]

For all participants, personal experiences in a voluntary community have inherent meaning above and beyond their instrumental value. Communalism is an ethical end where members derive personal support from others with whom they share this commitment. Students who participate in this type of schooling derive more from their education than just something to be endured now in order to get a good job in the future. Similarly, teachers' efforts in such environments involve more than earning an income to support out-of-work activities. Likewise, school administration takes on a distinctive character, where tending to the meaning-inducing quality of school life is a deliberate aim, on a par with concerns about the efficient organization of instruction. In such contexts, the managerial ethic of the bureaucracy is tempered by a personalism more characteristic of the family.

In sum, many desirable personal and institutional consequences derive from the organization of schools as voluntary communities. Nevertheless, we reiterate our doubts that the specific consequences found in Catholic high schools would appear more broadly should a market-based system of schooling emerge in the United States. In particular, without commitment to the specific values operative in the Catholic sector, we suspect that neither the quality of internal life found in these schools nor the more equitable social distribution of achievement would result. Rather, a market system seems likely to produce a highly differentiated set of schools, where educational opportunities would be even more inequitably distributed among individuals and communities than is already the case. We are reminded of Max Weber's famous prediction: "Capitalism stripped

---

[10]The role of teachers' beliefs and tacit understandings has become an important theme in research on teaching. See, for example, the review paper by Clark and Peterson (1986).

of its religious imperative is a cloak of steel, a cage of iron." A market system of schools, absent a vital moral imperative, would likely enact this image.

The High School as a Bridging Institution

Our research demonstrates that disadvantaged children can benefit from attending Catholic schools. The particular combination of organizational structure, social behavior, beliefs, and sentiments found in Catholic high schools constitutes a distinctive approach to the education of the disadvantaged, which we summarize in the idea of a "school as a bridging institution."

The philosophy of a bridging institution is dialogical. On one side is an empathetic orientation toward children and their families which is grounded in an appreciation of the dignity of each person without regard for outward appearances, customs, or manners.[11] The school welcomes all who want to come, and it conveys to parents and children a sense of security, personal well-being, and engagement. On the other side is a clear recognition of the demands of contemporary middle-class American life for which the school consciously seeks to prepare these children. From this perspective, the school is of value to disadvantaged students because it is culturally different. Specifically, school staff aim to provide an education that will enable each student to develop the knowledge, skills, dispositions, and habits necessary to function both effectively and critically in modern democratic society.

The tasks of the bridging institution involve constant tensions. While sensitive to the mores of family and community, it must also challenge behaviors and attitudes clearly at odds with the child's progress in school. While social idealism is a source of inspiration, the school and its students must also live in this world. While the school espouses a caring community, it also operates within a larger culture that values hard work, delayed gratification, and material success. While schools are committed to systematically preparing students with the intellectual and social competencies required for functioning in contemporary middle-class American life, they also seek to hone a critical consciousness toward social life as it should be.

Staff in a bridging institution seek to nourish and validate the best of family and community ties while also providing a link to a very different world. The transitions are difficult both for those individuals who seek

[11]For an account of this empathetic understanding as infused with Catholic values, see Coles's (1987) account of Dorothy Day's life in the Catholic Worker movement.

to ford it and for those institutions that seek to act as bridge. To be sure, the Catholic schools we studied were far from perfect in this regard. These concerns, however, were very alive in the conversations among school staff, and a collective moral voice made claims on school participants to act in accord with them.

As we begin to think about urban schools in these ways, we are reminded that all schools undeniably act as agents of socialization. This socialization role is especially salient in the inner city where the formation of a two-class society appears immanent. If real educational opportunities are to be afforded such disadvantaged students, they must have access to schools with strong institutional norms. In the Catholic schools that we studied, these norms were central to the schools' effectiveness in educating disadvantaged youth. Our findings link to a growing body of evidence that it is the disadvantaged in our society who benefit most from such strong institutions. For they, more than anyone else, must rely on the expertise, good intentions, and efforts of societal institutions for advancement. Anything less may resign large numbers of students to a permanent underclass.[12]

This line of analysis raises questions about whether Americans can obtain such moral aims as equality of educational opportunity without an enlivened moral discourse about the aims and methods of schooling. Public educational policy has instead searched for instrumental levers to advance moral purposes. In the recent past, busing programs, magnet schools, and individual educational plans have served as such levers. Now school improvement plans, accountability systems, and markets are offered as solutions. To be sure, different organizational arrangements can facilitate different consequences. Ultimately, however, it is school values, norms, and traditions that influence the selection of "appropriate structures" and create meaning for participants within whatever structure they happen to confront. Whatever specific reform initiative we choose to pursue, it must eventually be enacted by individuals in schools, each of whom draws his or her own personal beliefs but also must operate within a larger context where moral conversation holds a very uncertain status.

[12]The idea of an underclass has been developed by Wilson (1987), and subjected to considerable debate and scrutiny in an edited volume by Jencks and Peterson (1991). In brief, Wilson argues that economic and demographic forces reshaped many of our urban centers during the 1970s, creating a distinct separate underclass. We are now witnessing a secondary consequence of this phenomenon, as the children of the underclass are increasingly entering the public school system. Thus, what began as an economic and demographic problem (e.g., the movement of jobs and institutions to the suburbs) may now be beginning to manifest itself as a cultural issue.

Catholic High Schools and Urban School Improvement

Our investigation of Catholic high schools began in search of the key elements that contribute to the desired outcomes observed there. As this scientific work proceeded we gradually added a second focus on the nature of their institutional vision and the sources of hopefulness that ground the vitality of these communities and inspire human effort. We are convinced that if we are to have a renewed public philosophy for education in the United States—one that is capable of ennobling the work of faculty and staff and firing the hearts and minds of young people—it must involve more serious dialogue between the instrumental and evocative realms that interweave to create school life.

The Catholic schools that we have studied are relatively simple organizations with modest resources. Nonetheless, they manage to educate a broad cross section of Americans. We contend that many children who are currently undereducated in public schools would benefit from attending schools organized around the strong normative principles found in the Catholic sector. In this regard, I am reminded of the two central characters, Lafeyette and Pharaoh, in Alex Kotlowitz's *There are No Children Here.* In our field visits to Catholic schools, we were told about students enrolled in those schools whose home environment and community context were like Lafeyette's and Pharaoh's—chaotic, precarious, and often beyond their parents' control. We are convinced that many urban children like these can learn in an educational environment that combines a strong press toward academic work with a caring ethos that demands personal responsibility and the good efforts of all participants. In fact, it is not clear to us that public schools can better serve disadvantaged children who want to learn and also encourage larger proportions of the students to share these aims unless many more schools are transformed along the lines discussed above.

To be sure, not all students would benefit from such an educational experience. Some do fine in comprehensive high schools as currently operated. Others may require something more akin to a total institution, such as a boarding school, to significantly alter their life chances. We see the ideas offered by Catholic schools as of most value in the context of many diverse efforts now under way to reinvent urban public education. As we move to transform our large public school systems into systems of publicly supported schools, there is now more space for new schools, organized like Catholic schools, to emerge. For example, in the context of current efforts to break up large public high schools into smaller "schools-within-a-school," there are opportunities now to create more schools where a deliberately formed academic and social life creates strong educative institutions for the disadvantaged.

CATHOLIC SCHOOLS AND THE COMMON GOOD

In closing, I would like to note that in most public conversations, support for Catholic schools is typically posed as in opposition to public education. In my view, however, discussions about the future of Catholic and public schools in our major cities are really all of one fabric. The core idea here is quite simple. We live through our institutions. Many analyses of the problems of contemporary urban life point to the gradual erosion of local institutions of all kinds—economic, religious, social—that make communal life possible. Many Catholic schools are located in very troubled neighborhoods. Despite the best efforts of all involved with these schools, we will surely see more urban Catholic school closings in the next few years. It is hard to comprehend how the continued loss of these institutions can mean anything but a further erosion of urban life. At base here is the principle of subsidiarity. We need to preserve vital local institutions, such as urban Catholic schools, strengthen other institutions that are currently troubled, such as many of our public schools, and more generally promote local institution building of all kinds.

Contemporary Catholic schools are very different from those of 30 years ago. They now educate a very broad cross section of Americans of diverse race, ethnicity, and social class. They accomplish this with very modest fiscal resources and in the process extend significant educational opportunities to many. Instruction is not narrow, divisive, or sectarian, but rather is informed by a generous conception of democratic life in a postmodern society. Finally, these institutions serve an important public function in the communities of which they are a part. It is observations such as these that lead us to conclude that Catholic schools serve the common good, and the public has a stake in their preservation.

REFERENCES

Bryk, A. S., Carriedo, R. A., Holland, P. B., & Lee, V. E. (1984). *Effective Catholic schools: An exploration.* Washington, DC: National Catholic Education Association.

Bryk, A. S., Lee, V. E., & Holland, P. B. (1993). *Catholic schools and the common good.* Cambridge, MA: Harvard University Press.

Chubb, J. E., & Moe, T. M. (1990). *Politics, markets and America's schools*. Washington, DC: Brookings Institution.

Clark, C. N., & Peterson, P. L. (1986). Teachers' thought processes. In M. C. Whitrock (Ed.), *Handbook of research on teaching* (3rd ed., pp. 255–296). New York: Macmillan Co.

Cohen, D. K. (1988). Knowledge of teaching: Plus que ça change . . . In P. W. Jackson (Ed.), *Contributing to educational change* (pp. 27–84). Berkeley, CA: McCutcheon.

Coleman, J. S. (1987). The relations between school and social structure. In N. T. Hallinan (Ed.), *The social organization of schools: New conceptualizations of the learning process*. New York: Plenum Press.

Coleman, J. S., & Hoffer, T. (1987). *Public and private high schools: The impact of communities*. New York: Basic Books.

Coleman, J. S., Hoffer, T., & Kilgore, S. B. (1982). *High school achievement: Public, Catholic, and private schools compared*. New York: Basic Books.

Coles, R. (1987). *Dorothy Day: A radical devotion*. Reading, MA: Addison–Wesley.

Greeley, A. M. (1982). *Catholic high schools and minority students*. New Brunswick, NJ: Transaction Books.

Jencks, C., & Peterson, P. (Eds.). (1991). *Urban underclass*. Washington, DC: Brookings Institution.

Kotlowitz, A. (1991). *There are no children here*. New York: Doubleday.

Lee, V. E., & Bryk, A. S. (1988). Curriculum tracking as mediating the social distribution of high school achievement. *Sociology of Education, 61*(2), 78–94.

Lee, V. E., & Bryk, A. S. (1989). A multilevel model of the social distribution of high school achievement. *Sociology of Education, 62*(3), 172–192.

Lee, V. E., & Marks, H. M. (1991, April). *Which works best? The relative effectiveness of single-sex and coeducational secondary schools*. Paper presented at the Annual Meeting of the American Educational Research Association, Chicago.

Moles, O. C. (1988). *High school and beyond: Administrative and teacher survey (1985). Data file users' manual*. Washington, DC: Office of Educational Research.

National Center for Education Statistics. (1982). *High school and beyond 1980 sophomore cohort first follow-up (1982): Data file user's manual*. Washington, DC: National Center for Education Statistics.

Riordan, C. (1985). Public and Catholic schooling: The effects of gender context policy. *American Journal of Education, 5*, 518–540.

Wilson, J. T. (1987). *The truly disadvantaged*. Chicago: University of Chicago Press.

5

School Choice in New York City
Preliminary Observations

Peter W. Cookson Jr. and Charlotte S. Lucks

INTRODUCTION

When former New York City School Chancellor Joseph Fernandez initiated a citywide choice plan in 1992, he undertook a school reform of potentially great significance. He not only advocated greater freedom of choice for families, but implicitly called for the redesign of urban public education. Underlying his choice plan was the assumption that public education could not improve unless schools as well as families were granted more autonomy. In some ways, the Chancellor's plan emerged from a growing policy consensus that public education cannot be transformed unless educational governance structures are radically altered (Fernandez, 1993).

In this chapter we examine the underlying premises that informed the Chancellor's decision, place the plan in a historical and contemporary context, analyze the nature of the plan, and assess its probable impact on the city's schools. We also suggest how aspects of choice could improve urban education.

The data for this chapter are drawn primarily from research conducted in the early 1990s and preliminary research conducted in New York in 1994 (Cookson, 1994). In some ways, this paper should be viewed as a prologue to a larger study; there is a need for more systematic data

Peter W. Cookson, Jr.   Office of the Provost, Adelphi University, Garden City, New York 11530.   **Charlotte S. Lucks**   Hillcrest High School, Queens, New York 11432.

Restructuring Schools: Promising Practices and Policies, edited by Maureen T. Hallinan. Plenum Press, New York, 1995.

than are currently available. As we hope to demonstrate, the study of choice in large urban settings raises empirical and conceptual questions. In the end, we believe that choice can bring about greater family and school autonomy and by extension redesign elements of urban education, but without more resources choice by itself is not likely to improve student learning.

THE CHOICE MOVEMENT

During the latter part of the 1980s and the early 1990s, many school reformers and policymakers came to believe that unless public education was fundamentally restructured it would continue to produce students who were ill-prepared for the economic challenges of the future and for participation in civic life. Some reformers argued that the "public school monopoly" stifled the imagination of educators and limited the educational liberty of families. The school choice movement was born out of deep frustration with the status quo and a belief that consumer behavior is a superior mechanism for producing educational innovation than state-mandated reform. The term "school choice" covers a variety of policy options, all of which share a common characteristic: families must be given the option of choosing the school they wish their children to attend rather than being compelled to send their children to neighborhood schools. Public opinion polls generally show that parents are in favor of more choice, although other evidence indicates that there is still a great deal of support for the neighborhood school (Cookson, 1994). In general, the educationally disenfranchised (such as the poor inner-city minorities) are more in favor of choice than families who have good public schools available to them.

Choice, as a redesign strategy, is not monolithic in its underlying assumptions. Some school choice advocates argue that the fundamental problem with the governance of public education is that it violates free speech because it coerces children to attend schools that they might not attend unless they were compelled to do so (Arons, 1983). Some choice plans developed from an effort to bring about desegregation without forced busing. An early example of this type of "controlled choice" was in Cambridge, Massachusetts (Alves & Willie, 1987). A third perspective argues that the only effective cure for the educational malaise caused by public bureaucracies is to organize schools according to market principles (Chubb & Moe, 1990).

Essentially, the market argument hypothesizes that schools will improve when teachers and administrators meet the expectations of consumers because market principles provide incentives for change that demo-cratically organized schools do not (Chubb & Moe, 1990). This perspective challenges the very structure of public education and when taken to its logical conclusion suggests that until public education is deregulated there is little hope for genuine reform. This faith in markets is the core belief that is behind most voucher proposals including former President Bush's 1992 voucher initiative "G.I. Bill Opportunity Scholarships for Children."

The empirical evidence regarding the outcomes of school choice is inconclusive and sometimes is the subject of debate itself (Cookson, 1994). The school choice movement has not been fueled by statistical evidence of its efficacy but by a deep sense that public education is failing and that only choice provides a policy exit from the negative effects of the bureaucratic control of schools. The choice plan in New York City is constructed according to modified market principles; private schools are not included and there is very little incentive for weak schools to reform themselves. Thus, the New York choice plan can hardly be described as a redesigner's dream. There are many practical problems in implementing a choice plan in a school system that educates nearly one million students a year. For a market solution to bring about change it is necessary that certain "downside" risks be entertained (i.e., bad schools must close). The political reality in New York, however, is that the Board of Education cannot condone or encourage school closures where there are not educational alternatives, nor would the United Federation of Teachers be sympathetic to a reform plan that might put teachers out of work.

THE EMPIRICAL BACKGROUND

Essentially, there are four kinds of choice research: controlled experimental design, comparisons of public and private schools, qualitative studies of public school choice, and program evaluations. One of the earliest attempts to evaluate school choice occurred in San Jose, California, at the Alum Rock School District. The purpose of the experiment was to determine the educational and social effects of a voucher plan on enrollment patterns within a school system. Although the Alum Rock experiment was supposed to be a test case for systemwide vouchers, only the public schools of the district participated. The results of the Alum Rock experiment did not prove to be a test case for the efficacy of vouchers because of practical problems resulting from the implementation of the plan and its evaluation. There were some hopeful signs, however, that choice did encourage parental interest in education.

Most qualitative studies of choice involve observing and document-
ing the success or failure of magnet school programs. In general, research
has shown that magnet schools attract and hold students and increase
academic success. The success of magnet schools, however, often has
little to do with school choice *per se*. Blank (1989) reports that among the
magnet schools he studied, the best performance was achieved by those
that had strong central office support, energetic and able teachers, and
well-planned programs; characteristics that have little to do directly with
choice. Moreover, magnet schools usually have additional financial and
political support and more motivated students. Studies of controlled
choice, a plan that makes every school within a district a magnet school,
reveal that while choice is associated with increased learning within a
school district, poorly performing districts remain weak in comparison
with better performing districts that have no choice plan (Henig, 1994).

Comparative analyses of public and private schools indicate that
student achievement in private schools is higher, supporting the argument
that there is a private school "effect." In their research on high school
achievement in public, private, and Catholic schools, Coleman, Hoffer,
and Kilgore (1982) found that when they compared average test scores
of public and private school sophomores and seniors, there was not one
subject in which public school students scored higher. Of course, comparisons between public and private schools are not without conceptual and
methodological problems. For instance, how does one really control for
selectivity bias? Nonetheless, there is some reason to believe that the
organizational characteristics of private schools (i.e., size, basic curriculum, student discipline) do lead to better learning environments (Cookson & Persell, 1985).

Some researchers have argued that private schools are better because
they must respond to market pressures; in theory, market pressure eliminates mediocre schools leaving only academically superior schools. From
the research thus far, however, it cannot be concluded that market pressure alone improves student achievement, nor can it be shown that school
governance directly affects academic success (Cookson, 1994). Some schol-
ars have attempted to provide evidence that school governance influences
student cognitive outcomes, but with little success. Chubb and Moe (1990),
for example, make the claim that there is a positive relationship between
market-oriented schools and student achievement. Using a model that
compares achievement gains between public and private school students,
the authors argue that the characteristics of private schools are associated
with greater student learning. On reflection, the authors' argument seems
to lack empirical support, as their model only explains 5% of the variance
in achievement (Cookson, 1994, p. 86). The debate over the size and

meaning of the private school effect is far from closed; for instance, recent evidence seems to indicate that Catholic schools provide a sense of community that is directly related to positive student outcomes (Bryk, Lee, & Holland, 1993).

Program evaluations of school districts that have choice, such as East Harlem in New York, have yet to provide evidence that choice is related to measurable improvements in student learning. Of course, the major beneficial effect of school choice may only be indirectly related to student achievement. Choice may be a mechanism for creating more cohesive school communities and in the long run building parental and community support for schools, a redesign effect of real importance. In candor, however, one must admit that the empirical evidence that choice is the panacea for the improvement of schools is at best weak, at worst nonexistent, and, in general, so underdeveloped that strong conclusions cannot yet be drawn about the relationship of school choice to school improvement.

THE NEW YORK CONTEXT

New York is a prime example of the complexity of school reform in a large metropolitan area. With over 1000 public schools located in 32 community school districts, New York City has the largest school system in the United States. It is projected that by the year 2000 there will be nearly a million and a half public school students in the city (The University of the State of New York, 1993a). Many of the children who attend city schools come from poor backgrounds where English is a second language; 62% are eligible to participate in subsidized lunch programs (The University of the State of New York, 1993b). Approximately 73% of the students are either African-American or Hispanic. Many city students are recent immigrants; between 1983 and 1989, 55% of the families immigrating to New York were from the Caribbean, 16% from South America, and 13% from Asia. In fact, students attending New York City public schools represent over 80 languages. This racial and ethnic complexity confronts a school system badly in need of resources. There is virtually no resource that is not in short supply, including books, paper, and pencils.

Given these conditions, it is little wonder that the city's schools are struggling to deliver a quality education. Reform within this context is difficult to conceptualize let alone implement and achieve. Moreover, virtually all educational problems in the city are political problems; competing interest groups use the school system as a mechanism for expressing, but seldom resolving, deep philosophical and political differences.

Prior to the latter part of the 19th century, the city school system was a complex and generally unregulated collection of academies, religious schools, trade schools, and "public" schools (Cremin, 1988). By the 1880s, immigrants from Ireland, Italy, and Eastern Europe were changing the demographic and political characteristics of the city. Native Yankees, fearing that their political hegemony was threatened, began to cast about for ways of "Americanizing" the immigrants (Ravitch, 1983). This led to the expansion of the public school system; schools were seen as the most direct mechanism for socializing immigrant children (Cremin, 1988). At the same time, the Catholic Church established a large parochial school system that in some ways rivaled the public school system in terms of size and influence; low-cost, convenient school choice has been available to the city's Catholic population for over 100 years. Other religious groups have created their own parochial schools; ethnic groups still establish schools to maintain their cultural identities. Aside from religious and ethnically enriched schools, the city has scores of proprietary schools that claim to teach vocational skills and for the city's upper- and upper-middle-class families, there are a good number of socially elite private schools. As a consequence of this history, the city has a highly stratified private and public educational system that tends to reproduce existing social and educational inequalities.

SCHOOL CHOICE IN NEW YORK PUBLIC SCHOOLS

Most New York public school children attend "zoned" public schools; a zone is defined as a student catchment area. Catchment areas are established on the basis of population size and community need. Since similar groups tend to settle in the same neighborhoods, zoning tends to segregate the population. Even today, most children attend zoned schools, despite the fact that intradistrict choice, as a tool for integration, has been a policy of the Board of Education for nearly 30 years. Integration became a major issue for New York City public schools during the 1960s (Ravitch, 1974). In an attempt to address the issues raised by civil rights advocates, while placating the fears of middle-class parents, the Board of Education developed a plan to integrate city schools without forcing white middle-class children into schools located in minority neighborhoods (New York City Board of Education, 1984). Intradistrict choice allows parents to transfer their children from one school to another within their zone; however, there are several conditions imposed on participants. Receiving schools must have 55% or more white students. The sending schools must have student populations of which 90% or more are minority. Parents must choose one of several clusters of schools within a district. According to the Chancellor's memorandum on intradistrict choice, the plan involves only "those pupils whose participation will contribute to integration in both the designated sending schools and the receiving schools" (Cortines, 1994).

Most New York City high schools have magnet programs that are designed to promote integration. Some magnet schools such as the Bronx High School of Science were established to attract the gifted. A number of these schools have achieved a national reputation, but educate a relatively small number of city students. Recently, alternative public schools have increased in popularity. Some of these schools have been established for children with exceptional needs who are unable to cope in mainstream schools. Some alternative schools have been founded for families who are interested in progressive school environments.

The Central Park East Secondary School in East Harlem is an example of an alternative school. As the flagship school of District 4, Central Park East has been held up as an example of how choice can improve urban education (Cookson, 1994). There is some controversy concerning the educational effectiveness of the experiments in District 4 and whether or not the District's achievements can be attributed to choice (Harrington & Cookson, 1992). It could be reasonably argued that whatever educational successes have been achieved in District 4, they are attributable not so much to choice, but to charismatic leadership, smaller schools, and flexible, relevant curricula. The fact remains, however, that choice in District 4 seems to offer an alternative form of governance that combines educational freedom and academic achievement. In this sense, the innovations in District 4 paved the way for the citywide choice plan introduced by the Chancellor in 1992 (Fliegel, 1993).

CITYWIDE CHOICE

According to the Fernandez plan, parents of children enrolled in the New York City public school system have the right to transfer their children to any public school they choose, provided space is available (New York City Board of Education, 1993). No child can be discriminated against on the basis of race, ethnicity, gender, or special needs.

The rationale for this plan was based on five assumptions.

1.   The old structure of the city school system had created a bureaucratic environment that made reform impossible.

2.   City schools must be improved so that all children can be academically successful.

3.   All parents, irrespective of social and economic status, should have the right to choose where and how their children are educated.

4.   By forcing individual schools to compete in the educational marketplace, administrators and teachers gain the incentives and autonomy needed to develop innovative and creative educational programs.

5.   Schools should be held accountable. In theory, accountability forces teachers and administrators to improve curricula and pedagogy.

A parent who wants to take advantage of the interdistrict choice plan must contact the Board of Education in order to obtain a copy of the Chancellor's Choice Regulation. Parents are required to become familiar with a prospective new school's procedures and requirements. When a school is chosen, parents write a letter to the superintendent of the district where the school is located requesting the transfer. The time period in which the superintendent must respond is not specified. If a request is rejected, the parent has the right to appeal the decision to the Chancellor. There is no guarantee that siblings will be transferred to the same school and, most importantly, transportation is not provided.

Details of the program are found in the six-page regulation that was issued in February, 1993. Since that time, a new Chancellor has taken charge of the city's schools. He has been faced with so many difficulties that choice seems less urgent than the asbestos crisis, teacher contracts, reorganization of the Central Board, and budget cuts.

Following its official implementation, the response to school choice has been far from enthusiastic. There has been almost no publicity by the Board of Education or in the districts. In fact, the only detailed information available to the public is contained in a special *New York Newsday* "pull-out" section (1993). This newspaper article, titled "School Choice: A Guide to Picking a Public School for Your Child," gives a detailed overview of the schools in the 32 community school districts.

Parents may call the Board of Education parent advocate to gain information about the choice program. As part of the background for this chapter, Lucks called the Board of Education asking about procedures related to school choice. When asked if a child could be transferred to a very good school in Queens, the parent advocate responded: "If space is available you can move your child. The Superintendent is not mandated to make room for your child, nor will you be able to receive special transportation. I can't tell you for sure whether the school you choose will take your child. I do not want to tell you something and then disappoint you.''

The public response to school choice has been slow. Since it has not been enthusiastically promoted, many parents are unaware of its existence. An informal survey in a school in the East Bronx revealed that none of the parents had heard of the choice program. Since the process involves acquiring information, writing letters, and filing applications, it is likely that only parents who read and are able to fully comprehend the options available to them are taking advantage of school choice. As a consequence, the tendency is for more underprivileged children in the city to remain in their zoned schools; yet, it is these children whom it is believed would benefit most from the choice plan. The lack of transportation creates a major obstacle for parents who work or cannot afford independent transportation for their children. Moreover, many parents are uncomfortable with the prospect of sending their child far from home, preferring their child to be in close proximity in the event of illness or emergency.

The primary problem concerning choice is lack of space; districts cannot discriminate against students requesting transfers, but they do not have to accept a student when space is not available. Obviously, the better the school, the less space will exist for transfers. Moreover, to successfully implement change, schools must have the financial resources to develop innovative curricula and hire a creative and dynamic staff. Almost all funding in New York City is determined school by school based on the number of students enrolled. A small percentage of the overall budget is supplemented by federal funds such as those provided by Chapter 1. For this reason, there is a strong disincentive for schools to promote choice because if they lose students they lose funding.

Another impediment to choice is that in a decentralized system, neighborhoods and communities often think of schools as symbols of civic pride. To some extent the act of choosing can be seen as a form of disloyalty to a community that is struggling for identity and resources. The local political dimension of choice is seldom considered by its promoters. Moreover, a significant number of teachers are not willing to accept more responsibility than is presently required of them. Studies of school-based management have revealed that many teachers resist shared leadership if they must work outside of their contractual responsibilities and if they do not receive compensation. Choice implies that teachers must redefine their roles; in time, there seems little doubt that interdistrict choice will raise contractual issues between the Board of Education and the United Federation of Teachers.

There are certain obstacles for parents as well. The application process is not necessarily complex, but it is time-consuming and may be difficult for some parents. As of this time, intradistrict transfers and children living in a particular school's catchment area must be accepted over any interdistrict transfer. Parents may have to wait until the beginning of the school year to receive notification. For children, choice means going to schools outside their neighborhoods away from friends and homes. Parenthetically, one should also bear in mind that families make mistakes, not every choice is necessarily a good choice. For instance, there may be a significant discrepancy between a particular school's academic program and a transferring student's academic preparation and abilities.

POLICY IMPLICATIONS

Given the problems facing school choice in New York, it would be naive to expect a great deal of educational innovation and improvement. While it is unfair to judge the choice program at such an early date, a reasonable reflection should sober those who believe that choice is a reform panacea (Chubb & Moe, 1990; Rogers and Chuns, 1983). There is an abstract quality to many school choice plans that do not sufficiently take into account practical problems such as space, transportation, local politics, and the needs of small children.

Yet it would be a mistake to dismiss choice as another reform fad. While choice alone may not be a genuine strategy of reform, it can be a useful, and even necessary, tactic of reform. It seems likely that the current interdistrict plan in New York will not achieve its objectives because it is resource poor and so sweeping in its implications that it cannot be realized. Having established the principle of choice, it may be prudent to revise the policy along the following lines:

1. Phase in choice over a period of time. Choose a few districts to initiate choice, produce some positive results, and then implement the reform further.
2. Provide transportation, even on a limited basis. New York is a very large city, especially for a schoolchild. Without some reliable and free transportation, the city's poor families will be unable to send their children far from home.
3. Reserve space in each choice school for underprivileged children. If "good" schools effectively close their doors to students from other districts, choice will be a reform with no impact,

further spreading the general sense that urban schools cannot
be reformed.
4. Make the claims regarding the success of choice far more modest. Good schools don't magically appear because families
choose them, good schools need good teachers, good curricula,
and sufficient resources.

It seems unlikely that choice in New York will prove to be the single
reform that succeeds in saving city schools from the malaise created
by urban problems. School choice without good schools is meaningless.
Clearly, more research is needed.

Future investigators will study school choice in New York as the
plan develops; New York provides the opportunity to study what happens
when the theory of choice is tested against the realities of urban education
and life. As a case study, school choice in New York may provide important lessons about how urban schools can be improved through innovative restructuring principles.

REFERENCES

Alves, M. J., & Willie, C. V. (1987). Controlled choice assignment: A new and
more effective approach to school desegregation. *Urban Review, 19*(2), 67–87.
Arons, S. (1983). *Compelling belief: The culture of American schooling.* New York:
McGraw–Hill.
Blank, R. K. (1989). *Educational effects of magnet schools.* Madison, WI: University
of Wisconsin, National Center in Effective Secondary Schools, Wisconsin
Center for Educational Research.
Bryk, A. S., Lee, V. E., & Holland, P. B. (1993). *Catholic schools and the common
good.* Cambridge, MA: Harvard University Press.
Chubb, J. E., & Moe, T. M. (1990). *Politics, markets and America's schools.* Washington,
DC: Brookings Institution.
Coleman, J. S., Hoffer, T., & Kilgore, S. B. (1982). *High school achievement. Public,
Catholic, and private schools compared.* New York: Basic Books.
Cookson, P. W., Jr. (1994). *School choice: The struggle for the soul of American education.*
New Haven: Yale University Press.
Cookson, P. W., Jr., & Persell, C. H. (1985). *Preparing for power: America's boarding
schools.* New York: Basic Books.
Cortines, R. C. (1994, January). Chancellor's Memorandum Number 11: Free
Choice Program Instructional Manual.
Cremin, L. (1988). *American education: The metropolitan experience 1876–1980.* New
York: Harper & Row.
Fernandez, J., with Underwood, J. (1993). *Tales out of school.* Boston: Little, Brown.

Fliegel, S., with Macquire, J. (1993). *Miracle in East Harlem: The fight for choice in public education.* New York: Random House.

Harrington, D., & Cookson, P. W., Jr. (1992). School reform in East Harlem: Alternative schools vs. schools of choice. In G. A. Hess (Ed.), *Empowering teachers and parents: School restructuring through the eyes of anthropologists* (pp. 177–186). Westport, CT: Bergin & Garvey.

Henig, J. R. (1994). *Rethinking school choice: Limits of the market metaphor.* Princeton, NJ: Princeton University Press.

New York City Board of Education. (1984). Zoning of Schools: Number A-180. Brooklyn, New York.

New York City Board of Education. (1993). Interdistrict Parent Choice Transfers: Number A-181. Brooklyn, New York.

New York Newsday. (1993). School Choice: A Guide to Picking a Public School for Your Child.

Ravitch, D. (1974). *Great school wars, New York City 1805–1973: A history of the public school as a battlefield for change.* New York: Basic Books.

Ravitch, D. (1983). *The troubled crusade: American education 1945–1980.* New York: Basic Books.

Rogers, D., & Chuns, N. H. (1983). *110 Livingston Street revisited: Decentralization in action.* New York: New York University Press.

The University of the State of New York/The State Education Department. (1993a). Projections of Public and Non-Public School Enrollment.

The University of the State of New York/The State Education Department. (1993b). The State of Learning: A Report to the Governor and Legislature on the Educational Status of the State's Schools.

II

Organizing Students for Instruction

6

Tracking Students for Instruction
Consequences and Implications for School Restructuring

Adam Gamoran and Maureen T. Hallinan

Ability grouping or tracking is the assignment of students to groups for instruction based on their ability or academic achievement. The term *ability grouping* sometimes refers to within-class grouping, in which a class is divided into smaller instructional groups that are relatively homogeneous with respect to ability. Within-class ability grouping typically occurs in elementary schools, and most frequently in the areas of reading and mathematics. Tracking, or between-class ability grouping, refers to the practice of dividing a grade into classes on the basis of ability for instruction. Tracking is found most often in middle and secondary schools. Students generally are tracked for English and mathematics, and often for other subjects as well.

A number of mechanisms link ability grouping and tracking to student achievement. These mechanisms include instructional factors, such as the curriculum and pedagogical techniques, and social psychological factors, such as teacher expectations and student aspirations and self-esteem. These mechanisms trigger cognitive and social psychological processes that govern student attitudes and behaviors, and determine student outcomes. In principle, these effects may be positive, as, for example, when ability grouping allows teachers to gear instruction to the ability

Adam Gamoran   Department of Sociology, University of Wisconsin, Madison, Wisconsin 53706.   **Maureen T. Hallinan**   Department of Sociology, University of Notre Dame, Notre Dame, Indiana 46556.

Restructuring Schools: Promising Practices and Policies, edited by Maureen T. Hallinan. Plenum Press, New York, 1995.

level of the student, creating greater student engagement with the curriculum. However, these mechanisms also may generate negative outcomes, as, for example, when low-ability students are assigned uninteresting material that leads to their detachment from the learning process.

The effectiveness of ability grouping and tracking depends on how the practice is implemented and on the nature of the cognitive and social psychological processes it generates. Schools vary in the way grouping is practiced, in terms of the number of group levels, the permanence of placement, and the criteria for group assignment. Schools also vary in climate, which affects the social status associated with group assignment and student self-esteem. Identifying the predominant characteristics of a particular grouping structure and the climate in which it is implemented, should explain its effects on student achievement.

OVERVIEW OF STUDIES OF ABILITY GROUPING

Empirical studies of ability grouping can be organized around three themes: the effects of ability grouping on student achievement; the determinants of grouping assignments and the flexibility of those assignments; and the social psychological consequences of ability grouping. Most of the studies on the first theme, the effects of grouping on achievement, are surveys. Many of these studies rely on large, longitudinal data sets while others employ smaller longitudinal or cross-sectional data sets. Studies of the determinants of grouping assignments typically contain detailed information on a small number of schools. Research on the social psychological effects of ability grouping generally are case studies, relying on observational data from one or a few schools or classrooms.

Ability Grouping and Achievement

Most of the studies examining grouping effects on achievement either compare the average achievement of students in grouped schools with that of students in ungrouped schools, or compare student achievement across ability group levels with the same school. Recent reviews of these studies have been published by Slavin (1987, 1990), Gamoran and Berends (1987), and Hallinan (1990, 1994). Since only a small proportion of schools group students heterogeneously for English and mathematics, the samples for these studies tend to be small. In general, the studies are fairly consistent in showing no difference in the average achievement of students in schools with ability grouping and those without. Of course, the absence of a main effect of grouping does not preclude differences in the distribution of ability across students in grouped and ungrouped schools. Ability-grouped schools may have a wider distribution of achievement, with more very high and very low achievers, than ungrouped schools. Interestingly, these and other studies typically find no difference between the achievement of students assigned to the regular ability groups and that of students in ungrouped schools.

Considerably more research is available comparing the achievement of students across ability group levels and the growth in achievement of students in different ability groups. Again, the results of these studies are fairly consistent. They show that students in high-ability groups attain higher levels of achievement and learn at a faster pace than their peers in low-ability groups (e.g., Cochrane, 1961; Fogelman, Essen, & Tibbenham, 1978; Rosenbaum, 1976; Kerckhoff, 1986; Hallinan, 1994). Further, controlling for ability, student growth in achievement is faster in high groups than in low groups. The rate of growth and level of achievement of students in the regular group falls between that of those in the high and low groups. These studies point to several characteristics of grouping that explain the differential effects of grouping on students assigned to high and low groups.

Assignment to Ability Groups

The second theme around which ability grouping studies are organized concerns the factors that affect group assignments and the permanence of those assignments. School authorities rely on a number of criteria in assigning students to ability groups. The most commonly used criteria are relatively objective measures of ability or achievement, including standardized test scores and class grades. Other criteria include teacher and counselor recommendations, parent and student preferences, and scheduling constraints.

Empirical work has shown that objective measures of ability are strong predictors of group assignment. School personnel apparently view standardized test scores and subject grades as reliable indicators of student ability (Gamoran, 1992a). In addition, controlling for achievement test scores, prior group assignment is a significant determinant of group placement. This is particularly true at the transition from middle to secondary school (Gamoran, 1992a; Hallinan, 1992). A student assigned to a high track in middle school, regardless of achievement, has a significantly higher probability of assignment to a high track in secondary school. This dependence on prior track placement is not surprising, considering that a number of middle schools may feed into a single high school. Without knowing most of the students, high school personnel are apt to judge that a student who was successful at a particular group level in middle school is likely to succeed at that same level in high school.

Less objective measures of achievement, in the form of teacher and counselor recommendations and parental and student preferences, are given more weight as the student becomes better known in a school. A teacher's evaluation of a student's academic history, motivation, attitudes, behaviors, and aspirations is likely to influence course placement (Cicourel & Kitsuse, 1963; Oakes, 1985; Rosenbaum, 1976). Teacher expectations, shaped by countless influences, possibly including stereotypes based on gender, race, ethnicity, and social class, may influence a teacher's evaluation and affect group placement. Parental preference may take into account the academic and college or career aspirations of the student, as may student preference. Students may also request a particular course or group level in order to avoid schedule conflicts with other courses.

Background characteristics of students, including race, gender, and social class, affect group placement for both organizational and social reasons (Patchen, 1982; Vanfossen, Jones, & Spade, 1987; Hoffer & Kamens, 1992). Race can be a factor in ability-grouped schools if school authorities are trying to avoid the racial segregation that often accompanies ability grouping. For example, Hallinan and Sorensen (1985) found that some schools increase the size of high-ability groups to ensure that they are racially integrated. Gender may be a factor in assignment to English and mathematics tracks in middle and secondary schools if school personnel believe gender influences verbal and mathematical skills (Hallinan, 1991; Patchen, 1982). Since higher social class has been associated with higher group placement, it may be perceived as a measure of academic aspirations or ability.

One of the most serious charges critics level against ability grouping is that it locks students early on into a group or track level that may or may not benefit the student and that precludes subsequent change to a more appropriate group. Little research is available that examines the extent to which ability group assignments are permanent. Gamoran (1989) observed that in some cases, assignment to reading groups in second grade depended on where students had been assigned for reading in first grade, regardless of first grade achievement. Dauber (1994) noted that elementary school ability group positions affect placement in the transition to middle school. A few studies in the middle school also show that track assignments tend to be stable, although they differ across subject matter (Eder, 1981; Hallinan & Sorensen, 1985; Oakes, 1985). That is, students assigned to a particular track in English may or may not be assigned to the same track in mathematics. But track assignments in a subject are found to be fairly stable across middle school. In contrast, a recent study of track mobility in high school revealed considerable track mobility in both English and, to an even greater extent, mathematics (Hallinan, in press). Students were more likely to move to higher tracks than to lower ones, and to change track over the summer than during an academic year. Much of the mobility involved dropping out of the tracking system. School differences occurred in the extent to which track reassignment was permitted. Additional studies are being designed to replicate these findings.

Social Psychological Consequences of Tracking

The final theme that research examines is the social psychological consequences of ability grouping. Grouping affects students' attitudes toward schooling, their motivation and effort to learn, their self-image, their evaluation of their peers, and their choice of friends. Most of the empirical studies that investigate the relationship between grouping and these social psychological outcomes are based on fieldwork, and tend to be case studies of students in ability-grouped schools. The data are obtained primarily through observation, and occasionally by interviews and questionnaires.

According to this research, ability grouping generates a number of social psychological processes that produce various student outcomes (Oakes, 1985; Patchen, 1982; Rosenbaum, 1976, 1980; Metz, 1978). Ability grouping defines a status hierarchy based on group level and identifies academic achievement as the basis for status. School authorities and many students view students assigned to high groups as successful and those in lower groups as academically inferior. Students in high groups are likely to receive more respect and esteem from their peers than those in lower groups. They also receive academic rewards and recognition from their teachers and peers more frequently than their peers. Low-ability-grouped students have less social status and receive fewer academic awards for their academic efforts. Schools differ in the significance attached to academic success and in the basis for student status. The stronger the academic climate of a school, the greater is the salience associated with scholastic success or failure and the greater the likelihood that academic achievement is the primary basis for social status.

Qualitative studies provide evidence that ability group assignment affects a student's self-image (Oakes, 1985; Patchen, 1982; Rosenbaum, 1976, 1980). Students assigned to lower-ability groups form a poor image of their abilities and develop low expectations for their achievement. In so doing, they may be reacting to the low expectations teachers tend to have for students in low-ability groups (Oakes, Gamoran, & Page, 1992). A loss of self-confidence weakens motivation and effort, which, in turn, produces lower achievement. Further, low self-confidence is associated with student detachment from the instructional process and disruptive behavior in the classroom. A cyclical process develops in which negative attitudes and behaviors lead to lower academic achievement, which further decreases motivation and weakens self-image. The reverse process is seen in the high-ability groups where academic achievement builds self-confidence, which increases effort to attain further success.

Ability grouping also affects students' social relationships and, in particular, their choice of friends (Cusick, 1973; Hallinan & Sorensen, 1985). Students assigned to the same group engage in more interaction and shared academic activities with each other than with those in different groups. While these students already have similar ability levels, their frequent within-group interactions create new similarities and foster friendships. Further, students may form a subculture within a group, which may or may not be consistent with the academic climate of the school. A shared subculture becomes an added factor in the formation of within-group friendships. These friendships, in turn, are likely to affect students' attitudes toward learning and their behavior in school.

In summary, the empirical literature on the effects of ability grouping is fairly consistent in supporting three main findings. First, ability grouping has differential effects on high- and low-ability students, providing learning advantages to students assigned to high groups and disadvantages to those placed in low groups. Second, group assignments are heavily determined by previous academic achievement and group placement, but teacher and counselor recommendations and parental and student preferences also play a role, as do background characteristics. Further, while group assignments tend to be more stable in the middle school, they are quite flexible in secondary school, permitting change across tracks both within and across school years. Finally, grouping assignments affect students' attitudes and behaviors in such a way as to influence their motivation, effort, educational aspirations, and academic achievement.

IMPLICATIONS FOR SCHOOL DESIGN

What do these finding imply for school restructuring? One common response has been to argue that tracking and grouping should be eliminated, or at least minimized. Because ability grouping contributes to inequality in cognitive and noncognitive outcomes, adherents of this view demand that students be taught along with classmates of varying ability levels. Other persons concerned with education—particularly teachers and parents—claim that without some degree of grouping, academic diversity among students is too great to permit successful teaching. Imagine confronting a class of ninth graders, some of whom are struggling with arithmetic, and others who have mastered algebra. The gap is too wide, many believe, to make effective progress at both ends of the math ability spectrum in a single instructional context.

We respond to these findings and concerns in two ways. First, we argue that certain forms of grouping and tracking, which are associated with the strongest negative consequences, should be eliminated. Second, to the extent that some forms of grouping remain, we assess the prospects for more effective implementation than has typically occurred in the past.

Eliminate Rigid Tracking

To an important degree, the negative effects of tracking stem from the breadth, permanence, and inflexibility with which it is commonly implemented.

Assignment for Many Subjects on a Single Criterion

Often, elementary school students are assigned to a class based on a single test score such as IQ or reading comprehension (Slavin, 1987). Students assigned to a class in this manner differ widely in skills not directly addressed by the test. For example, students assigned on the basis of reading scores are greatly heterogeneous in math skills. Any possible advantages of homogeneity are lost in curricular areas not directly incorporated in the skills used for assignment. The same phenomenon occurs when students are assigned to a curricular track (e.g., the college-preparatory track, the general track) which dictates all of their courses. This procedure ensures that classes in particular subjects will be heterogeneous, and no positive effects of tracking can be realized.

To bring out any positive effects of homogeneous classes, it is essential that the classes be homogeneous on criteria that are relevant to the curriculum of the class (Slavin, 1987). Thus, separate assignment decisions are required for each subject that is to be taught in homogeneous classes.

Persistence of Track Assignment

Assignment to a particular track or ability group level tends to persist over time, particularly in elementary and middle schools, though to a lesser extent in high school (Gamoran, 1989, 1992a; Hallinan, 1990, 1994). Even when students' academic growth rates vary, track assignments typically remain stable. For example, Gamoran (1992a) observed that students in honors English classes in eighth grade who maintained high test scores had about an 87% likelihood of entering the honors class in ninth grade, while students who were not in honors classes in eighth grade but who performed equally well on tests had only a 59% chance of entering the honors class in ninth grade. Because of this persistence, what are supposedly homogeneous classes are bound to become more heterogeneous over time, so any instructional advantages of homogeneity are diminished, yet the social disadvantages of labeling and hierarchy are preserved.

Lack of mobility across ability groups exacerbates achievement inequality (Gamoran, 1992b). This may occur because permanent tracks tend to foster highly differentiated friendship groups (Sorensen, 1970), or because instruction cannot be adjusted to students' needs when movement between tracks is rare. To accommodate students' changing needs, flexibility in track assignment is required.

In some cases, the desire for flexibility has been taken to an extreme. Gamoran and Nystrand (1990) observed a middle school in which students were assigned to heterogeneous English classes, and then regrouped by ability for reading, writing, spelling, and sometimes for literature. Students were assigned to different groups for each topic, and generally several topics were covered each day. The result was chaotic classrooms, with students (and often the teachers) not knowing where they were supposed to be at a given moment, and much instructional time lost in transition. Hence, the need for flexibility and mobility in ability-group assignment must be balanced with the need for an orderly and efficient classroom.

Eliminate "Teacher Tracking"

Qualitative as well as survey evidence suggests that more qualified teachers tend to teach high-track classes while low-track classes are taught by less qualified teachers. Finley (1984) observed that teachers compete with one another for the opportunity to teach the honors class, and those with the best reputations often win out. Principals may use assignment to the honors class as a reward for favored teachers (Becker, 1973). In a national survey, Talbert (1990) found that about one-third of teachers mainly instruct classes of a single ability level, but this probably occurs more in some schools than others; Rosenbaum (1976) observed a school in which most teachers taught in a single track. Using national data,

Oakes (1990) found that high-track math and science classes are taught by teachers who are more experienced and better qualified in their subject matter. From another national survey, Hoffer and Gamoran (1993) found that high-track math teachers more often had math majors than teachers in other tracks, but the finding did not hold for science.

Schools that repeatedly assign more qualified or more effective teachers to the high track obviously exacerbate the effects of tracking on inequality. Not only do equity demands call for teachers of similar quality across tracks, but circulating teachers among tracks may help break the vicious cycle of low expectations, in which low-track teachers hold low expectations, producing poor performance among students, which reinforces the teachers' low expectations (Oakes, Gamoran, & Page, 1992).

Toward More Effective Grouping

Eliminating the most rigid forms of tracking and rotating teachers among track levels would mitigate tracking's impact on inequality. Quantitative research on tracking and achievement suggests that the more similar the quality of academic experiences in different tracks, the less tracking tends to magnify achievement differences. But is it possible to provide equally high-quality instruction in all tracks? What evidence, if any, suggests that it is feasible to sort students for instruction by academic performance, without reinforcing the achievement gaps between tracks?

Grouping in Elementary Schools

Slavin (1987) concluded that in some cases, ability grouping produces higher achievement than mixed ability teaching in elementary schools. To be successful, he noted, a grouping plan must reduce heterogeneity in the skill taught, allow teachers to move students among groups as performance levels change, and teachers must "vary the pace and level of instruction to correspond to students' levels of readiness and learning rates" (Slavin, 1987, p. 322). Our assessment of the evidence is consistent with these conclusions.

One approach that consistently had positive effects was within-class grouping. This approach avoids the features of ability grouping that exacerbate inequality the most. First, the same teacher instructs all of the groups, so there is no "teacher tracking." Second, students are assigned to within-class groups for particular subjects on the basis of subject-specific criteria. Third, consistent with Slavin's conclusions, teachers tend to vary the pace of instruction with different groups. However, there is some evidence that differences between groups in curricular coverage are often wider than they need to be, and this tends to limit the achievement of students in low groups. In a comparison of 45 first-grade reading groups in 12 classes, Gamoran (1984) observed that gaps between groups in content coverage were very wide in some classes and narrower in others; these differences were not always related to ability differences among students in different groups. The narrower were the gaps in coverage, the lower the inequality of achievement. Hence, the challenge for teachers is to sustain narrow gaps in instructional coverage while maintaining high standards.

In addition, some teachers may exacerbate inequality by showing obvious favoritism for the higher groups. For example, some teachers devote more time and attention to the top group, and others provide more positive labels for higher-ranked groups (e.g., Rist, 1970; Weinstein, 1976; Gamoran, 1984). Effective within-class grouping clearly demands that teachers refrain from these practices.

Between-class grouping in elementary schools shows little evidence of positive effects overall, and it may enhance inequality of achievement among students assigned to different classes. However, when students are assigned to ability-grouped classes for particular subjects, and when this is combined with multiage grouping, test scores appear higher (Slavin, 1987). In this approach, also, grouping is implemented without its most rigid features.

Grouping in Middle and High Schools

Research to date has uncovered little evidence of successful ability grouping at the secondary level. Case studies of Catholic schools suggest that by emphasizing academic rigor at all ability levels, the harmful effects of tracking may be mitigated (Valli, 1990; Camarena, 1990). Survey evidence is consistent with this claim, indicating that tracking's effects on inequality are smaller in Catholic than in public schools (Gamoran, 1992b).

Gamoran (1993) examined 24 eighth- and ninth-grade low-track English classes, and found only 2 that appeared successful, in the sense that high-quality instruction seemed to help students keep pace with their higher-achieving peers. Both classes were in Catholic schools, as one might have expected based on Valli's (1990) and Camerena's (1990) findings. Gamoran concluded that successful low-track classes shared four characteristics: (1) high teacher expectations, manifested in a refusal to relinquish the academic curriculum as commonly occurs in other low-track classes; (2) extensive oral interaction between teachers and students, in contrast to reliance on worksheets as has been reported elsewhere for low tracks (e.g., Page, 1991); (3) extra exertion by teachers to keep students interested and on task; and (4) the absence of a schoolwide system of assigning weak or inexperienced teachers to low-track classes. Whether these characteristics can be transferred to public schools has yet to be demonstrated.

Recently, several states and school districts have attempted to raise academic standards for low-achieving high school students. For example, educators in New York and California have created "transition" math courses, which are supposed to bridge the gap between elementary and advanced mathematics (White, 1994). The aim of these courses is to lead greater proportions of students into college-preparatory mathematics, and ultimately to eliminate the general track. This is essentially a tracking program, in that students may be assigned to general, transition, or college-preparatory math courses. However, the transition courses are "upgraded" in the sense that they are more challenging academically and they prepare students for higher math instead of being terminal, even though they are targeted to a low-achieving (and usually low-income) population of students. Research on students' course-taking patterns indicates that students who enroll in transition courses have much better odds of ultimately completing a college-preparatory sequence than students who enroll in the general track (White, Gamoran, & Smithson, 1994). This finding holds even among students with similar grades and test scores prior to high school. Hence, results from the transition math programs suggest that courses for low-achieving students can be improved, and if so they yield better results.

The Problem of Incentives

A major problem in reducing inequality of results among students enrolled in different tracks may be that incentives for academic performance are not the same in all tracks. In particular, students who are not planning on attending college have little reason to do any more than pass the course and accumulate enough credits to graduate (Rosenbaum, 1989; Bishop, 1993). Among those who have a diploma, success in the job market has little visible connection to school performance. By contrast, students in honors classes may be aiming for elite colleges, so their grades and accumulated knowledge and skills have a recognizable payoff beyond high school. Under these conditions, improving the quality of instruction in low-track classes may do little to reduce inequality of achievement between students in high and low tracks.

Explaining track inequality as an incentives problem is consistent with some of the evidence we have reviewed. Evidence of successful low tracks in Catholic secondary schools may reflect the fact that these schools are typically populated by middle-class students who are planning on attending college. Low-achieving students in Catholic schools may be more motivated than the typical low-track public school student.

An emphasis on incentives is also consistent with evidence on the effectiveness of curricular upgrading. When students who would typically be assigned to low tracks are instead placed in courses that lead to a college-preparatory curriculum, they tend to succeed, even though the transition courses are more challenging and demanding than general-track courses. This may occur not only because of improvements in curriculum and instruction, but because students view these classes as more meaningful.

In countries outside the United States, students' academic performance has consequences for their lives after high school. In Japan, for example, high school grades are an important criterion for employer decisions on job offers (Rosenbaum, 1989). In England, students take a national examination at age 16 (American Federation of Teachers, 1994). Performance on the exam has consequences not only for admission to postsecondary schooling, but also for employment opportunities. In these cases, students at all track levels have incentives to work hard during secondary school. No matter one's location in the academic hierarchy, the better one performs, the better one's chance of success after high school. This is not the case in the United States. National or state-level examination systems, which are being widely discussed at present, could change the incentive structure and make tracking less potent in producing inequality. The Commission on Skills of the American Workforce (1990), for example, has advocated a "certificate of initial mastery" to be earned by age 16. The certificate would signify competence in essential academic subjects, and would have value for subsequent opportunities both inside and outside the educational system. The introduction of performance standards of this type, if tied to benefits that are relevant for all students, could reduce or eliminate discrepancies in incentives between tracks that may now exist.

SOCIAL AND POLITICAL CONTEXTS AFFECTING GROUPING REFORM

Plans to alter school design to improve educational practice typically meet resistance. In particular, proposals to change ability grouping and tracking practices provoke strong feelings and vigorous debate. As Oakes argues, ability grouping and tracking exist in a social and political context that creates barriers to educational change (Oakes, 1994; see also Oakes & Lipton, 1992).

One of the factors that makes change in current ability grouping policies difficult is the belief of many educators and parents that intelligence is fixed and can easily be measured. Those who hold this belief find the academic criteria that teachers employ in assigning students to group levels appropriate. Further, to those who think that intelligence is unidimensional, the current practice of using verbal and mathematics scores on standardized achievement tests to assign students to tracks in various subjects seems justified. The assumption that intelligence is a fixed trait and that student growth in achievement is linear makes permanent assignments reasonable. Recent advances in the study of intelligence and learning contradict these beliefs, demonstrating that intelligence is multidimensional and that learning is nonlinear (Gardner, 1993). However, until this research gains wider acceptance, many will fail to understand the limitations that many grouping practices impose on student learning.

Observations in highly restructured schools suggest that secondary school mathematics instruction may be most resistant to organizational change. In a study of highly restructured schools, 12 of 16 secondary schools maintained ability grouping in math even when other subjects were mixed-ability. In 2 of the secondary schools that formed heterogeneous classes for math, teachers complained that they were unable to meet the needs of all students (Gamoran and Weinstein, 1995).

Similarly, in the study of upgrading the math curriculum for low-achieving students, teachers and administrators emphasized the value of new alternative curricula, asserting that simply mixing low-achieving students together with other students in college-preparatory classes was not a workable solution (White *et al.*, 1994). Despite new standards proposed by the National Council of Teachers of Mathematics (1989), most teachers appear to view mathematics as a hierarchical subject matter. According to this conception, mathematics must be learned in sequence; students who have not mastered arithmetic, for example, should not study algebra. A softer version of this position holds that students who have not mastered arithmetic can study algebra, but they should do so in a separate group from those who have mastered arithmetic, so instruction in each context can take advantage of students' strengths and address their weaknesses.

Despite the resistance of many educators and community members to altering ability grouping and tracking practices, the political and social climate of the schools and communities is changing in such a way as to support moderate reform efforts. While national reports on education in the 1980s emphasized educational excellence (e.g., National Commission on Excellence in Education, 1983), the present focus seems to have shifted to incorporate educational equity. Without abandoning efforts to foster scholastic excellence, educators and community members are struggling to ensure that the learning needs of all students are taken into account.

Emphasis on equity can be seen in several national and statewide reform efforts. One of these reforms aims at refinancing the public schools by redistributing taxes or other monies to provide a more equal allocation of funds across all schools in a state. Another reform that is sensitive to equity is Goals 2000, which proposes national standards and assessments for all students, to be met by providing a challenging academic curriculum and quality training for the work force. The assumption underlying Goals 2000 is that all students can learn and attain high standards with appropriate support from school and community.

Similarly, the Reauthorization of the Elementary and Secondary Education Act addresses equity by focusing on reducing minority group isolation and providing funds to help states achieve greater equity in the distribution of educational resources and opportunities across all students. A fourth reform motivated partly by equity considerations is school choice, designed to give students access to any public, and in some cases, private, school within a school district or state.

A second change in climate is manifested in the recognition by states and districts that too often, low-ability groups, remedial classes, and low-track classes are dead ends for students. In response, many of these classes are being eliminated. While some schools simply detrack and create heterogeneous classes, many schools are replacing low groups by alternate programs. Of growing popularity in both the education and business community are school-to-work programs that directly prepare students for the labor market (see Rosenbaum, this volume, Chapter 11). One of these programs, Tech Prep, has already been implemented in a majority of states. Transition math courses that aim to bridge the gap between basic and college-preparatory math are another example of alternative courses for low-achieving students (White et al., 1994).

Given a better understanding of the limitations of current ability grouping and tracking practices, new research that provides a broader understanding of the nature of intelligence and learning, and a recognition that the current political and social climate may be supportive of educational reform, the conditions seem to exist to make possible fundamental change in the way students are organized for instruction. The current political and social climate seems conducive to educational reform that emphasizes equality of educational opportunity for all students without undermining the efforts that have been made to promote educational excellence.

To eliminate the inequities and deficiencies of ability grouping and tracking, Oakes and Lipton (1992) argue that a culture of detracking is needed. By this they mean a climate in which ability grouping and tracking are eliminated as part of a broader educational reform that includes fundamental change in school organization, practice, and policy. Such change would require the definition of new teacher roles, the promulgation of democratic values, new patterns of communication among educators, parents, and students, and a renewed emphasis on intellectual curiosity and learning.

While the idea of creating a culture of detracking is appealing, in practice it often leads to no more than simply eliminating tracking. Fundamental restructuring of instruction and the curriculum rarely accompanies the organizational change. As a result, detracking may be no more effective than ability grouping. Rather than a culture of detracking, it may be more useful to think of a culture of schooling, which emphasizes excellence as well as equity, which acknowledges differences among students, and which supports whatever approach best meets all students' educational needs.

Efforts must be made to deal with the very real problems that ability grouping was designed to address. Regardless of how students are organized for instruction, a diversity of students are found within each school, and some way must be found to meet students' varied needs. Since some degree of student diversity exists regardless of how students are assigned to instructional groups or classes, the problem transcends the organizational arrangement of students for instruction. Thus, the focus of reform must be to design a curriculum and pedagogical practices that address the real learning needs of students regardless of how they are grouped.

The solution may lie in some combination of mixed-ability and homogeneous grouping. When students are assigned to mixed-ability groups, they can benefit from the intellectual diversity of their peers, from strong learning models, from opportunities to tutor and be tutored by peers, and from the absence of stigma associated with assignment to a low-ability group. What they are missing is an instructional processin which the curriculum is presented at a rate and level that best fits their learning abilities. When students are assigned to ability groups or tracks, they receive instruction that is adapted to their learning abilities. However, as our review indicated, ability grouping often results in a lower-quality instruction for low-achieving students. Also, grouping is often accompanied by a social elitism that creates social barriers among students and stigmatizes those assigned to low groups. To assign students to some mixed classes, in subjects where the curriculum is accessible to a wide variety of learning levels, and to some ability groups, where the curriculum is tapered to student needs, may provide a balance absent in detracked or strictly ability-grouped schools. Assigning students to both ability-grouped and mixed classes has the advantage of promoting academic excellence, especially among high-achieving students, in certain subjects, while at the same time providing a variety of learning opportunities and settings for all students. Furthermore, the social hierarchy created by strict ability grouping is likely to be weakened, since all students will belong to some mixed classes. However, it is essential to ensure that in subjects that continue to be ability grouped, high standards are established for instructional quality in low-ability classes.

Regardless of the basis of group assignment, further reform efforts must be aimed at increasing the quantity and quality of instruction in all classes. This involves curriculum reform, aimed at defining a body of information that is relevant, interesting, and of consequence to the students. It also involves implementing new pedagogical techniques and methods of instruction to better engage students in the learning process (e.g., Newmann, 1992). Finally, it requires increasing the exposure of students to the curriculum and instruction, to maximize the length of time students are actually engaged in the learning process.

Our argument is consistent with Oakes and Lipton's (1992) view that a change in ability grouping and in tracking systems must occur in the context of broader curriculum change, including presentation of learning tasks as complex problems with multiple right answers, in meaningful contexts, and where knowledge can be socially constructed by students as well as teachers. The difference between our view and Oakes's is that we support making these broad curricular changes in ability-grouped or mixed-ability classes, wherever they can best succeed.

ACKNOWLEDGMENTS.   Support was provided by the Center on Organization and Restructuring of Schools, funded by the U.S. Department of Education (Grant #R117Q00005-94); the Office of Educational Research and Improvement, U.S. Department of Education (Grant #R117E10139-01); and the National Science Foundation (Grant #RED-9311800). Findings and conclusions are those of the authors and do not necessarily represent the views of the supporting agencies.

REFERENCES

American Federation of Teachers. (1994). World class standards. *American Educator, 18*(1).

Becker, H. (1973). *Outsiders* (rev. ed.). New York: Free Press.

Bishop, J. (1993). *Incentives to study and the organization of secondary instruction.* Ithaca, NY: Center for Advanced Human Resource Studies. Cornell University, Working Paper 93-08.

Camarena, M. (1990). Following the right track: A comparison of tracking practices in public and Catholic schools. In R. Page & L. Valli (Eds.), *Curriculum differentiation: Interpretive studies in U.S. secondary schools* (pp. 159–182). Albany, NY: SUNY Press.

Cicourel, A., & Kitsuse, J. (1963). *The educational decision makers.* Indianapolis: Bobbs-Merrill.

Cochrane, J. (1961). Grouping students in junior high school. *Educational Leadership, 18,* 414–419.

Commission on Skills of the American Workforce. (1990). *America's choice: High skills or low wages!* Rochester, NY: National Center on Education and the Economy.

Cusick, P. A. (1973). *Inside high school.* New York: Holt, Rinehart & Winston.

Dauber, S. (1994). *Tracking and transitions through the middle grades: Channeling educational trajectories.* Paper presented at the annual meeting of the American Sociological Association, Los Angeles.

Eder, D. (1981). Ability grouping as a self-fulfilling prophecy: A micro-analysis of teacher–student interaction. *Sociology of Education, 54,* 151–162.

Finley, M. K. (1984). Teachers and tracking in a comprehensive high school. *Sociology of Education, 57,* 233–243.

Fogelman, K., Essen, J., & Tibbenham, A. (1978). Ability-grouping in secondary schools and attainment. *Educational Studies, 4,* 201–212.

Gamoran, A. (1984). *Teaching, grouping, and learning: A study of the consequences of educational stratification.* Ph.D. dissertation, Department of Education, University of Chicago.

Gamoran, A. (1989). Rank, performance, and mobility in elementary school grouping. *Sociological Quarterly, 30,* 109–123.

Gamoran, A. (1992a). Access to excellence: Assignment to honors English classes in the transition from middle to high school. *Educational Evaluation and Policy Analysis, 14,* 185–204.

Gamoran, A. (1992b). The variable effects of high school tracking. *American Sociological Review, 57,* 812–828.

Gamoran, A. (1993). Alternative uses of ability grouping in secondary schools: Can we bring high-quality instruction to low-ability classes? *American Journal of Education, 101,* 1–22.

Gamoran, A., & Weinstein, M. (1995). *Differentiation and opportunity in restructured schools.* Paper presented at the annual meeting of the American Sociological Association, Washington, DC, August 1995.

Gamoran, A., & Berends, M. (1987). The effects of stratification in secondary schools: Synthesis of survey and ethnographic research. *Review of Educational Research, 57,* 415–435.

Gamoran, A., & Nystrand, M. (1990). *Tracking, instruction and achievement.* Paper presented at the World Congress of Sociology, Madrid.

Gardner, (1993). *Multiple intelligences: The theory in practice.* New York: Basic Books.

Hallinan, M. T. (1990). The effects of ability grouping in secondary schools: A response to Slavin's best-evidence synthesis. *Review of Educational Research, 60*(3), 501–504.

Hallinan M. T. (1991). School differences in tracking structures and track assignments. *Journal of Research on Adolescence, 1*(3), 251–275.

Hallinan, M. T. (1992). The organization of students for instruction in the middle school. *Sociology of Education, 65,* 114–127.

Hallinan, M. T. (1994). Tracking: From theory to practice. *Sociology of Education, 67*(2), 79–91.

Hallinan, M. T. (in press). Track mobility in secondary school. *Social Forces.*

Hallinan, M. T., & Sorensen, A. B. (1985). Ability grouping and student friendships. *American Educational Research Journal, 22*(4), 485–499.

Hoffer, T., & Gamoran, A. (1993). *Effects of instructional differences among ability groups in middle-school science and mathematics.* Paper presented at the annual meeting of the American Sociological Association, Miami.

Hoffer, T., & Kamens, D. (1992). *Tracking and inequality revisited: Secondary school course sequences and the effects of social class on educational opportunities.* Paper presented at the annual meeting of the American Sociological Association, Pittsburgh.

Kerckhoff, A. C. (1986). Effects of ability grouping in British secondary schools. *American Sociological Review, 51,* 842–858.

Metz, M. H. (1978). *Classrooms and corridors: The crisis of authority in desegregated secondary schools.* Berkeley: University of California Press.

National Commission on Excellence in Education. (1983, April). *A nation at risk: The imperative for educational reform.* Washington, DC: U.S. Government Printing Office.

National Council of Teachers of Mathematics. (1989). *Curriculum and evaluation standards for school mathematics executive summary.* Washington, DC: Author.

Newmann, F. (Ed.). (1992). *Student engagement and achievement in American secondary schools.* New York: Teachers College Press.

Oakes, J. (1985). *Keeping track: How schools structure inequality.* New Haven: Yale University Press.

Oakes, J. (1990). *Multiplying inequalities: The effects of race, social class, and tracking on opportunities to learn mathematics and science.* Santa Monica: RAND.

Oakes, J. (1994). More than misapplied technology: A normative and political response to Hallinan on tracking. *Sociology of Education, 67*(2), 84–89, 91.

Oakes, J., Gamoran, A., & Page, R. N. (1992). Curriculum differentiation: Opportunities, outcomes, and meanings. In P. W. Jackson (Ed.), *Handbook of research on curriculum* (pp. 570–608). New York: Macmillan Co.

Oakes, J., & Lipton, M. (1992, February). Detracking schools: Early lessons from the field. *Phi Delta Kappa,* 448–454.

Page, R. N. (1991). *Lower track classrooms: A curricular and cultural perspective.* New York: Teachers College Press.

Patchen, M. (1982). *Black–white contact in schools: Its social and academic effects.* West Lafayette, IN: Purdue University Press.

Rist, R. (1970). Social class and teacher expectations: The self-fulfilling prophecy in ghetto education. *Harvard Education Review, 40*, 411–451.

Rosenbaum, J. E. (1976). *Making inequality: The hidden curriculum of high school tracking.* New York: Wiley.

Rosenbaum, J. (1980). Social implications of educational grouping. In D. C. Ben-linger (Ed.), *Review of research in education* (Vol. 7, pp. 361–401). Washington, DC: American Educational Research Association.

Rosenbaum, J. E. (1989). What if good jobs depended on good grades? *American Educator, 13*(4), 10–43.

Slavin, R. E. (1987). Ability grouping and achievement in elementary schools: A best-evidence synthesis. *Review of Educational Research, 57*, 293–336.

Slavin, R. E. (1990). Achievement effects of ability grouping in secondary schools: A best-evidence synthesis. *Review of Educational Research, 60*, 471–499.

Sorensen, A. B. (1970). Organizational differentiation of students and educational opportunity. *Sociology of Education, 43*, 355–376.

Talbert, J. (1990). *Teacher tracking: Exacerbating inequalities in the high school.* Paper presented at the annual meeting of the American Educational Research Association, Boston.

Valli, L. (1990). A curriculum of effort: Tracking students in a Catholic high school. In R. N. Page & L. Valli (Eds.), *Curriculum differentiation: Interpretive studies in U.S. secondary schools* (pp. 45–65). Albany, NY: SUNY Press.

Vanfossen, B., Jones, J., & Spade, J. (1987). Curriculum tracking and status maintenance. *Sociology of Education, 60*(2), 104–122.

Weinstein, R. S. (1976). Reading group membership in first grade: Teacher behaviors and pupil experience over time. *Journal of Educational Psychology, 68*, 103–116.

White P. (1994). *Upgrading instruction and achievement in high school: The implementation of state, district, and school policies to upgrade the math curriculum.* Madison, WI: Consortium for Policy Research in Education.

White, P., Gamoran, A., & Smithson, J. (1994). *Upgrading the high school math curriculum: Math course-taking patterns in New York and California.* Madison, WI: Consortium for Policy Research in Education.

7

Local Constraints on Opportunity to Learn Mathematics in High School[1]

Jennifer S. Manlove and David P. Baker

Perhaps the longest running and most salient political fault line in the historical development of education in the United States is the clash between locally administered schooling and a national educational establishment bent on reform. Repeatedly, over the past century and a half, constituencies from these two arenas have been in conflict over a number of educational issues. The outcomes of these struggles have helped form the structure of U.S. schooling. The development of the age-graded school, the Carnegie unit and the core academic curriculum, school racial desegregation, and ability grouping are some examples of defining educational issues that have been filtered through the unique American split between national and local interests (for other examples see Firestone, 1994; Mirel, 1994; Ogawa, 1994; Tyack & Tobin, 1994).

Educational reform in the United States has emerged from conflicts between multiple interest groups. In more centralized, corporatist coun-

[1]This research was supported by a research fellowship (for Jennifer Manlove) and a senior fellowship (for David Baker) from the American Educational Research Association, which receives funds for its "AERA Grants Program" from the National Science Foundation and the National Center for Education Statistics (U.S. Department of Education) under NSF Grant #RED-9255347. Opinions reflect those of the authors and do not necessarily reflect those of the granting agencies.

Jennifer S. Manlove   Child Trends, Inc., Washington, D.C. 20008.   **David P. Baker** Department of Sociology, The Catholic University of America, Washington, D.C. 20064.

Restructuring Schools: Promising Practices and Policies, edited by Maureen T. Hallinan. Plenum Press, New York, 1995.

tries, school reform has resulted from large-scale battles between powerful central ministries, national educational interests such as teachers unions, and pervasive and national business organizations (Rubinson, 1986). In U.S. schools, however, our battles are fought between local school interests and national interests, and among national interests themselves. Our system pits a host of local concerns, resources, and political orientations against often competing education professionals and loosely linked national business and national political parties (e.g., Angus, Mirel, & Vinovskis, 1988; Kliebard, 1987; Richardson, 1986; Tyack & Hansot, 1982; Wrigley, 1982). Given the many local and national factions influencing the U.S. school system, it is not surprising that many unintended outcomes occur with wide local variation.

Nowhere is this arrangement more evident than in the current efforts toward educational *restructuring* and concern over educational quality in U.S. schools. Fueled by international achievement comparisons and an image of failing economic competitiveness, there is a pervasive national vision that our schools are in the midst of a crisis in quality leading to many calls for change and national plans for reform (NCEE, 1983). This cycle is not new: U.S. education has periodically gone through similar phases of crisis–reform–restructure at various points over the last 150 years. What is new in the current round is the pace of reform. Our educational system had just finished (some would say it is still in progress) adjusting to a wave of national concerns over equal educational opportunity in the late 1960s and 1970s when the current concern for educational quality came to the forefront. The result has been a dual track of national interest in both equal opportunity and quality (e.g., Mirel & Angus, 1994; Oakes, Gamoran, & Page, 1992).[2] Even the federal government is captured by these dual, and perhaps competing, concerns as witnessed by the official slogan of the Clinton Department of Education: "Our Mission is to Ensure Equal **Access** to Education and to Promote Educational **Excellence**" (emphasis theirs).

The concern over quality has generated a number of nationally based reforms aimed at establishing some type of a national curriculum, particularly in core academic areas of mathematics, reading, and science. For example, in the field of mathematics, national organizations such as the National Council of Teachers of Mathematics (NCTM) have begun a campaign to develop national mathematics standards and are working in conjunction with other national and state organizations to have these

[2]Compare, for example, the contrasting messages in Kozol's *Savage Inequalities* (1991) with McKnight and colleagues' *The Underachieving Curriculum* (1986); the former depicts a deepening crisis of unequal educational opportunity and the latter describes an inefficient and ineffective mathematics curriculum across the nation's schools.

guidelines adapted within schools' curriculum (NCTM, 1989; Blank & Dalkilic, 1990). The logic behind this work is perhaps best evoked by NCTM's summary in its standards report which combines equality of opportunity with educational quality:

> Creation of a society where equal opportunity exists in access to mathematics has become an economic necessity. . . . In sum, the overall objective of teaching mathematics should be to develop in each and every student an understanding of mathematics that lasts a lifetime and grows to meet changing demand. [NCTM, 1989, p. 11]

At the same time, concern over educational equality alone continues on a national level. For example, the Office of Civil Rights in the U.S. Department of Education began a watchdog program to legally challenge local districts and schools in which ability grouping or curricular tracking practices are deemed to lead to racial inequality of educational opportunities. There is an accompanying national debate among education researchers and policy analysts about tracking and educational equality. For example, in a recent exchange that captures much of the tone of the larger debate, Oakes (1994) argues against tracking, insisting that the practice "builds inequality into schools." In short, she issues a call to national reform. Taking a different approach, Hallinan (1994) argues that, done correctly, tracking can add to educational quality without inequality and that (as we show in terms of curricular opportunity below) many local conditions of our schools shape whether or not the practice produces positive outcomes.

These kinds of proposals and counterproposals for sweeping, national reform, often with some inherent contradiction within and between them, fall onto an extremely decentralized school system. Often there has been less appreciation of the way in which a local school system will adjust to and modify national reforms than for the issues behind the reforms themselves. It is really this "localizing" process that shapes the nature of our schools. But sensitivity to the way local districts and schools adjust to various national concerns and local conditions in the United States escapes most participants in debates about national educational concerns.

Those who have taken a broader view of the U.S. educational reform process have noted a defining difference between the way education is structured nationally as an institution and locally as an organization (Meyer, 1986; Meyer & Scott, 1983; Meyer & Rowan, 1978; Tyack & Hansot, 1982). Our educational system is decentralized organizationally, but not institutionally. On a national, institutional level, U.S. educational reforms organize around heavily symbolic battles whose immediate goals are political: to change the rules of the national institution, but not necessarily to reshape organizational features. Reforming institutional rules, such as equality or quality, is of primary importance; making them uniform organizational realities comes later, if at all (Meyer, 1986). U.S. national educational reform works through "social movements" within the educational establishment.

In part, this is because the United States does not have a top-down mechanism of organizational control, and national reform does not easily translate into specific organizational realities. On the local level, our schools are organizationally decentralized with a fair amount of governance autonomy. Individual states and school districts provide the majority of funding and control over educational policies in schools. Administrative responsibility for many key instructional and curricular decisions is spread over 50 states and some 15,000 school districts. Decisions and implementation of policy for local distribution of educational opportunity and instructional quality are the domain of schools and their immediate administrative environments. This means that national reforms filter through many levels simultaneously, independently of each other, in an uncoordinated and decoupled fashion (Meyer, 1986; Weick, 1976).

Local actors in schools and districts make policy decisions in a complex environment and are influenced by numerous local constituencies; parents, businesses, and other local interest groups have relatively direct access to educational issues in local settings. At the same time, local school officials are aware of, and to a degree are part of, the national social movement aimed at reform. Local variation in the basic inputs to schooling also heavily influences the organization of any particular school. For example, in case studies of three comprehensive high schools, Oakes & Guiton (1995) conclude that high schools take an eclectic approach to tracking decisions by responding to these multiple and often competing influences. They argue that the resulting tracking policies and practices can work to the advantage of the most privileged students.

LOCAL CONDITIONS FOR CURRICULUM REFORM

The remainder of this chapter illustrates the local school conditions that specific reforms filter through. The chapter focuses on opportunity to learn mathematics and the structure of the mathematics curriculum in U.S. public high schools. The complex set of contrasting pressures described above influences local school policy in crucial areas and can easily produce a compromise curriculum (Oakes, Gamoran, & Page, 1992). The combination of competing forces that influence school policy helps determine the curricular opportunities available to students. These conditions and processes are, and will continue to be, the local forces that shape the eventual outcomes of the national restructuring reforms over curricular issues, which are so central to the educational quality and equality issues. Three questions are addressed by the analyses.

1. What is the nature of the distribution of opportunity-to-learn in a decentralized, local educational system?
2. What school-level factors influence opportunity-to-learn?
3. What are the implications of variation of local opportunity-to-learn for educational equality and quality?

These questions are answered from the viewpoint of the school (i.e., curricular policy) instead of the individual student (i.e., course taking) or national program (i.e., content of national curricular reform). The central organizing influence of the school on curricular matters that affect opportunity-to-learn has in the past been understudied compared with studies of student course taking or curricular content. This weakness in the literature is acute since the school is the main organizational controller and interpreter of curricular issues leading to classroom-level opportunity-to-learn.

OPPORTUNITY-TO-LEARN AND SCHOOL ORGANIZATION

Opportunity-to-learn (OTL) is fast becoming a popular term in U.S. education, and represents a simple idea, namely that students can learn only what is made available to them through direct or indirect means. OTL, which originated as a concept from the design of several international achievement studies in the early 1980s, puts agency into the idea of a curriculum in the schooling process. This implies that a school's curriculum is a resource that is distributed across its students. Sometimes OTL has been used to refer to the final point of implementing (i.e., teaching) a curriculum in a classroom, but it contains the larger idea of the whole process by which a curriculum is placed before the student, including class scheduling, instruction, and course groupings by ability. Here we take OTL to mean the process of how a curriculum is organized into a set of courses by certain policies and practices at the school level. Students' course-taking decisions are based on the curricula offered to them. Stevenson, Schiller, and Schneider (1994) argue that student course taking locks them into a sequence of OTLs that may influence their educational outcomes.

The locally organized school system in the United States shows a high degree of variation in OTL. For example, Stevenson and Baker (1991) found that cross-nationally, U.S. schools have more variation between mathematics classrooms in what is taught, how much is taught, and the pace at which the subject is taught than do other countries. The amount of an intended mathematics curriculum that is actually taught in our classrooms depends more on local school and teacher factors than in most other countries. Only other decentralized educational systems such as those of England and Wales have similar levels of between-classroom variation in curriculum. In more centralized systems like Japan or France, variation between classrooms was comparatively small, and any existing variation had nothing to do with local factors.

In the United States this variation is built directly into the governance of schools. For example, a study of five U.S. states showed that 70% of the school districts in these states had their own official, and differing, curriculum and 55% of the districts had their own timetable for the implementation of the curriculum (Floden *et al.*, 1988). In a study of schools in two midwestern cities, Hallinan (1992) found that the local organizational constraints of different schools influenced their curricular offerings.

DATA

Data for these analyses are based on a U.S. Department of Education Fast Response Survey System (FRSS) of High School Curricular Options. The National Center for Education Statistics designed this survey to collect information on the types of curricular policies and practices in public high schools. The FRSS is a stratified sample of public schools selected from approximately 5000 eligible schools from the 1991 Schools and Staffing Survey (SASS). Data were collected from 912 public secondary or combined schools that provide instruction in grades 9 through 12, with a response rate of 92%.[3]

Data were collected on the schools' stated tracking policy, the amount of mobility between tracks, teacher and student assignments, and the

---

[3]Ten of the thousand schools were no longer at the same location or serving the same population, so the response rate is based on the 990 eligible schools in the sample.

types of courses offered in the core curriculum in mathematics and English. Schools listed all of the courses they offered in mathematics during the fall of 1993. The course listing included course titles, ability level of students for which the courses were designed (high, average, low, or widely differing), and the percentage of students enrolled in each course. The analyses examine two aspects of the curricular structure of schools as they pertain to OTL: the number of mathematics classes available to students and the ability level of mathematics courses. The data were merged with SASS to include information on school characteristics such as location and diversity. The reported data here are weighted to provide national estimates.

DISTRIBUTION OF OPPORTUNITY-TO-LEARN

Examples of Curricular Offerings in Selected Schools

As an illustration of the local nature of the distribution of OTL, Table 1 presents the combination of tenth grade mathematics courses offered in four schools from the sample that typify the major patterns in the data. Table 1 lists the courses that are either stratified (high, average, or low abilities) or unstratified (widely differing abilities). First, the schools are classified into three general tracking policies, based on their combination of stratified and unstratified courses offered: schools that offer only courses that are stratified by ability are classified as "traditionally tracked" (e.g., School 1); schools that offer only courses that are unstratified by ability are classified as "untracked" (e.g., School 4); and schools that offer a combination of both stratified and unstratified classes are classified as "mixed" (e.g., Schools 2 and 3).[4] The values are the percentage of all tenth grade students taking a particular class, adding up to approximately 100%.[5]

These example schools help diagram the range of options available to students in different schools and demonstrate the wide variety of mathe-

---

[4]This categorization of schools considers only the types of mathematics courses offered and does not include other measures of tracking policy. Another study by NCES (1994), *Curricular Differentiation in Public High Schools*, finds that when considering whether or not students are allowed to choose classes, only 15% of schools fit the traditionally tracked category.
[5]The percentages may not total 100% because some schools offer classes to a small percentage of "atypical" students.

Table 1. Four Example Schools Representing Main National Patterns of Curricular Offerings and Opportunities to Learn Tenth Grade Mathematics[a]

School	Classification	Higher Abilities	%[b]	Average Abilities	%[b]	Lower Abilities	%[b]	Widely Differing Abilities	%[b]
1	Traditional track	Geometry	25%	Intermediate Algebra	45%	Technical Math Transition Math	15% 10%		
2	Mixed	Honors Algebra II	4%	Advanced Algebra II Advanced Geometry	13% 5%	Algebra I Algebra I-4	32% 4%	Algebra II Geometry	18% 24%
3	Mixed	Algebra II/Trig	10%	Algebra I Applied Math	60% 8%			Consumer Math	16%
4	Untracked							Geometry Algebra 1	90% 10%

[a]This table represents the curricular offerings of four sample schools that represent major patterns in U.S. schools.
[b]Percentage of students enrolled in each course.

matics programs available in public schools in the tenth grade. Each school offers different combinations of courses and has different percentages of students enrolled in each ability-group type, showing how opportunity to learn mathematics is organized locally. Schools vary, to some extent, on student assignment to courses; however, the vast majority of schools (85%) have policies of open student choice (NCES, 1994).

The opportunities available to students would vary dramatically across these four schools. School 1 is an example of a traditionally tracked mathematics curriculum, offering a total of four courses, all of which are stratified by ability. Approximately a quarter of its students are enrolled in the high-ability mathematics class (Geometry) and another quarter of students attend one of two lower-ability classes (Technical Math or Transition Math). The remaining students are enrolled in a class designed for students with average abilities (Intermediate Algebra). This particular school is large and suburban, offers no classes that are unstratified by ability, and its official policy is that it assigns students to courses according to their ability level. This kind of school is often assumed to be the standard model of curriculum differentiation in the United States, but, in actuality, there are a variety of school types (see discussion of Table 3).

At the other extreme is School 4, which has a completely untracked curriculum and offers only courses to students with widely differing abilities. This school has two undifferentiated courses: one is a geometry course, enrolling 90% of the tenth grade students, and the other is Algebra 1, enrolling the other 10% of students. Students are allowed to take either class, if they have taken the prerequisite(s). This is an example of a school that offers no courses organized for students with different abilities. This particular school is a small, rural, primarily white school.

Students with similar ability levels would face different opportunities depending on the type of school they attend. For example, high-ability students in School 4 have no access to courses designed primarily for high-ability students, while high-ability students in School 1 may be placed in an advanced mathematics course. Research on the influence of tracking on outcomes shows some support for the finding that students in high-ability classes show achievement gains (Oakes et al., 1992). Thus, parents of a high-ability student may prefer having their child in a class targeted to students of similar ability levels. On the other hand, students with lower ability levels, who show some losses in attainment if placed in low-ability tracks, may benefit from their location in a mixed-ability class in School 4, while lower-ability students in School 1 may be disadvantaged because of less-demanding courses.

Schools 2 and 3 are examples of schools with mixed curricula. These schools offer courses that are *both* stratified and unstratified by ability;

the difference is the degree in which both kinds of courses occur in the curriculum. School 2 offers classes for students with widely differing abilities, as well as courses targeted to all three ability groups, although most of its enrollment is either in the lowest ability class or in the widely differing ability class. This particular school is large and in the central city, offers a total of seven courses, and seems to offer "something for everyone." Its assignment policy allows students open choice of the type of class they take, even to the stratified courses.

The number and levels of mathematics courses in School 2 represent a maze of course-offerings that some students and parents must negotiate to get through tenth grade. The type of mathematics course a student enrolls in will influence the sequence of opportunities available to them throughout high school (Stevenson *et al.*, 1994). School 2 has the advantage of providing a large number of courses in a range of different categories; however, it expects students and their parents to help choose which course is optimal for the student. Working-class parents and minority students may not have as much access to the information regarding which class would benefit them the most. Thus, this curricular structure may produce unintended inequalities in OTL.[6]

School 3 has a mixed curriculum that offers fewer courses that are stratified by ability level and more that are unstratified. This particular school no longer offers classes to students with lower abilities, but has introduced courses to students with widely differing abilities. This is an example of a school that offers an unstratified mathematics course, but this course—Consumer Math—seems to be targeted to vocational students. Some schools now label vocational courses or low-ability courses as widely differentiated-ability mathematics classes. Again, in this situation, parents and students must consider an assortment of classes, and higher-SES families may be more able to place their children in courses that will improve their OTL.

These example schools show the amount of local variation in opportunities to learn mathematics. Schools 2, 3, and 4 design some or all of their classes for students with a wide range of abilities, which seems to indicate

---

[6]The names of courses alone vary from school to school and demand parental knowledge of the local system. For example, higher-ability-level classes sometimes have very general names, such as, "Course I, Course II, Course III, Math 10, Math 2, Math 201, Math III, Math Analysis, Sequential Math." Higher-ability classes often have "geometry" or "algebra" in the title, such as "Enriched Geometry, Geometry, Honors Geometry" or "Advanced Algebra, Algebra 1 , Algebra 2, Algebra 3–4, Algebra II, Enriched Algebra, Honors Algebra." Classes targeted to students with average, low, or widely differing abilities have similar course titles to higher ability courses.

that schools may be making their mathematics curricula more open.[7] Students in an "untracked" school, on the other hand, also may have limited OTL as the price for equality of opportunity. They have few course options, and students of widely differing abilities attend classes in which there is a limit on the amount of mathematics curricula provided to the whole class. Some schools with primarily stratified course offerings are opening up their curricula to offer courses to students with widely differing abilities. Students in these schools often must choose between an untracked set of courses and a stratified set of courses. In some schools, high-ability students may be placed in, or choose, a class targeted to their ability. In other schools, high-ability students may be in classes with students with a range of abilities.

Student Choice

Schools vary, to some extent, on student assignment to courses. The majority of U.S. public schools surveyed in this sample (85%) offer students open access to any class provided they have taken the prerequisite(s), regardless of the curriculum that is offered (NCES, 1994). This implies that students and parents have an influence over the types of courses in which students enroll. While there is some debate about the amount of student input into course-taking decisions (e.g., Oakes *et al.*, 1992), this study assumes that school policies of open choice allow students and their parents some control over course decision-making.

Table 2 presents the percentage of schools allowing students an open choice of classes, by general tracking classification. All "untracked" schools that offer only undifferentiated courses have open student choice policies. A higher percentage of "mixed" schools that offer both differentiated and undifferentiated courses have open student choice policies (86.5%) than schools with "traditionally tracked" curricula (80.8%). Still, the vast majority of all schools (85.0%) offer schools a choice of courses, given they have taken the prerequisite(s). Increasing students' choice of

[7]There seem to be three different types of classes that fit under this definition. Some schools, like School 4, place a large proportion of their students into an algebra or geometry class targeted to students with widely differing abilities. These classes seem to be part of a higher-level mathematics sequence. Another type of school, like School 3, claims that its vocational classes are targeted to students with a range of abilities. In addition to these types of schools, it also seems that some schools which no longer offer classes for students with low ability are simply replacing these classes with classes designed for a range of students. These decisions are made on a school-by-school level, with no consistent definition of a widely differing ability class.

Table 2.   Percentage of Schools Allowing Student Choice of Classes, by School Curricular Offerings[a]

	Traditional Track	Mixed	Untracked	Total
Student choice	80.8%	86.5%	100.0%	85.0%
No student choice	19.2%	13.5%	0.0%	15.0%

[a]Schools were classified as allowing student choice if they answered that students have open access to any course provided they have taken prerequisite(s).

courses requires added input from students and parents. Families who are less knowledgeable about their school's curricular offerings may rely on teacher and counselor recommendations instead of considering what might be the best course available for their child's abilities.

Profile of U.S. Schools

Literature on tracking considers traditionally tracked schools to be the modal pattern of curriculum differentiation in the United States, but this study finds a number of other patterns of school curricular offerings. Table 3 further describes the distribution of OTL in U.S. public high schools by presenting patterns across the entire distribution of schools. It demonstrates the large variety of combinations of curricular offerings in mathematics across schools. Students have different opportunities to take courses depending on what type of school they attend. Once again, schools are categorized as "traditionally tracked," "mixed," or "untracked" based on the combination of courses they offer. Schools are divided according to whether or not they offer any courses (at least one) in each of the stratified ability levels (high, average, and low) or in unstratified ability levels (all abilities), and patterns within categories are shown with an "X" placed in columns of course offerings available.

The first two school types in Table 3 (A and B) represent the "traditionally tracked" schools which offer only stratified courses. These schools offer no courses designed for students with widely differing abilities. Type A schools offer at least one course each to students with high, average, and low abilities. This school type represents what is considered the dominant pattern of curriculum differentiation in the United States. However, according to these data, only 39.1% of schools fit into this category of a traditionally tracked school which offers differentiated classes to students in high-, average-, and low-ability groups. The data

Table 3. National Distribution of Schools, by Ability Group of Mathematics Courses Offered (National Estimates Based on 912 Schools)

School Type	Classification[a]	Course Offerings	Ability Groups				% Schools
			High	Avg.	Low	All	
A	Traditional track	3 ability groups	X	X	X	X	39.1%
B	Traditional track	Combination of 2 ability groups	X		X		18.3%
			X	X	X		
C	Mixed	3 ability groups + range of abilities	X	X	X	X	10.7%
D	Mixed	Range of abilities + 1 ability group	X	X		X	7.0%
					X	X	
E	Mixed	Range of abilities + 2 ability group	X		X	X	10.4%
			X	X	X	X	
F	Untracked	Range of abilities		X		X	13.5%

[a]Classification of schools into "traditional track," "mixed," and "untracked" is based only on types of courses offered. This classification does not take into consideration schools' stated policies on student access to courses. Another study with these data by NCES (1994) finds that when considering whether or not students are allowed to choose classes, only 15% of schools fit the traditionally tracked category.

do not include other measures of tracking, such as whether students are assigned to courses or have a choice of what course they take.

Type B schools (18.3%) are also traditionally tracked, but these have some combination of courses designed for students from just two of the ability groups (e.g., high and average, high and low, or average and low abilities). The largest category within this group is schools that offer only high- and average-ability-level courses (10.4%), which shows a trend away from offering low-ability classes. Low-ability students in school types A and B may encounter different opportunities to learn, depending on whether low-ability students are placed in a separate class or are included in the average-ability-level classes. Students whose families are looking for an untracked curriculum have no access to courses targeted to multiple ability students in either of these school types.

In an apparent response to national calls for schools to detrack, schools are beginning to include courses offered to students with widely differing abilities. Note the large percentage of schools (41.6%—types C–F) offering at least one class to students with widely differing abilities. These courses are often within a mathematics curriculum that also has some classes stratified by ability (the mixed schools); only a small percentage (13.5%—type F) of schools offer all classes targeted to students with a wide range of abilities. Untracked schools in type F are overwhelmingly small, rural schools that offer very few courses and probably a restricted range in the coverage of mathematics content.

School types C, D, and E—the mixed schools—include at least one unstratified class (available to students with all types of abilities) and at least one class offered to students who are stratified by abilities (high, average, and/or low). These kinds of course mixes appear as un-wieldy curricular structures. Mixed schools allow students to take classes that are stratified by ability or to be in untracked classes open to a range of student abilities. Students have a much greater range of opportunity to learn in these schools, but may face the difficult task of determining which course is best suited to their abilities. More and more curricular decisions are being placed on the students. For these mixed schools the "school as shopping mall" approach has filtered into the curricular structure.

Table 3 only includes broad categories of course offerings, but each school type has a huge assortment of numbers and types of courses offered to each ability level. The vast range of types of class offerings available at the local level shows the need for students and their families to understand local school policies. Students may attend schools with only untracked courses or with only courses that are stratified by ability. A large percentage of schools offer some combination of the above. This range of course offerings, combined with a large percentage of schools allowing students an open choice of courses, demonstrates the array of local variation in opportunities to learn that may present difficulties for students and parents in choosing courses.

SCHOOL-LEVEL FACTORS THAT INFLUENCE OPPORTUNITY-TO-LEARN

To examine the effects of local school characteristics on curricular OTL, we did an analysis of the number of tenth grade mathematics courses schools offer. The number of a school's course offerings gives information on the range of choices available to students. Schools that offer only one or two courses provide fewer opportunities for their students than schools that offer a greater number of courses. There is wide variation in the number of courses offered to students who attend U.S. high schools. Public schools offer an average of 4.28 mathematics courses to tenth grade students, with the number of mathematics courses offered ranging from 0 to 17. Eighteen and a half percent of schools offer 2 or fewer classes and 25.0% of schools offer 6 or more mathematics courses. Thus, students may have either a wide variety of mathematics courses to choose from or almost no options. And, as we saw from the previous tables, students with similar ability levels may have different opportunities available to them depending on the school they attend.

The question is, to what degree do local school factors shape the size of mathematics course offerings? Table 4 regresses the number of courses offered by various indicators of school size and diversity to see whether certain types of schools offer a greater or lesser number of mathematics courses. We control for number of students in school and test whether measures of school location, student characteristics, or the categories of curricular offerings are related to numbers of courses offered and thus opportunities to learn. The explanatory variables are defined in Table 5.

The models show that, even after controlling for school size, the number of courses offered varies by school location and diversity. First, as would be expected, the number of courses offered is strongly related to school size. Each additional student attending grades 10–12 in a school increases the number of courses offered by 0.001. But, net of school size, urbanicity, region, and school level also affect course offerings. Schools located in the suburbs and in towns (population of 2500 or greater) have on average three-quarters of a mathematics course more than rural schools. Central city schools, however, do not have a significantly different number of courses than rural schools. Students who attend schools located in the

Table 4. Number of Mathematics Courses Offered Regressed on Selected School Characters (OLS Coefficients) ($N = 912$)

Model	1	2	3
Number of students	0.001***	0.001***	0.001***
Location[a]			
Central city	0.063	0.159	−0.002
Suburbs	0.753***	0.513	0.345
Town	0.796***	0.688***	0.517***
Region[b]			
Midwest	−0.736***	−0.657***	−0.602***
Southeast	−0.219	0.008	−0.004
West	−0.268	−0.145	0.020
School level[c]			
Combined elementary and secondary	−0.802***	−0.693***	−0.517**
School characteristics			
% student lunch		−0.009**	−0.008**
Teacher education		0.001	0.001
% minority teachers[d]			
0%		−0.374*	−0.268
5–20%		−0.074	−0.081
20.01–50%		−0.812**	−0.558*
50.01–100%		−1.160***	−0.754*
Tracking classification[e]			
Mixed			0.165
Untracked			−1.642***
Intercept	5.267***	5.523***	4.326***
Adjusted R^2	0.291	0.320	0.387

[a]Reference category is Rural Schools.
[b]Reference category is Northeast.
[c]Reference category is Secondary Only.
[d]Reference category is 1–5% Minority Teachers.
[e]Reference category is Traditional Track.
  *$p < 0.05$.
  **$p < 0.01$.
  ***$p < 0.001$.

midwest have almost three-quarters of a class fewer mathematics offerings than do students attending a northeastern school. Finally, schools that combine elementary and secondary grades have 0.802 fewer classes than schools that include only secondary grades.

Model 2 adds other measures of school diversity. These measures include the percentage of students receiving free lunches, the percentage of teachers with degrees past a B.A., and the minority composition of

Table 5. Variable Definitions of School Characteristics

Variables	Variable Definitions	Range	Mean (S.D.)
# of math courses	Number of math courses offered	0–17	4.28 (2.02)
# of students	Number of students in grades 10–12	0–3033	519 (487)
Location			
Central city	A central city of a Standard Metropolitan Statistical Area (SMSA)	0–1	0.12 (0.33)
Suburbs	An urban place within an SMSA of a large or midsize central city	0–1	0.17 (0.37)
Town	Population >2500 not in an SMSA	0–1	0.26 (0.44)
Rural	Population <2500	0–1	0.45 (0.50)
Region			
Northeast	CT DC DE MA MD ME NH NJ NY PA RI VT	0–1	0.15 (0.36)
Midwest	IA IL IN KS MI MN MO ND NE OH SD WI	0–1	0.33 (0.47)
Southeast	AL AR FL GA KY LA MS NC SC TN VA WV	0–1	0.34 (0.47)
West	AK AZ CA CO HI ID MT NM NV OK OR TX UT WA WY	0–1	0.18 (0.38)
School level			
Secondary only	School has only secondary students	0–1	0.86 (0.35)
Combined	School has both elementary and secondary students	0–1	0.14 (0.35)
% Student lunch	Percentage of students receiving free school lunches	0–1	0.26 (0.23)
Teacher education	Percentage of teachers who have degrees past a bachelor's	0–1	0.50 (0.25)
Minority composition of teachers			
0% minority	0% of teachers black, Hispanic, or American Indian	0–1	0.48 (0.50)
1–5% minority	1–5% of teachers black, Hispanic, or American Indian	0–1	0.19 (0.39)
5–20% minority	5.01–20% of teachers black, Hispanic, or American Indian	0–1	0.21 (0.41)
20–50% minority	20.01–50% of teachers black, Hispanic, or American Indian	0–1	0.08 (0.27)
50–100% minority	50.01–100% of teachers black, Hispanic, or American Indian	0–1	0.04 (0.35)
Tracking classification			
Untracked	Offers unstratified courses only	0–1	0.13 (0.34)
Mixed track	Offers a combination of stratified and unstratified courses	0–1	0.28 (0.45)
Traditionally tracked	Offers only stratified courses (high, average, or low ability)	0–1	0.57 (0.49)

teachers.[8] These measures of school diversity show strong relationships with the number of opportunities available to students and improve the fit of the model. Lower-SES schools (as measured by the free lunch program) offer significantly fewer courses than higher-SES schools, net of school size and location, and show a disadvantage in OTL in these types of schools.

The percentage minority teachers shows an interesting association with numbers of courses offered.[9] Schools with mostly white teachers (48% of schools have no minority teachers) or mostly minority students (a total of 12% of schools had between 20.01 and 50% or 50.01 to 100% minority teachers) offer significantly fewer classes than racially mixed schools (1–5% minority teachers), but it is unclear exactly what this local effect means.[10]

The final model includes our earlier classification of schools into traditionally tracked, mixed, and untracked schools (the reference category is traditionally tracked). Net of school size and diversity, students who attend untracked schools have 1.64 fewer courses offered than students in traditionally tracked schools, net of numbers of students in school. Course offering size in mixed schools does not significantly differ from traditionally tracked schools, however. This indicates that schools that have detracked their curricula and provide only undifferentiated courses offer fewer courses and perhaps fewer opportunities for students than other schools.

Students who attend schools with a wide range of options have the advantage of choosing a course that will fit their needs and abilities, but this choice comes with the responsibility of deciding among a maze of options. The unintended consequence of opening up student choice places the burden of determining the most appropriate course on students and their parents.

POLICY IMPLICATIONS

National school reforms concerning educational quality and equality filter through diverse local school systems and influence the range of

---

[8]An earlier analysis included the minority composition of students and found that this was strongly related to the minority composition of the teachers. In these models, we only use the percentage of minority teachers in each school.

[9]Note that the majority of schools have either no minority teachers or 1–5% minority teachers.

[10]Racial composition of teachers and students was highly correlated. This result may indicate that schools with racially diverse faculty and students offer a greater variety of courses to meet a range of student needs.

curricular opportunities available to students. The current distribution of opportunities for students in U.S. public high schools shows a great amount of local variation in curricular offerings reflective of an organizationally decentralized educational system. While a core group of schools offers stratified classes targeted only to students with high, middle, and lower abilities, the analyses show that there is no single, standard type of curricular offering in our public high schools. There is no standard size for a curriculum, nor a standard approach to students with different abilities, nor even a similar set of course names. This varying number of courses and course contents provides a smorgasbord of curricular approaches through which students with similar abilities face very different OTL depending on the school they attend. The issue of what opportunities students have in their local schools in the United States is further complicated by the fact that so many local, and perhaps seemingly unrelated factors, help determine actual OTL for students.

Issues of both educational equality and quality are easily entangled in this maze of local conditions. For example, the detracking movement, which emphasizes educational equality, in combination with reforms toward increased quality, has mobilized competing forces that influence the curricular offerings in local schools. The analyses show an "opening up" of school curricula with the inclusion of some or all classes designed for students with a range of abilities. Untracked classes are often offered in conjunction with ability-grouped classes so that a large group of schools offer a range of both stratified and unstratified courses. This large category of "mixed" schools suggests the emergence of a "compromise curriculum" in response to multiple pressures from local constituencies and national movements for educational reform.

The broad range of course offerings, combined with policies that indicate open student choice of courses, results in the responsibility for course decision-making being placed on students and their families. As others have also shown, students and their parents must now navigate mathematics curricula at their individual schools. There are serious implications of this process. Families with lower levels of involvement in the school system may have a more difficult time placing their child in the best course for their abilities. Lareau (1989) suggests that working-class parents already have fewer cultural and material resources than middle-class parents that facilitate their being involved in their children's education. Lower-SES parents may have even fewer resources to assist their children in choosing curricular courses as the mix of ability grouping, curricular size, and coverage of content becomes more complex. This arrangement drives up the overall level of necessary parental involvement within the U.S. school system, which may unintentionally hurt some families, as well as take time that could be used in other equally important familial pursuits.

This chapter points out the need to more clearly understand the local conditions through which national educational reform movements filter down to school curricular policies. A victory at the national level for curricular standards or detracking does not necessarily translate into a simple outcome at the school level. The educational establishment must also consider unintended consequences of reforms that may increase educational inequality and jeopardize educational quality.

REFERENCES

Angus, D. L., Mirel, J. E., & Vinovskis, M. A. (1988). Historical development of age stratification in schooling. *Teachers College Record, 90,* 211–236.

Blank, R., & Dalkilic, M. (1990). *State indicators of science and mathematics education.* Washington, DC: CCSSO, State Education Assessment Center.

Firestone, W. A. (1994). Redesigning teacher salary systems for educational reform. *American Educational Research Journal, 31*(3), 549–576.

Floden, R., Porter, A., Alford, L., Freeman, D., Irwin, S., Schmidt, W., & Schwille, J. (1988). Instructional leadership at the district level. *Educational Administration Quarterly, 24,* 96–124.

Hallinan, M. T. (1992). The organization of students for instruction in the middle school. *Sociology of Education, 65*(2), 114–127.

Hallinan, M. T. (1994). Tracking: From theory to practice. *Sociology of Education, 67*(2), 79–83.

Kliebard, H. (1987). *The struggle for the American curriculum, 1893–1958.* London: Routledge & Kegan Paul.

Kozol, J. (1991). *Savage inequalities: Children in America's schools.* New York: Crown Publishers.

Lareau, A. (1989). *Home advantage: Social class and parental intervention in elementary education.* Philadelphia, PA: Falmer Press.

McKnight, C. C., Crosswhite, F. J., Dossey, J. A., Kifer, E., Swafford, J. O., Travers, K. J., & Cooney, T. J. (1986). *The underachieving curriculum.* Champaign, IL: Stipes.

Meyer, J. (1986). The politics of educational crises in the United States. In W. Cummings, E. Beauchamp, S. Ichikawa, V. Kobayashi, & M. Ushiogi (Eds.), *Educational policies in crisis: Japanese and American perspectives* (pp. 44–158). New York: Praeger.

Meyer, J., & Rowan, B. (1978). The structure of educational organization. In M. Meyer *et al.* (Eds.), *Environments and Organizations* (pp. 78–109). San Francisco: Jossey–Bass.

Meyer, J., & Scott, R. (Eds.). (1983). *Organizational environments.* Beverly Hills: Sage.

Mirel, J. (1994). School reform unplugged: The Bensenville New American School Project, 1991–93. *American Educational Research Journal, 31*(3), 481–518.

Mirel, J., & Angus, D. (1994). High standards for all? The struggle for equality in the American high school curriculum, 1890–1990. *American Educator,* (Summer), 4–42.

National Center for Education Statistics (NCES). (1994). *Curricular differentiation in public high schools.* Washington, DC: U.S. Department of Education, NCES 95–360.

National Commission on Excellence in Education. (1983). *A nation at risk: The imperative for educational reform.* Washington, DC: U.S. Government Printing Office.

National Council of Teachers of Mathematics. (1989). *Curriculum and evaluation standards for school mathematics executive summary.* Washington, DC: Author.

Oakes, J. (1994). More than misapplied technology: A normative and political response to Hallinan on tracking. *Sociology of Education, 67*(2), 84–88, 91.

Oakes, J., & Guiton, G. (1995). Matchmaking: The dynamics of high school tracking decisions. *American Educational Research Journal, 32*(1), 3–33.

Oakes, J., Gamoran, A., & Page, R. N. (1992). Curriculum differentiation: Opportunities, outcomes, and meanings. In P. W. Jackson (Ed.), *Handbook of research on curriculum* (pp. 570–608). New York: Macmillan Co.

Ogawa, R. T. (1994). The institutional sources of educational reform: The case of school-based management. *American Educational Research Journal, 31*(3), 519–548.

Richardson, J. (1986). Historical sequences and the origins of common schooling in the American states. In J. Richardson (Ed.), *Handbook of theory and research for the sociology of education.* New York: Greenwood Press.

Rubinson, R. (1986). Class formation, political organization, and institutional structures: The case of schooling in the United States. *American Journal of Sociology, 92,* 519–548.

Stevenson, D. L., & Baker, D. P. (1991). State control of the curriculum and classroom instruction. *Sociology of Education, 64*(1), 1–10.

Stevenson, D. L., Schiller, K. S., & Schneider, B. (1994). Sequences of opportunities for learning. *Sociology of Education, 67*(3), 184–198.

Tyack, D., & Hansot, E. (1982). Managers of virtue: Public school leadership in America, 1820–1980. New York: Basic Books.

Tyack, D., & Tobin, W. (1994). The "grammar" of schooling: Why has it been so hard to change? *American Educational Research Journal, 31*(3), 453–480.

Weick, K. (1976). Educational organizations as loosely coupled systems. *Administrative Science Quarterly, 21* (March), 1–19.

Wrigley, J. (1982). *Class politics and public schools: Chicago, 1900–1950.* New Brunswick, NJ: Rutgers University Press.

III

Classroom Processes

8

Talking and Working Together
Conditions for Learning in Complex Instruction

Elizabeth G. Cohen, Rachel A. Lotan, and Nicole Holthuis

Psychologists, curriculum developers, and reformers of mathematics and science education recommend active learning in which students in small groups talk and work together. Small groups provide an opportunity for students to construct their own knowledge in a way that develops conceptual learning and higher-order thinking skills. Noddings (1989) sees this latter school of thought as originating in the work of Dewey and the social constructivism of Vygotsky (1978). Educators and researchers belonging to the "constructivist" school of thought assume that suitable discourse or conversation within the small groups and/or a process of discovery is a prerequisite for conceptual learning.

We would agree that interaction among the members of cooperative small groups is indeed central to conceptual learning. However, there are some key sociological conditions that must be met before the cognitive benefits of interaction can be realized. In this chapter we will test the hypothesis that when there are true group tasks that feature ill-structured problems, interaction will predict learning that involves higher-order thinking skills. Moreover we would only expect to see this relationship when students have been adequately trained to interact cooperatively.

In a classroom, the stage must be set for interaction to take place in groups. Unless the teacher delegates authority to groups while holding

Elizabeth G. Cohen, Rachel A. Lotan, and Nicole Holthuis   School of Education, Stanford University, Stanford, California 94305.

Restructuring Schools: Promising Practices and Policies, edited by Maureen T. Hallinan. Plenum Press, New York, 1995.

them accountable for performance, one may see little on-task interaction within the groups. Even more basic to the fostering of interaction is the division of students into sufficiently small groups so that everyone has potential "air time" for expressing their ideas.

After showing how we derive these propositions from sociological theory and past classroom research, we will put them to a test with observational data from middle school classrooms, all of which were using a strategy called *complex instruction*. Complex instruction is designed for heterogeneous classrooms where the teaching objectives are conceptual and stress higher-order thinking. Students use each other as resources in cooperative groups, working on demanding, open-ended tasks requiring a wide range of intellectual abilities and skills.

THEORETICAL FRAMEWORK

The hypotheses in this research are derived from a combination of organizational theory and social psychology. They also stem from empirical research on cooperative learning in classrooms. These particular hypotheses have been tested previously on elementary school data on complex instruction. We examine the generalizability of these propositions to a different age group, school setting, and different curriculum subjects.

Interaction and Learning in Small Groups

A number of research studies have correlated observed interaction within cooperative groups and achievement, holding constant prior achievement. However, this literature presents a most interesting inconsistency. Webb (1983, 1991) showed that in a set of studies of mathematics classes, the simple frequency of interaction did not predict achievement. Most of these studies were conducted in mathematics classes where students had problems to solve and were told to work together as a group, helping each other, and asking the teacher for help only when no one in the group could assist. She argued that only certain types of interaction—giving and receiving elaborated explanation—were critical for learning.

In contrast, research on complex instruction at the elementary level has consistently documented the positive relationship between frequency of task-related interaction and gains on standardized and content-referenced tests at the individual as well as at the classroom level (Cohen, 1984; Cohen, Lotan, & Leechor, 1989; Leechor, 1988). What differences between these two bodies of studies could account for the differential effectiveness of simple interaction? The first difference lies in the working relationships between the group members. In the case of the group assignments in mathematics, the tasks could have been carried out by individuals. They were not inherently *group tasks*. A *group task* is a task that requires resources (information, knowledge, heuristic problem-solving strategies, materials, and skills) that no single individual possesses so that no single individual is likely to solve the problem or accomplish the task objectives without at least some input from others (Cohen & Arechavala-Vargas, 1987). The tasks in complex instruction fit this definition of a group task. When working on a group task, members are interdependent in a reciprocal fashion. In other words, each actor must exchange resources with others before the task can be completed. This contrasts with many routine tasks used in cooperative learning where achievement depends on the stronger students helping the weaker students. This arrangement is also interdependent, but the interdependence is *sequential* as opposed to reciprocal, e.g., one student's performance is dependent on another's, but the reverse is not true.

In the case of complex instruction, reciprocal interdependence is also produced by the system of classroom management in which each student is responsible for helping to ensure the success of all members. Each student has a role that has to do with the functioning of the group. Moreover, the students experience a week of skill-building activities in which they internalize norms of mutual assistance. Lastly, specific steps are taken to prevent the better students from doing all of the helping and weaker students from accepting all of the help (Cohen & Cohen, 1991). In the studies reviewed by Webb, there was no such system of classroom management nor was there any special training for cooperative relationships.

The second important difference lies in the nature of the work assigned to the groups. Computational or algorithmic mathematics assignments typically have a right answer that can be reached in well-structured ways while open-ended and discovery tasks such as those used in complex instruction do not have one right answer and are ill-structured problems; they are nonroutine problems for which there are no standard recipes or procedures. Under the conditions of a true group task and an ill-structured problem, interaction is vital to productivity (Cohen & Cohen, 1991). Because group members need each other to achieve the best possible product, they must interact with one another in order to achieve their potential. There are at least two ways in which classroom groups can use each other in the course of problem-solving: (1) those students who do not read or compute will have access to the resources of students with better academic skills; (2) the exchange of ideas and information enables group members to find creative solutions to their assignment or to discover underlying principles. In the case of a classroom setting, productivity is often defined in terms of achievement gains. This conditional relationship between interaction and productivity may be stated as a more general proposition:

> Given an ill-structured problem and a group task, productivity will depend on interaction.
>
> More specifically: Given a problem with no one right answer and a learning task that will require all students to exchange resources, achievement gains will depend on the proportion of students who are talking and working together.

Delegation of Authority

If interaction is critical for achievement, then the job of the teacher is to foster and maximize this interaction. Obviously, when students are working independently in small groups, the teacher's role changes. She or he cannot be everywhere at once telling people what to do; whenever the teacher tries to tell the class something directly, the interaction in the small groups comes to an abrupt halt. Within small groups, the self-directed nature of student talk tends to disappear when the teacher arrives (Harwood, 1989).

The extent to which the teacher applies direct supervision (the obverse of delegation of authority) will diminish the possibilities and opportunities of students communicating with each other. If the teacher, as an authority figure, takes responsibility for their task engagement, students will not assume responsibility for solving problems related to the task. In two data sets, based on classrooms using complex instruction, Cohen *et al.* (1989) found that the rate at which the teacher used forms of direct instruction when students were working in small groups was *negatively related* to talking and working together among the students. This research provides support for a general sociological principle formulated by Perrow (1967). Once technology has become more uncertain, two necessary changes should be made in order to maintain or increase organizational productivity: (1) delegation of authority to the workers and (2) more lateral communication among the workers. In educational terms, this means that when cooperative learning tasks are nonroutine, problem-solving or discovery tasks, it is necessary for the teachers to avoid direct supervision and to foster talking and working together within the small groups.

This discussion leads to the second hypothesis:

Given uncertain group tasks, the rate of direct supervision by the teacher will be negatively related to the proportion of students talking and working together on task.

Differentiation of the Technology

The management of cooperative learning requires the teacher to deal with instruction that has become quite complex; instead of the whole class working on the same task, there may be as many as six or seven groups working at their own pace, or in the case of complex instruction, each group is working on a different task. The sociologist refers to the latter pattern of work as a highly differentiated technology.

What do teachers do when faced with such a complex mode of instruction? A highly differentiated technology could lead to several alternative methods of supervision. From the teacher's point of view and according to organizational sociologists, one alternative is to use direct supervision; the teacher can manage and guide the students' behavior through detailed rules and schedules. However, this solution assumes that workers are facing tasks that are relatively certain. Comstock and Scott (1977) summarized this argument:

But when work is not predictable, performance programs cannot be developed and individuals must be called upon to make the best judgments of which they are capable. When different groups of workers are carrying out different and uncertain tasks, it is more efficient if they have a clear sense of authority and can make their own decisions, and can learn from their own mistakes. [p. 177]

Assuming that efficiency is a concern, under conditions of uncertainty, it follows that differentiation will be positively associated with delegation of authority.

In classroom terms, when there are multiple groups each working on different problems with ill-structured solutions, we have a situation that is both highly differentiated and uncertain. In actual practice, the most efficient and productive response to this challenge is not always implemented. Teachers vary in how many small groups they employ. They sometimes try to simplify the technology by cutting down on the number of groups so that they can use direct supervision. They may also simplify the situation so that all groups are carrying out the same task. It is then much easier to make sure that each group is solving the problem in a standardized fashion. Even if they try neither of these simplifying strategies, rather than delegating authority, teachers may try to race from group to group to make sure that each task is being done properly and in the manner that they prefer. The sheer impracticality of this latter solution when six groups are carrying out very different tasks pushes teachers toward delegation of authority. At the elementary school level, we found in two data sets taken from classrooms using complex instruction that the larger the number of groups that a teacher is trying to manage, the lower is the probability that she will use direct instruction and direct supervision in which she exerts detailed control over how tasks are executed (Cohen *et al.*, 1989).

In the case of the middle school data, there was variation in how many different activities were in simultaneous operation. One classroom with six groups might have had six different activities while another might only have had three different activities. This leads to the third hypothesis:

> Given uncertain group tasks, the number of different activities in simultaneous operation in a classroom will be negatively related to the use of direct supervision.

A final proposition concerns the effect of the size of groups. When there are fewer, larger groups in a classroom, the opportunities for individuals to talk are limited by the "air time" available for a given member of the group. Obviously, there is not as much air time for students in larger groups as in smaller groups.

The fourth and final hypothesis follows:

> The size of the small groups will be negatively related to the percentage of students observed talking and working together in the classroom.

From an educational perspective, the importance of these factors that affect the amount of interaction in groups, such as delegation of authority and differentiation of the technology, lies in the relationship of interaction to learning outcomes. Teachers who have too few groups or who try to use direct supervision when students are working cooperatively unwittingly sabotage the attainment of their objectives. By inhibiting the process of talking and working together, they prevent the students from developing a good grasp of concepts or from discovering things for themselves.

DESIGN OF THE STUDY

Although all of the middle school classrooms in this study used complex instruction, there were important classroom differences in the number of activities, in the size of small groups, in the extent to which teachers used direct supervision when students were working in groups, and in the proportion of students talking and working together when groups were in operation. We test the hypotheses by correlating these classroom statistics with each other and with the average classroom gains in a test of higher-order thinking skills.

All of the teachers were using specially prepared curricula in social studies/language arts, mathematics, and human biology that provided activity cards for each group. The tasks, in each case, fit the definition of group tasks. Moreover, the tasks were open-ended and uncertain, thereby fulfilling criteria for problems with ill-structured solutions. For example, students in social studies were asked to design a Crusader castle they could defend or to create a role play on how the Crusader Handbook was used to recruit peasants for the Crusades. Students in mathematics read a story about two tug-of-war matches involving giant frogs, athletic grandmas, and a frisky kangaroo. In the story the students find that an even tug-of-war is five grandmas of equal strength pulling against four giant frogs, also of equal strength. Another even match results when the kangaroo pulls against two grandmas and a giant frog. The group's task is threefold: (1) to use characters from the story to create a tricky tug-of-war match that would not come out even, (2) to provide a written account of two different ways to verify mathematically which side would win the tug-of-war it had created, and (3) to make a poster that presents its tug-of-war problem for others to solve.

All of the teachers received the same type of staff development and classroom follow-up. They attended a two-week workshop on complex instruction followed by systematic classroom observations of their classrooms. After three observations on a given classroom, staff developers provided feedback to the teachers in which they discussed the results of observations, using a bar graph presentation. Teachers received between one and three such feedback visits. The students were prepared for cooperative learning with a set of skill-building experiences. The aim of some of these skill-builders was to improve the character of group discussion by training the students to present their rationales and ideas in a more articulate fashion.

All of the variables with the exception of learning outcomes were measured with systematic observations. Achievement data for this study only include tests on the social studies units. We used correlations and multiple regressions to test the hypotheses at the classroom level. The hypothesis concerning interaction and achievement outcomes was tested only on the social studies classrooms where we had achievement measures. The other hypotheses concerning the predictors of direct supervision and interaction were tested on the larger sample of classrooms in the three subject matters.

SETTING AND SAMPLE

During the 1991/92 school year, we worked with five middle schools from five districts in the larger Bay Area. The student population at all of these schools was racially and ethnically mixed, a fair representation of California's present student demographics. All of these schools had made a commitment to untrack in all subject matters. They had also integrated social studies and language arts in their seventh grades and had assigned two- or three-period sessions to a "core" subject.

For each participating teacher, we selected (where possible) two kinds of classrooms for closer follow-up. Based on the students' existing reading scores on standardized tests, we constructed a profile to reflect the academic range in the classroom. Although the schools considered themselves to be detracked, we found that some classrooms had a wider range than others, i.e., were more heterogeneous than others. We then selected (where possible) one heterogeneous and one more homogeneous (high or low) classroom for each teacher to be included in our sample. We analyzed the predictors of direct supervision and interaction in a sample of 42 classrooms in all three subject matters. The data for the analysis of achievement and interaction come from a subset of that sample—the 22 social studies classrooms.

MEASUREMENT

Observation Data

We were able to collect complete sets of observation data in 42 classrooms across the three subject matters (social studies, human biology, and mathematics). We used the teacher observation instrument to record the rate of teacher facilitating, instructing, and disciplining—indicators of direct supervision. Facilitation includes telling students how to get through the task or asking procedural questions such as "Did you read the resource cards? Does the group know what you are supposed to do?" There were a total of 246 such teacher observations. For purposes of this study, we counted only teacher behaviors during the time that students were at the learning stations, when delegation of authority is required.

We measured interscorer reliability by calculating the percentage agreement between the scoring by the rater and the criterion scorer. Reliability on this observation instrument was 93.64%. We standardized the rates of teacher talk by the number of minutes for each observation and averaged all of the observations of a particular teacher to construct an index of direct supervision. The index of direct supervision was the average rate of teacher talk in the total of the following categories: Teacher Facilitates, Teacher Instructs, and Teacher Disciplines. To check whether there was greater variation among the teachers in a sample than there was among the observations of a particular teacher, we performed ANOVAs for the combined total of these three categories for each observation. The ANOVA showed significant teacher effects for this index ($F = 1.623$; $p = 0.013$).

We used the whole class instrument to obtain measures of differentiation, number of students per learning station, and the proportions of students talking and working together. This instrument consists of a grid representing grouping and activity patterns of students. The observers counted the number of students who were engaged in various activities such as talking, manipulating the materials, looking and listening, or disengaged at the learning stations and sometimes away from the centers (in transition/on business, wandering, playing). Observers also recorded the number of different learning stations and the number of different kinds of curricular materials in use. The whole class instrument is like a snapshot of all of the students and the teacher at a given time. There were 502 such observations for the classrooms of this study always taken when the students were working at the learning stations—after the initial orientation to the lesson and before the final wrap-up. Interscorer reliability on this instrument was 94.42%.

We constructed the relevant statistics for the purposes of this analysis as follows: The proportion of students talking and working together was the average percentage of students checked off in the "Talking" or "Talking and Manipulating Materials" categories over a set of observations for a given classroom. Students who were in engaged in nontask talk were not included. The measure of differentiation was the average number of different activities in simultaneous operation, as noted in the whole class instrument. The number of students per group was a grand mean of the average number of students per learning station for each observation of a given classroom. As with the teacher observation instrument, we performed ANOVAs on the variables of interest before aggregating across observations. The F values of these analyses were as follows: For percentage talking and working together, $F = 2.605$ ($p = 0.000$); for number of different activities, $F = 10.617$ ($p = 0.000$); for students per learning station, $F = 9.347$ ($p = 0.000$).

Achievement Tests in Social Studies

The multiple choice tests for the seventh and eighth grade in social studies had two major sections: factual information and higher-order thinking. When designing test items, we carefully consulted the state-approved textbooks and tests published to accompany the textbooks because we planned to administer the tests in both CI classrooms and comparison classrooms where students did not have access to the CI curricula. Each test item reflected content in all classrooms. We wanted all students taking the test, regardless of their exposure to CI curricula, to have a reasonable chance of answering the questions correctly. For the factual information items, we used as many questions from the textbook's published tests as possible. We composed new higher-order thinking questions. The same test form was used for pre- and posttests.

The test for the eighth grade included 40 items: 30 factual and 10 higher-order thinking items. It covered materials on the following topics: Manifest Destiny, the Civil War, and the Rise of the Industrial Era. All of these topics are part of the California State Framework and all are covered in the textbook. Seven teachers reviewed a prototype of the eighth grade test; with their comments and critique, we revised the test.

The seventh grade test had 50 items, 33 factual and 17 higher-order thinking items. It covered materials on the following topics: Feudal Japan, the Crusades, the Maya, and the Reformation. All topics are part of the California Framework, and all are covered in the textbook most frequently used in California schools.

All of the students present in the selected classes took the whole test early and late in the school year. For the purposes of the analyses reported in this chapter, we constructed a gain score for each student who took the pre- and the posttest and calculated the average gain score per classroom based on individual gain scores.

RESULTS

Table 1 shows the means and standard variations for the variables used to test our hypotheses. As indicated, the average number of different activities occurring at one time was 4.11. The analysis of variance tests indicated that this average varied significantly by class ($F = 10.62$, $p < 0.001$) as well as by subject ($F = 108.99$, $p < 0.001$).

Direct supervision on the part of the teacher was relatively high. Teachers averaged 13.39 remarks during 10 minutes of observation. Some teachers made numerous short remarks, thus boosting the total. The average number of students per group was 3.75. The range of this variable indicates that none of the groups was very large. In fact, many of the groups had three or less students.

The percentage of students talking and working together was, on average, 36.45%. There was great variation in this measure among the classrooms (S.D. = 8.80). Lastly, the classrooms tested gained an average of 12.14% of the total number of items between the pre- and posttest. This was computed by subtracting each individual's total pretest score from their total posttest score. The standard deviation for this mean was 7.50, indicating considerable variability in achievement as well. While not directly relevant to the analysis described in this chapter, it is of interest to note that these classrooms did significantly better than comparison

Table 1. Descriptive Statistics for Variables in the Path Model

Variable	Mean	S.D.	Min./Max.	Number of Classrooms
Number of different activities[a]	4.11	1.93	1.00/8.00	42
Teacher direct supervision[b]	13.39	3.70	6.92/21.75	42
Number of students per group[c]	3.75	0.31	3.07/4.50	42
% talk/work together[d]	36.45	8.80	17.13/56.48	42
Gain scores[e]	12.14	7.50	−4.80/29.80	22

[a]Average of the number of different activities implemented simultaneously.
[b]Total of the average rate of the following behaviors of teacher per 10-minute observation while children were at the learning centers: teacher facilitates, instructs, and disciplines.
[c]Average of the ratio of the number of students to the number of learning centers.
[d]Average percentage of students talking and working together in the classroom.
[e]Percentage gained on social studies test.

classrooms in which the same topics were covered without complex instruction.

Testing the Hypotheses

The four hypothesized relationships discussed earlier all show statistically significant correlation coefficients (see Table 2). First, the average amount of interaction per classroom as measured by the percentage of students talking and working together is positively correlated with average achievement gains per classroom ($r = 0.50, p < 0.01$). Those classrooms where students were more actively engaged in talking about the task gained more than those classrooms with smaller percentages of students talking and working together. The correlations support the second hypothesis regarding the relationship between the measures of direct supervision and interaction as well: There is a statistically significant negative correlation between the average rate of direct supervision and percentage of students talking and working together ($r = -0.52, p < 0.001$). In other words, those teachers who tended to engage in direct instruction while students were in groups had fewer students talking and working together than those teachers who interfered with the groups less. Third, the number of different activities in simultaneous operation is negatively related to the use of direct supervision ($r = -0.40, p < 0.01$). Teachers who were working with a smaller number of activities were more likely to engage

Table 2.   Intercorrelation of Indicators of Differentiation, Size of the Groups, Direct Supervision, and Interaction ($N = 42$)

	Number of Different Activities	Teacher Direct Supervision	Number of Students per Group	% Talk/ Work Together
Number of different activities[a]	1.00			
Teacher direct supervision[b]	−0.40**	1.00		
Number of students per group[c]	0.28*	−0.26*	1.00	
% talk/work together[d]	0.47**	−0.52***	0.40**	1.00

*$p < 0.05$.
**$p < 0.01$.
***$p < 0.001$.

in direct supervision than teachers who used as many as six groups each with different activities.

Lastly, the size of the small groups is directly related to the percentage of students observed talking and working together ($r = 0.40$, $p < 0.01$). However, it should be noted that this last correlation is in the opposite direction from that predicted. Instead of finding that larger groups cut down on the number of students interacting, the results show that the greater the size of the group, the larger the proportion of students interacting.

There are other interesting correlations not previously hypothesized. For example, the smaller the size of the groups, the higher was the rate of direct supervision ($r = -0.26$, $p < 0.05$). Also, the amount of interaction was positively related to the number of different activities ($r = 0.47$, $p < 0.01$). Finally, when there were more different activities, there were somewhat larger groups ($r = 0.28$, $p < 0.05$).

The Path Model

Figure 1 presents the path model depicting the hypothesized relationships between status, interaction, and learning. We were not attempting to model a phenomenon in this path analysis. Rather, we were testing a specific theoretically driven argument. Thus, the detailed causal model in Figure 1 presents the particular indicators of basic concepts that are relevant to the data set. If we were modeling the phenomenon, we would include some of the additional relationships just noted in the matrix of correlations. Table 3 presents the separate regression analyses used to estimate the path coefficients for the model. Included in the table are the standardized coefficients, the standard error, and the value of R^2.

The quantities reported over the arrows in Figure 1 are the path coefficients or standardized regression coefficients taken from the equations reported in Table 3. As expected, teachers in classrooms with greater

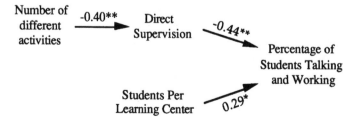

Figure 1.   Path model of antecedents of gains in learning.

Table 3. Standardized Regression Coefficients and Standard Errors (in Parentheses)
for Equations in the Path Models ($N = 42$)

Dependent Variables/ Predictors	Teacher Direct Supervision	% Talk/ Work Together
Number of different activities	−0.40** (0.28)	
Teacher direct supervision		−0.44** (0.32)
Number of students per group		0.29* (3.80)
$R^2 = 0.16$		

*$p < 0.05$.
**$p < 0.01$.

differentiation had lower rates of direct supervision ($r = 0.50$, $p < 0.01$). In addition, both direct supervision and the number of students per group are independent predictors of the percentage of students talking and working together. A regression of the percentage of students talking and working together on both direct supervision and number of students per group indicates that both variables are significant predictors. The path model shows a statistically significant negative coefficient between direct supervision and student interaction ($r = -0.44$, $p < 0.01$). There is a significantly positive coefficient—the opposite from what we expected—between the number of students per group and interaction ($r = 0.29$, $p < 0.05$). In turn, interaction is a positive predictor of learning gains in social studies ($r = 0.50$, $p < 0.01$).

DISCUSSION AND IMPLICATIONS

There was general support in the data for all but one of our hypotheses. As we have indicated, there was a positive, rather than negative, relationship between the size of the group and the percentage of students talking and working together. That is, we found that the larger the average size of the groups, the greater was the percentage of students talking and working together. This is understandable when we consider the size range of the groups in these classrooms. Few, if any, groups were larger than five students. In fact, groups often consisted of three or fewer students. Thus, air time was not the critical issue. These activities are characteristically challenging, multiple ability, and interdependent—we suspect that groups of two or three did not have the intellectual resources within the group to complete the activity. As a result, students in these groups may have either quietly or disruptively given up.

As reported, the number of different activities implemented simultaneously varied by subject and by class, thus producing the variability in differentiation. The math units, for example, did not always provide a variety of activities in simultaneous operation as did the social studies units. Rather, each group did the same activity with only some slight variation, if any, in the product required. In some classrooms, in an effort to simplify the implementation, teachers reduced the number of different activities occurring simultaneously. The consequences for student learning are apparent: the fewer the number of activities, the greater the level of direct instruction, and the lower the interaction.

As we have seen, the level of direct instruction is not the only predictor of interaction—the size of the group is important as well. What, then, is the optimal size of the groups? Considering our results, it would appear there is both an upper and lower limit to the size of the groups. On the one hand, groups of only two or three may be appropriate for a somewhat simpler task such as completing a worksheet, studying for a spelling test, or performing a scientific lab, but are not large enough for the stimulating, challenging activities in complex instruction curricula. On the other hand, groups larger than five do not provide all students with the chance to contribute as individuals compete for scarce time to talk and work together. Additionally, students in such large groups are unable to make eye contact with all members of the group or are physically isolated because of the size of the table necessary to hold all members. There are a number of practical implications of these findings. In the first place, interaction in the groups is unlikely to be a direct precursor of learning unless there are true group tasks and uncertain problems. In creating curricula, we have found that tasks that are open-ended and contain a healthy level of uncertainty facilitate student talk. In addition, the tasks must also be conceptually challenging—students may learn vocabulary words for a unit of the Maya civilization or the structures of the eye best via a lecture or an individual worksheet. Group tasks, in contrast, should pose or ask students to pose provocative and challenging problems that require four or five minds to solve the problem collectively and to create a product.

Second, it is necessary to set the stage for the desired interaction to take place. Teachers have to learn how to delegate authority to groups and to avoid direct instruction when groups are in operation. Curriculum developers would do well to create different activities for different groups so as to push the teacher to avoid direct instruction.

This work also has direct implications for teachers. Teachers can increase the amount of student-to-student interaction by minimizing the amount of direct supervision when students are working in their groups. When a teacher facilitates, disciplines, or provides direct instruction, it has the effect of shutting down the student talk. While it is sometimes necessary to intervene with the work of a group, high levels of direct instruction will lead to low levels of interaction among students.

However, lowering one's level of direct instruction is not necessarily easy or natural. Thus, we suggest increasing the number of *different* activities simultaneously being implemented. If, for example, each group in the class is working on a different activity related to the digestive system, the teacher will be unable to interrupt the groups with directions about how far they should be on the activity and what they should do next. Rather, as teachers delegate authority to the groups, students become responsible for monitoring themselves and completing the task successfully.

Finally, this work has implications for ways in which the organization of schools support teachers. Most of the available curriculum materials for small groups do not meet the criteria of true group tasks and uncertain problems. Teachers will need assistance with acquiring and adapting curriculum materials. Learning how to delegate authority while holding groups and individuals accountable requires more than the typical workshop in cooperative learning. Research has shown that proper implementation requires follow-up and systematic feedback for teachers in their own classrooms (Cohen, Lotan, & Morphew, forthcoming). Furthermore, work arrangements in the school must become more collaborative. Teachers will need to talk and work together with their colleagues and principals if they are to be able to solve problems that arise with this more complex and sophisticated technology of teaching (Cohen *et al.*, forthcoming).

CONCLUSION

We have been able to demonstrate the generalizability of propositions concerning effective conditions for group interaction and learning from the elementary to the middle school. In both settings, it has been shown that given true group tasks and problems with ill-structured solutions, there is a strong and significant relationship between interaction and learning. It is also the case that direct supervision is counterproductive when groups are in operation in that interaction and, therefore, learning outcomes are weakened. Finally, the level of differentiation of the technology will push teachers to use less direct supervision. We have shown these propositions to hold despite the major differences in the age of the student, the organization of the school, and the subject matter of the curricular tasks.

Organizational theory has powerful and practical implications for the use of cooperative learning in classrooms. However, relevant sociological theory and research are largely unfamiliar to those educators attempting to restructure classrooms. Reformers, curriculum developers, and teachers hope to hear students in groups constructing their own knowledge as they solve open-ended problems in mathematics or experiment and discover scientific principles. But they will not be successful without taking into account the necessary conditions for interaction among students to result in desired learning gains. Thus, sociological knowledge must find a way to enter the arena of changing policy on classroom instruction, an arena where its usefulness is still unrecognized.

REFERENCES

Cohen, B. P., & Arechavala-Vargas, R. (1987). *Interdependence, interaction and productivity.* Working Paper 87-3. Stanford University, Stanford, CA: Center for Sociological Research.

Cohen, B. P., & Cohen, E. G. (1991). From groupwork among children to R&D teams: Interdependence, interaction and productivity. *Advances in Group Processes,* Vol. 8, pp. 205–226. Greenwich, CT: JAI Press.

Cohen, E. G. (1984). Talking and working together: Status interaction and learning. In P. Peterson, L. C. Wilkinson, & M. Hallinan (Eds.), *Instructional groups in the classroom: Organization and processes* (pp. 171–188). New York: Academic Press.

Cohen, E. G., Lotan, R., & Leechor, C. (1989). Can classrooms learn? *Sociology of Education, 62,* 75–94.

Cohen, E. G., Lotan, R., & Morphew, C. (forthcoming). Beyond the workshop: Evidence from complex instruction. In C. Brody, N. Davidson, & C. Cooper (Eds.), *Professional development for cooperative learning.* New York: Teachers College Press.

Comstock, D. E., & Scott, W. R. (1977). Technology and the structure of subunits: Distinguishing individual and work group effects. *Administrative Science Quarterly, 22,* 177–202.

Harwood, D. (1989). The nature of teacher–pupil interaction in the active tutorial work approach: Using interaction analysis to evaluate student-centered approaches. *British Educational Research Journal, 15,* 177–194.

Leechor, C. (1988). *How high achieving and low achieving students differentially benefit from working together in cooperative small groups.* Unpublished doctoral dissertation, Stanford University.

Noddings, N. (1989). Theoretical and practical concerns about small groups in mathematics. *Elementary School Journal, 89,* 607–623.

Perrow, C. (1967). A framework for the comparative analysis of organizations. *American Sociological Review, 32,* 194–208.

Vygotsky, L. (1978). *Mind in society.* Cambridge, MA: Harvard University Press.

Webb, N. (1983). Predicting learning from student interaction: Defining the interaction variable. *Educational Psychologist, 18,* 33–41.

Webb, N. (1991). Task-related verbal interaction and mathematics learning in small groups. *Journal of Research in Mathematics Education, 22,* 366–389.

9

Academic Challenge, Motivation, and Self-Esteem
The Daily Experiences of Students in High School

Barbara Schneider, Mihaly Csikszentmihalyi, and Shaunti Knauth

Secondary school students are assigned to various programs and classes that offer them different opportunities for learning (Hallinan, 1994; Oakes, 1985, 1992). A considerable number of studies have examined how students are assigned to programs and classes and what effect these different opportunities have on students' academic performance, social behaviors, and educational aspirations (for a review of these studies, see Oakes, Gamoran, & Page, 1992). One persistent question is whether the quality of students' daily experiences varies from class to class. For example, do students feel more challenged, motivated, and self-assured when they are in academic classes, compared to other classes directed at special activities such as band, or classes directed toward work such as computer processing? We suspect that the quality of students' daily experiences is likely to affect their attitudes toward education and influence their tolerance for and perseverance in schooling.

Success in school depends in part on how well students are able to persevere on tasks that they may find difficult (Carroll, 1963). One

Barbara Schneider   National Opinion Research Center, The University of Chicago, Chicago, Illinois 60637.   **Mihaly Csikszentmihalyi**   Committee on Human Development, The University of Chicago, Chicago, Illinois 60637.   **Shaunti Knauth**   Department of Education, The University of Chicago, Chicago, Illinois 60637.

Restructuring Schools: Promising Practices and Policies, edited by Maureen T. Hallinan. Plenum Press, New York, 1995.

explanation for persevering with difficult tasks may be related to a student's self-esteem, that is, whether the student perceives that he or she is meeting personal expectations as well as the expectations of others. The importance a student places on a particular activity will undoubtedly affect a student's tolerance for schooling. Classes that trigger high internal expectations are likely to be less enjoyable than classes where students do not feel the pressure to succeed. For some students the long-term effects of not meeting expectations may be an unwillingness to persevere in school after high school graduation.

Vocational classes may produce different psychological effects than academic classes. The content of vocational classes may be more directly tied to the future goals of the students. For example, if a student intended to enter the labor force directly after high school graduation and enrolled in classes that helped him or her to prepare for future employment, the student's self-esteem may be higher in those classes than in academic classes that are seen as less salient to future goals. Yet there may be a problem with such classes that promote high self-esteem at the expense of intellectual challenge. In fact, recent criticisms of vocational classes have been directed at the lack of attention to cognitive complexity (Secretary's Commission on Achieving Necessary Skills, 1991). Students may graduate from high school and move into the labor market feeling good about themselves but having had few opportunities in school that were intellectually challenging.

It has been suspected that students not interested in pursuing a postsecondary experience after high school graduation are tracked into non-college-preparatory programs that provide fewer opportunities for learning than do college-preparatory programs (Oakes, 1990, 1992). These restricted opportunities for learning have been shown to negatively affect students' self-esteem, academic achievement, and educational aspirations (Oakes *et al.*, 1992). However, recent evidence from the National Education Longitudinal Study of 1988 (NELS:88) suggests that conventional definitions of high school program track are not as revealing regarding variation in learning opportunities as course sequences (Stevenson, Schiller, & Schneider, 1994). For example, many students in the college-preparatory track were not taking high-level mathematics and science courses, whereas students in the general and vocational track were. Thus, course taking in high school among some subject areas is not closely tied to high school program track as was previously assumed.

Studying what happens to students in their various classes in high school takes us one step further in understanding how schools structure different opportunities for learning. Assessing the quality of the day-today experiences students have in their classes allows us to look at the types of classes in which students feel they are meeting the expectations of themselves and others and are also intellectually challenged. We suspect that the quality of experiences will vary systematically by the type of class a student is in, i.e., academic, nonacademic, or vocational classes.

In this chapter we explore the quality of experience for high school students while they are in the classroom. To examine variation in students' experiences we use as a measure of curricular differentiation whether students' high school courses were strictly academic or also included vocational course work. To gain a view of the students' responses to the teaching and learning process we focus on three aspects of students' experiences: the level of intellectual press, or challenge, that students find in the classroom; students' tolerance for schooling, that is, whether they find schooling an experience they endure or enjoy; and the extent to which they feel successful at the tasks at hand.

FACTORS CONTRIBUTING TO VARIATIONS IN DAILY HIGH SCHOOL EXPERIENCES

How students feel in their high school classes depends to a large extent on three major factors. The first is the structural qualities of the learning opportunities which occur primarily through curricular differentiation. Differences in the knowledge presented to the students, instructional strategies, and classroom climates are likely to vary from class to class even within the same academic subject. Second, the classes students attend will vary in their focus on academic challenge, emphasis on motivation, and effects on self-esteem. Third, students have certain predispositions about their classes that stem from their families, peer groups, and prior experiences in school.

Curricular Differentiation

Students occupy certain positions in the curricular structure. The allocation of students to courses, whether on the basis of program or ability level, is likely to provide students with different educational experiences. For example, students in more advanced-level courses are more likely to receive better instruction (Gamoran & Mare, 1989), spend more time on learning (Hallinan & Sorenson, 1986), and be held to higher standards (Oakes, 1985). Students in lower-level courses are less likely to receive a quality education because their opportunities for learning are constrained by their placement (Hallinan, 1994; Oakes, 1994).

Students' curricular placement in high school has been shown to influence their academic performance, postsecondary plans, attendance, and educational attainment (Oakes *et al.*, 1992). Controversy over the interpretation of these findings continues to persist. In the past the debate primarily focused on whether student differences were the consequences of curricular differentiation or the result of inadequate controls for differences among students in different tracks (Alexander & Cook, 1982). Today the debate is primarily concerned with how to restructure schools to minimize differences in learning opportunities among various programs (Hallinan, 1994; Oakes, 1994).

In the not too distant past, high schools would typically identify their curricular programs as college preparatory, general comprehensive, or vocational. National survey data indicate that most high school administrators define their curricular programs as essentially college preparatory (Schiller, 1995). Criticisms regarding the lack of learning opportunities associated with high school tracking have made many schools reluctant to differentiate among their programs. Moreover, the increasing variation in high school course offerings (Powell, Farrar, & Cohen, 1985) also makes it difficult to accurately identify which courses are part of which programs.

Since 1970, secondary vocational education programs have been steadily contracting. Currently high school students are taking fewer vocational courses than in the early 1980s (National Assessment of Vocational Education, 1994). Analyses of NELS:88 find smaller numbers of students being enrolled in vocational tracks than were found in *High School and Beyond* (1982), another national longitudinal study of high schoolers (Rasinski, Ingels, Rock, & Pollack, 1993).

Why students are taking fewer vocational courses is uncertain. Some explanations have attributed these low enrollments to the poor quality of some vocational programs to adequately prepare students seeking full-time employment after high school graduation (Secretary's Commission on Achieving Necessary Skills, 1991). In response to low enrollments and concerns over the quality of vocational programs, many school districts are now attempting to make vocational courses more relevant for the needs of today's labor force. In a number of school districts, traditional vocational courses have been replaced with Tech-Prep classes, which merge academic course work and career preparation (Knauth, 1994). Tech-Prep classes are usually open to all students, including those interested in entering a postsecondary institution after graduating from high school.

Recent changes in the curricular structure of vocational classes have important implications for identifying students as being in a vocational track. While there is some indication that students have misperceptions regarding their high school track (Rosenbaum, 1976), students tend to be better at identifying what course they are in and its respective level of difficulty. West, Miller, and Diodato (1985) found that while students tended to report taking more difficult courses than listed on their transcripts, the differences between the student reports and transcripts were minor.

To gain an understanding of who takes vocational courses and how they feel when they are in these classes, it is important to look at the type of classes in which students are enrolled. Being able to obtain information regarding what a person is doing when he or she is in class and how one feels at the time provides an important window into how students are experiencing various learning activities. One activity of some vocational courses is work-related internships.

Typically, work-related internships involve having the student work at a job site for part of the high school day. Students in these programs receive high school graduation credits for their work-related activities. Since these internships are one component of vocational course experiences, we have also obtained information on how students feel when they are at those job sites for which they will receive high school graduation credit.

Academic Challenge, Motivation, and Self-Esteem

One of the major educational reform strategies being widely advocated today is the development of classroom instruction techniques that engage students in higher-order thinking, are active rather than passive in their orientation, and are directly relevant to students' lives (Newmann & Wehlage, 1993). In classrooms with these qualities, one might expect that on a daily basis students would be more likely to feel intellectually challenged, sufficiently skilled to handle academic problems, motivated to achieve, and able to concentrate on their learning tasks.

It has been argued that students who are interested in seeking employment after high school are more likely to perceive academic courses as unimportant to their future goals. Moreover, if they were engaged in activities that related more to their future expectations they would find school more rewarding (Hamilton, 1990). It is not yet at all clear, though, that when students are in courses that are directly related to employment, such as mechanical drafting, they feel more challenged and see their experiences as more salient to their future goals than when they are in their primarily academic courses.

The quality of students' experiences in vocational classes is unknown. A recent study of vocational programs, the National Assessment of Vocational Education (1994), criticized secondary school vocational courses as having some academic content, but not enough to meet the intellectual demands of a future labor force. The report specifically cited vocational courses as lacking academic rigor and being organized to cover irrelevant subject matter. For example, students in vocational courses were involved with computers, but the emphasis appeared to be on learning word processing skills, rather than on learning computer skills that would lead to employment beyond word processing. Given these conditions, one might expect that students taking vocational classes might find them less challenging than academic classes.

How students feel in school from day to day is likely to affect their future goals. We would expect that students who feel challenged and motivated at school would be more willing to invest in future schooling. In contrast, students who have the daily experience of feeling bored, disinterested, and unable to make connections between what they are doing and their futures are less likely to feel committed to stay in school. Even though most students report wanting to attend college (Rasinski *et al.*, 1993), one would suspect that curricular differences may mediate these expectations.

Family Influences

Students receive a variety of messages about their futures from their teachers, peers, and parents (Bidwell, Csikszentmihalyi, Hedges, & Schneider, 1992). What students expect of themselves and what others expect of them are significant motivators of performance. For example, Muller (1993), using data from NELS:88, found that low parental educational expectations have deleterious effects on their children's academic test scores and grades.

Family expectations are clearly a fundamental factor in shaping students' future educational expectations. However, they can be mediated by day-to-day experiences in school. A highly motivated and informed teacher can help to reshape the expectations students have for themselves regardless of their parents' expectations. Students whose parents have high educational expectations for them may feel more anxious and competitive in classrooms than their classmates whose parents have lower expectations. On the other hand, students whose parents have lower expectations may be influenced more by the attitudes of their classmates and actions of their teachers than by parental expectations. Such students may be more likely to become bored, and, consequently, feel less motivated to achieve when they are placed in classes that are not challenging.

THE QUALITY OF EXPERIENCE IN CLASSES

Our data come from an ongoing study of adolescent development funded by the Alfred P. Sloan Foundation (Bidwell *et al.*, 1992). The study involves a series of surveys and interviews with adolescents in 12 school-based sites across the country. For this chapter, we examine data on 376 students who represent 13 high schools across 9 states and 12 cities. Students were randomly selected from class lists in grades 10 and 12, stratified by gender, race and ethnicity, and ability level. The sites were selected to represent variation in urbanicity, race and ethnicity, and labor force composition and participation. Further details concerning the sampling design and procedures can be found in Bidwell *et al.* (1992).

The quality of the day-to-day experiences students have in their classes is difficult to determine through conventional research methods such as surveys or case studies. On the day of a test a student may feel especially anxious, rather than relaxed as on a day when the class is seeing a movie. Surveying the student on a test day may produce different results than surveying the student on the day of a movie. Characterizing the classroom setting as one that is likely to produce feelings of anxiety or relaxation over time can be problematic even with case studies that rely on the observations of an observer who has to make indirect assumptions rather than obtaining direct information from the students.

Having a tool that can capture the feelings associated with the learning experience makes it possible to obtain direct measures of student interpretations of their classroom activities, even the tacit messages of peers and teachers, which are often masked through observations. The Experience Sampling Method (ESM) is particularly valuable for studying the quality of students' daily experiences. Developed by Mihaly Csikszentmihalyi (Csikszentmihalyi, Larson, & Prescott, 1977), ESM is used for examining the objective aspects of experience (what a person is doing, where he or she is located, who he or she is with) and the subjective aspects of experience (mood, motivation, self-esteem) of students in their normal routines at random points in time. In comparison to surveys, the ESM produces a daily log of experiences over an extended period of time. Thus, it is possible to determine how experiences vary from one class or activity to another and how consistent the experiences are over time. We use ESM data here to examine the quality of experience students report during different high school classes.

To carry out ESM, students were provided with digital wristwatches that were programmed to emit signals at random times over a 1-week period. They were also given corresponding self-report forms that were to be completed immediately following each signal. The self-report forms contain a series of both open-ended and scaled items (for validity and reliability information on the ESM, see Csikszentmihalyi & Larson, 1987). Over the 7-day period, students were randomly signaled by their watches eight times daily between the hours of 7:30 a.m. and 10:30 p.m. The stratified random schedule of signals was designed to be unpredictable to the students, while at the same time providing a representative sample of each subject's moods and activities for that week.

Students also completed a questionnaire that replicated a number of items used in the NELS:88 Base Year and First Follow-Up, a friends sociometric form, and a career orientation survey. In addition, the students were interviewed in person for approximately an hour. Selected items from these instruments are used for the analyses reported in this chapter.

In selecting ESM variables for our analyses, we assumed that in academic classes students would be experiencing high levels of intellectual press, which could be measured by the quality of experience levels of challenge, competition, and anxiety. To examine tolerance of schooling, that is, whether students find schooling an experience they endure or enjoy, we used a composite measure, namely, motivation. Finally, we suspected that living up to one's expectations and the expectations of others might also be higher in nonacademic classes where there is less fear of failure. Expectations, salience of the task to future goals, and being in control were examined through the composite measure self-esteem. Construction of the quality of experience variables and composites is described in the Appendix.

We also wanted to learn if students in more traditional academic programs experience academic classes differently than students who are also taking some vocational courses. Because of the reluctance of schools to identify student programs, and the lack of clarity reported by students in identifying their own programs, we chose to separate students according to how they reported their everyday experiences on the ESM instruments. Students who reported that they were in vocational classes and who also reported doing vocational-type activities were classified as students whose academic program had some aspect of vocational experiences. Students who reported not participating in any of these experiences were categorized as taking a more traditional high school college-preparatory program. Responses of students on the ESM were also verified with survey items in which students identified their high school programs.

There are three components to our examination of students' experiences. For our first step, we use students' ESM reports to determine the proportions of time spent in different activities while in academic classes. We then turn to examining the quality of experience students report having in academic and nonacademic classes, and whether this varies by program placement. Nonparametric statistics were used to determine whether mean levels of challenge, competitiveness, anxiety, motivation, and self-esteem vary by classroom environment and by program placement.

For our final analysis, we conduct two sets of ordinary least squares (OLS) regressions. The first estimates individual experiences for challenge, motivation, and self-esteem while in academic classes, controlling for a variety of background variables. The second estimates students' expectations for educational attainment, again controlling for a variety of background variables and including individual experiences (i.e., relaxation, cooperation, and motivation) while in class.

Pervasive Idleness: How Students Spend Their Time in Academic and Nonacademic Classes

Our first step was to determine what students were doing when they were in academic classes. We examined what classes students reported being in when they were beeped. Academic classes included mathematics, English, sciences, foreign languages, and social sciences, as well as some more advanced-level courses such as political science, philosophy, and humanities. Nonacademic classes included physical education, music, driver's education, and the arts. Vocational classes included agriculture, shop, vo-tech, domestic arts, business skills, and work experience during school hours.

We then constructed a list of what the students reported they were doing in their classes. As there were no predesignated "doing" codes, we developed activity codes based on who was involved: the individual student, teacher and student, and student and classmates; and the nature of the activity: listening to a lecture, taking a test or quiz, participating in a class discussion, studying, talking to friends, and daydreaming.

Examining what students are doing in their academic classes (see Figure 1), we find that a little over a third of the students' time is spent doing individual seat work and listening to the teacher lecture. More than twice as much time is spent talking to friends (10.7%) as compared to participating in class discussions (4.5%). Nearly as much time is spent listening and taking notes (5.0%) as watching films or TV (4.5%). Similar amounts of time are spent taking tests or quizzes (7.6%) and doing laboratory work in science (7.5%). But what seems most disconcerting is that slightly over 10% of students' time in academic classes is spent in the "other" category, which consists primarily of "downtime," such as waiting to do something, standing, or walking. The proportion of passive waiting time is three times greater than the proportion of time spent daydreaming.

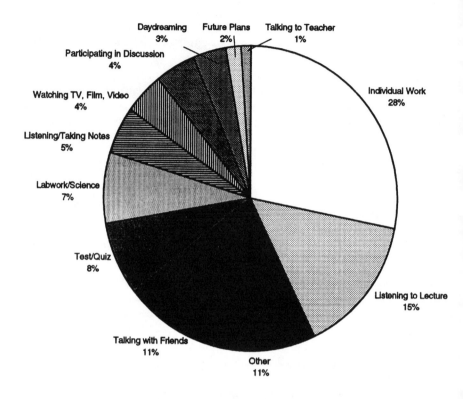

Figure 1.   Proportion of time spent in academic classes by type of activity (academic classes include time spent in English, science, mathematics, and social studies). "Other" includes activities such as sitting, standing, walking, and life maintenance.

These percentages seem to indicate that, at least in academic classes, high school students are spending only about a third of their time on independent work that can be thought of as intellectually challenging (individual work, 28.0%, and tests and quizzes, 7.6%). One-quarter of their time is spent in relatively autonomous passive activities (i.e., listening to the teacher lecture, 14.7%, and waiting to do something, 11.2%). Considerably less time is spent on activities that could be considered as more engaging, such as listening and taking notes (5.0%), watching TV or films (4.5%), or participating in class discussions (4.5%). A little less than a quarter of the students' time is spent interacting with classmates either around social or academic matters (talking with friends, 10.7%, labwork,

7.5%, and participating in class discussions, 4.5%). And regardless of the type of class, few moments are spent talking with the teacher individually.

How Students Feel in Academic and Nonacademic Classes

We then turned to examining how students in academic high school programs and students in vocational programs felt when they were in academic classes versus their nonacademic classes. We defined academic classes as mathematics, English, sciences, foreign languages, and the social sciences; and nonacademic classes as physical education, music, driver's education, and the arts. Looking at Table 1 (left side), we find that students taking the more traditional high school college-preparatory program report higher levels of intellectual press in their academic classes compared to their nonacademic classes. They report higher levels of challenge and feel less relaxed in academic classes than in nonacademic classes. As expected, their level of motivation is higher in nonacademic classes than in academic classes.

Comparing the quality of experience that vocational students have in academic versus nonacademic classes, we find similar patterns although significance levels differ (Table 1, right side). Students taking both academic and vocational classes appear to have more challenging experiences in academic classes compared to nonacademic classes. In addition, they find their academic courses to be significantly more important to their future goals than their nonacademic courses. These results are similar to those of students taking only academic classes.

In Table 2, we examine the quality of experience reported by vocational students in their academic classes versus their vocational classes. In Table 1 we compared all students in the sample ($n = 376$) as to the quality of experience in academic versus nonacademic classes. In this analysis we look only at students with vocational experiences ($n = 77$) and compare the quality of experience in academic classes versus only vocational classes. Academic classes are defined as described above; vocational classes include agriculture, shop, vo-tech, domestic arts, business skills, and work experience during school hours. Not included in the academic or vocational column are experiences while in nonacademic classes, that is, physical education, music, driver's education, and the arts.

Looking at Table 2, we see a somewhat consistent pattern emerging. Students taking academic and vocational classes report slightly significant differences between the intellectual press in their academic classes and their vocational classes. Students have higher challenge in the academic classes. What perhaps is most disconcerting is that when students are

Table 1. Quality of Experience in Academic and Nonacademic Classes by Students in Academic Programs and Students in Vocational Programs[a]

Quality of Experience	Students Taking Academic Classes (N = 299)		Students Taking Academic and Vocational Classes (N = 77)	
	Academic Classes	Nonacademic Classes	Academic Classes	Nonacademic Classes
Challenge[b]	4.71	4.17**	4.59	4.26*
Cooperation/competition	4.33	4.09**	4.51	4.41
Relax/anxious	4.37	4.75**	4.53	4.90
Motivation	4.49	5.59**	4.82	5.65
Future importance	5.11	4.59**	4.82	4.37*
Self-esteem	6.23	6.59	6.21	6.49

[a]Academic classes are defined as mathematics, English, sciences, foreign languages, and social sciences. Nonacademic classes are defined as physical education, music, driver's education, and the arts.

[b]Cooperation/competition and relax/anxious are on a 7-point scale; the remaining variables are on a 9-point scale.

*$p < 0.05$, **$p < 0.001$.

Table 2.   Quality of Experience in Academic and Vocational Classes[a] by Students in Vocational Programs ($N = 77$)

Quality of Experience	Academic Classes	Vocational Classes
Challenge	4.59	4.53*
Cooperation/competition	4.51	4.39
Relax/anxious	4.53	4.29
Motivation	4.82	5.09
Future importance	4.82	4.29
Self-esteem	6.21	6.40

[a]Academic classes are defined as mathematics, English, sciences, foreign languages, and social sciences. Vocational classes include agriculture, shop, vo-tech, domestic arts, business skills, and work experience during school hours.
[b]Cooperation/competition and relax/anxious are on a 7-point scale; the remaining variables are on a 9-point scale.
*$p < 0.05$.

having vocational experiences, which theoretically are preparing them for work after high school, they do not find those experiences to be more important to their future goals than their experiences in academic classes.

Who Finds Schoolwork Challenging?

For our next set of analyses we look more specifically at what types of students are likely to find academic course work intellectually challenging, motivating, and salient, taking into account their gender, race and ethnicity, family background factors, parent expectations, grades, and type of classes they are currently enrolled in. One would suspect that over time the content of the courses in which a student is enrolled, the type of activities the student is expected to perform in class, and how he or she feels when in class, would have a direct effect on student educational expectations. By delving into how students feel when they are in different types of classes, we can learn more about how these factors influence future educational decisions. We looked particularly at the differences between students taking vocational classes or engaged in work activities during school hours, and students who reported taking only academic classes.

Our three dependent measures are challenge, motivation, and self-esteem. In our final model we examine how the quality of experience variables affect educational aspirations. Table 3 shows the standardized coefficients of these three separate OLS regressions.

Table 3.   OLS Regressions Estimating Challenge, Motivation, and Self-Esteem While in Class ($N = 376$)

	Standardized Coefficients		
	Challenge	Motivation	Self-Esteem
1. Female	−0.140***	0.064	0.056
2. Asian	0.059	0.003	−0.042
3. Hispanic	−0.062	0.098*	−0.033
4. African-American	−0.018	0.026	0.068
5. Two-year college parent	0.011	−0.004	−0.010
6. College graduate parent	0.012	−0.007	0.082*
7. Graduate degree parent	−0.023	0.074	0.035
8. Parent expects student to complete college	−0.020	−0.140*	0.083
9. Parent expects student to attend graduate school	−0.026	−0.017	−0.000
10. Student expects to attend college	0.049	0.015	0.041
11. Student expects to attend graduate school	−0.029	−0.013	0.024
12. Prior grades	0.012	0.025	−0.046
13. Student takes vocational classes	0.049	0.007	−0.037
14. Student is in academic class	0.090*	−0.270****	0.020
15. Relax	−0.175***	0.110*	0.219****
16. Skill	−0.069	−0.049	0.446****
17. Cooperation	−0.100*	0.003	0.073*
18. Challenge		0.046	0.105**
19. Motivation	0.053		0.281****
20. Esteem	0.163**	0.375****	
21. Future importance	0.373****	0.181***	0.012
r^2	0.20	0.31	0.49

*$p < 0.05$, **$p < 0.01$, ***$p < 0.001$, ****$p < 0.0001$.

Feeling Challenged

Examining challenge, we find that students feel the highest level of challenge in their academic classes, regardless of their high school program. Students are less likely to feel relaxed when challenged, probably as a consequence of the anxiety associated with cognitive tasks perceived as important to the individual's personal expectations and the expectations of others. Students are also less likely to feel cooperative when challenged. As expected, it appears that challenge is more associated with individual competition and being anxious than being cooperative and relaxed. From our analysis of classroom activities, we find that students spend a considerable proportion of their time in individual activities. We suspect that there are few opportunities in high school classrooms that link cooperation and challenge.

We find positive associations between students' reports of challenge and self-esteem, and the extent to which students feel that their classroom activities are related to future goals. Self-esteem is a composite variable that reflects in part the extent to which students feel that they are living up to their own and others' expectations. The positive associations of future importance and self-esteem with challenge suggest that a sense of challenge may be related to the immediate quality of a task, and to its relationship to a larger framework of goals and expectations.

With respect to demographic characteristics, results show that females report feeling less challenged than males in academic classes. Females may feel less excited and involved in academic classes because they do not feel encouraged to participate in class activities. Other research has shown that teachers tend to call on and respond to males more often (Sadker, Sadker, & Klein, 1991; Sandler, 1987). This aspect of teachers' behavior may lessen females' opportunities for involvement during school. It may also be that females, knowing that they are less likely to receive encouragement to participate, internalize a sense of disengagement and consequently are less excited while in class.

Being Motivated

Motivation is a composite variable, calculated as the mean of the variables "wish to be doing present activity," "enjoy what you are doing," and "activity is interesting to you." Thus, not surprisingly, feeling relaxed is positively associated with motivation. As with challenge, motivation is positively associated with self-esteem and future goals. We suspect that enjoyment of a school activity is linked with the importance and relevance the activity has to the individual.

There is, however, a strong negative relationship between being in an academic class and feeling motivated. We suspect this finding is the consequence of most academic classroom activities being unenjoyable and uninteresting.

And finally, we find that only Hispanics are likely to report being motivated in their classes. Perhaps Hispanics find that classwork is more enjoyable than activities outside of school. Analyses of national data bases indicate that Hispanic teenagers are less likely than other racial and ethnic groups to work for pay and participate in extracurricular activities (Ingels, Schneider, Scott, Plank, & Wu, 1994; Fejgin, 1993). Compared to other racial and ethnic groups, they tend not to enjoy spending time with their families (Rich & Schmidt, 1994).

Self-Esteem

Feeling relaxed, being motivated, and using a high level of skill are highly positively associated with self-esteem. Challenge and cooperation are also positively associated with self-esteem. The only quality of experience variable not associated with self-esteem is future importance. This may imply that global self-esteem is distinctively different from the importance an individual places on a specific single activity. Type of class or program is also not associated with self-esteem, suggesting that global self-esteem may not be significantly affected by school-related experiences.

Educational Expectations

In our last OLS analysis (see Table 4), we examine how background characteristics, skill, prior performance, academic program, and experi-

Table 4. OLS Regressions Estimating Students' Expectations for Educational Attainment ($N = 376$)

	Standardized Coefficients
1. Female	−0.013
2. Asian	0.051
3. Hispanic	−0.073
4. African-American	0.076
5. Two-year college parent	0.148**
6. College graduate parent	0.113*
7. Graduate degree parent	0.142**
8. Parent expects student to complete college	0.258***
9. Parent expects student to attend graduate school	0.589****
10. Prior grades	0.130**
11. Student takes vocational classes	−0.104*
12. Relax	0.049
13. Skill	−0.005
14. Cooperation	−0.006
15. Challenge	0.020
16. Motivation	−0.044
17. Self-esteem	0.005
18. Future importance	0.039
r^2	0.28

*$p < 0.05$, **$p < 0.01$, ***$p < 0.001$, ****$p < 0.0001$.

ences in academic classes affect educational expectations. Not surprisingly, high parent educational attainment and high parent educational expectations are positively associated with high student educational expectations. Students whose parents have a college or advanced graduate degree report higher educational expectations than students whose parents have lower levels of education (i.e., less than a college degree). A similar pattern occurs with parents' expectations for their children's education. Students are more likely to have high educational expectations when their parents have high educational expectations for them.

Students who do well in school are more likely to report wanting to continue with their education beyond high school. Prior academic achievement, as measured by students' reports of their recent grades, is positively associated with higher educational expectations. Students who report taking vocational classes have significantly lower expectations than other students.

The quality of daily experiences is not significantly positively or negatively associated with educational expectations. It is important to note that the overall educational expectations of high school students are generally very high, that is, over 80% of high school sophomores expect to graduate from college (Rasinski et al., 1993). It would appear that how one feels on a daily basis in school is neither a deterrent nor an enhancer of educational expectations. However, the rewards of schooling, that is, grades and varied learning opportunities in different classes, appear to be significantly related to future educational plans.

TOLERANCE FOR SCHOOLING

Bidwell and Friedkin (1988) suggest that those students who persevere in school are those who tolerate the conditions of schooling. These data allow us to look more closely into what those conditions of schooling may be for students in academic and vocational classes in high school. Our first set of analyses conform to what Goodlad and Sizer argue in their reviews of high school classes (Goodlad, 1984; Sizer, 1984). Schooling for high schoolers is primarily a passive, independent activity. Students spend more time listening to the teacher and waiting for something to happen than they spend even on independent seat work. Despite the seemingly uninteresting nature of the activities that students are engaged in, they still feel more challenged in their academic classes than in other classes.

While students may feel more challenged in their academic classes, they do not appear to find these classes interesting or enjoyable. Time spent in academic classes is positively associated with challenge, but negatively associated with motivation. These results are consistent with findings from other studies that examined the experiences of talented teenagers (Csikszentmihalyi, Rathunde, & Whalen, 1993).

The findings concerning challenge and motivation seem to raise the question of whether academic classes can be academically demanding and at the same time be motivating. The repetitive, passive, routine nature of activities in academic classes certainly contributes to the feeling that schooling is something to be endured and persevered rather than motivating.

Yet, challenge in class is positively associated with self-esteem. This finding seems to suggest that classroom activities that require high challenge are also perceived as meeting high personal expectations, as well as the expectations of others. Thus, challenging activities are perceived as "real" or "authentic" school tasks. By high school, students may have a strong sense of what constitutes schooling, and how they should behave in that context even if they do not enjoy it.

The different relationships of academic class to challenge, motivation, and self-esteem point to the importance of making academic classes more intellectually engaging, enjoyable, and salient. One of the current educational reforms being proposed is to blend vocational experiences into academic courses for students in vocational programs. Our results show that students in vocational programs do not find their academic or vocational courses intellectually challenging. If these new courses are not challenging intellectually, or do not match students' expectations of schooling, these proposed reforms may be even less effective than traditional programs for preparing high school students for work or postsecondary education.

The Secretary's Commission on Achieving Necessary Skills (1991) recommended that vocational classes equip students with the cognitive skills necessary for undertaking the type of work and life-styles projected for the 21st century. The explosion of technology places intellectual demands on students regardless of the type of job they will hold in the future. If high school classes were more intellectually challenging and motivating, perhaps students' tolerance for schooling and learning in general would increase.

APPENDIX: DESCRIPTION OF VARIABLES

Experience Sampling Method (ESM) Data

The ESM variables measure an aspect of the students' experiences while they were engaged in a particular activity. The variables used here are on a seven- or nine-point scale in which 1 is the lower, or negative, end of the scale and 7 or 9 the higher or positive end.

Challenge is the extent to which students felt the activity they were doing made them feel "excited or makes you want to get involved." *Skill* is the extent to which students felt that they were using their skills; *Relax* is the extent to which students felt relaxed rather than anxious; and *Cooperation* is the extent to which they felt cooperative rather than competitive. *Future importance* is the extent to which students felt that their present activity related to their future goals. *Motivation* is a composite variable calculated as the mean of the variables "wish to be doing present activity," "enjoy what you're doing," and "activity is interesting to you." *Self-esteem* is again a composite calculated as the mean of living up to others' expectations, living up to your own expectations, feeling good about yourself, feeling successful at the current activity, and feeling in control.

Academic class specifies whether students were in academic classes, nonacademic classes, or vocational classes when responding to the ESM forms.

The variable *Voc* was used to determine which students were in programs that included vocational course work. The data used for this variable were taken from ESM responses and cross-checked with responses from the modified version of NELS:88.

Background Characteristics

These variables were obtained from a modified version of NELS:88 completed by the students. *Race* and *Gender* were thus obtained from student reports, confirmed by school records. *Prior grades* is a continuous measure of a student's grades on prior report cards, using a scale that runs from "mostly A's" to "mostly D's and below." *Parent's education* gives the highest level of education of either parent in the household. *Parental expectations for student's education* is based on students' reports of the level of schooling their parents expect them to achieve. *How far in school a student expects to go* is the level of schooling a student expects to achieve.

ACKNOWLEDGMENTS.   This work is supported by a grant from the Alfred P. Sloan Foundation for The Study of Youth and Social Development. The views expressed here are those of the authors and do not represent the Foundation. Special thanks to Kim Maier for her assistance in several of the analyses reported herein.

REFERENCES

Alexander, K. L., & Cook, M. A. (1982). Curricula and coursework: A surprise ending to a familiar story. *American Sociological Review, 47,* 626–640.

Bidwell, C., & Friedkin, N. (1988). The sociology of education. In N. Smelzer (Ed.), *Handbook of sociology* (pp. 449–471). Newbury Park, CA: Sage.

Bidwell, C., Csikszentmihalyi, M., Hedges, L., & Schneider, B. (1992). *Studying career choice.* Chicago: Ogburn–Stouffer Center, University of Chicago/ NORC.

Carroll, J. B. (1963). A model of school learning. *Teachers College Record, 64,* 723–733.

Csikszentmihalyi, M., & Larson, R. (1987). Validity and reliability of the Experience-Sampling Method. *The Journal of Nervous and Mental Disease, 175,* 525–536.

Csikszentmihalyi, M., Larson, R., & Prescott, S. (1977). The ecology of adolescent activity and experience. *Journal of Youth and Adolescence, 6,* 281–294.

Csikszentmihalyi, M., Rathunde, K., & Whalen, S. (1993). *Talented teenagers: The roots of success and failure.* London: Cambridge University Press.

Fejgin, N. (1993). *High school competitive sports: Who participates and what are the benefits?* Unpublished manuscript, The University of Chicago.

Gamoran, A., & Mare, R. (1989). Secondary school tracking and educational inequality: Compensation, reinforcement or neutrality? *American Journal of Sociology, 94,* 1146–1183.

Goodlad, J. (1984). *A place called school: Prospects for the future.* New York: McGraw–Hill.

Hallinan, M. (1994). Tracking: From theory to practice. *Sociology of Education, 67,* 79–84.

Hallinan, M., & Sorenson, A. (1986). Student characteristics and assignments to ability groups: Two conceptual formations. *The Sociological Quarterly, 27,* 1–13.

Hamilton, S. (1990). *Apprenticeship for adulthood: Preparing youth for the future.* New York: Free Press.

Ingels, S., Schneider, B., Scott, L., Plank, S., & Wu, S. (1994). *A profile of the American high school sophomore in 1990.* Washington, DC: National Center for Education Statistics, U.S. Department of Education.

Knauth, S. (1994, April). *Vocational education from the students' view: Using the Experience Sampling Method.* Paper presented at the annual meeting of the American Educational Research Association, New Orleans.

Muller, C. (1993). Parent involvement and academic achievement: An analysis of family resources available to the child. In B. Schneider & J. Coleman (Eds.), *Parents, their children, and schools* (pp. 77–113). Boulder, CO: Westview Press.

National Assessment of Vocational Education. (1994). *Interim report to Congress.* Washington, DC: Office of Educational Research and Improvement, U.S. Department of Education.

Newmann, F. M., & Wehlage, G. G. (1993). Five standards of authentic instruction. *Educational Leadership, 50,* 8–12.

Oakes, J. (1985). *Keeping track: How schools structure inequality.* New Haven: Yale University Press.

Oakes, J. (1990). *Multiplying inequalities: The effects of race, social class, and tracking on opportunities to learn math and science*. Santa Monica, CA: Rand.

Oakes, J. (1992). Can tracking research inform practice? Technical, normative, and political considerations. *Educational Researcher*, 12–21.

Oakes, J. (1994). More than misapplied technology: A normative and political response to Hallinan on tracking. *Sociology of Education, 67*, 84–89.

Oakes, J., Gamoran, A., & Page, R. (1992). Curriculum differentiation: Opportunities, consequences, and meanings. In P. Jackson (Ed.), *Handbook of research on curriculum: A project of the American Educational Research Association* (pp. 570–608). New York: Macmillan Co.

Powell, A. G., Farrar, E., & Cohen, D. K. (1985). *The shopping mall high school: Winners and losers in the educational marketplace*. Boston: Houghton Mifflin.

Rasinski, K., Ingels, S., Rock, D., & Pollack, J. (1993). *America's high school sophomores: A ten year comparison*. Washington, DC: National Center for Education Statistics, U.S. Department of Education.

Rich, G., & Schmidt, J. (1994, February). *Hispanic student identity and career development*. Paper presented at the meeting of the Society for Research on Adolescence, San Diego, CA.

Rosenbaum, J. E. (1976). *Making inequality: The hidden curriculum of high school tracking*. New York: John Wiley & Sons.

Sadker, M., Sadker, D., & Klein, S. (1991). The issue of gender in elementary and secondary education. In G. Grant (Ed.), *Review of research in education* (Vol. 17, pp. 269–334). Washington, DC: American Educational Research Association.

Sandler, B. R. (1987). The classroom climate: Still a chilly one for women. In C. Lasser (Ed.), *Educating men and women together: Co-education in a changing world* (pp. 113–123). Urbana: University of Illinois Press.

Schiller, K. (1995). *Organizations' uncertainty and information: The transition of students to high school*. Unpublished dissertation, The University of Chicago.

Secretary's Commission on Achieving Necessary Skills. (1991). *What work requires of schools: A SCANS report for America 2000*. Washington, DC: U.S. Department of Labor.

Sizer, T. (1984). *Horace's compromise: The dilemma of the American high school*. Boston: Houghton Mifflin.

Stevenson, D., Schiller, K., & Schneider, B. (1994). Sequences of opportunities for learning. *Sociology of Education, 67*, 184–198.

West, J., Miller, W., & Diodato, L. (1985). *An analysis of course taking patterns in secondary schools as related to student characteristics*. Washington, DC: National Center for Education Statistics.

IV

School-to-Work Transitions

10

Reforming Education
A Critical Overlooked Component

Alan C. Kerckhoff

The idea that we need to "do something" about the U.S. educational system is a very popular one. Ever since the publication of "A Nation At Risk" (U.S. Department of Education, 1983), momentum has been building to introduce some kind of reform. In 1994 the Goals 2000: Educate America Act, introduced by President Bush, was signed into law by President Clinton, and the Clinton administration has been attempting to build up the Department of Education. Support for federal action has come from both political parties.

A centerpiece of almost all recently suggested education legislation is the establishment of a set of national standards for student performance in basic academic subjects (Ravitch, 1992). Often linked with this is the idea of a national curriculum. The proposed actions reflect a growing sense that we need to raise the level of performance of American students. It is not always clear, however, whether the focus should be on the lower-performing students, or the best and brightest, or on simply raising the overall level of performance. Part of that lack of clarity comes from the fact that at least two rather different forces seem to be driving the proposals. One is the relatively poor showing of American students in international studies of academic performance. This tends to direct our attention to the upper part of the distribution. The other force comes from the often-heard complaint that American students are not sufficiently well

Alan C. Kerckhoff   Department of Sociology, Duke University, Durham, North Carolina 27708.

Restructuring Schools: Promising Practices and Policies, edited by Maureen T. Hallinan. Plenum Press, New York, 1995.

educated to take on the kinds of jobs being created by our changing economy. This tends to direct our attention to the lower part of the distribution.

National standards and curricula are presented as ways in which (1) we can ensure that all of our students are offered an opportunity to learn and (2) we can more adequately monitor how well they are learning as they pass through the system. Such proposals do not call for any change in the way our educational system is organized or in the forms of public recognition the system gives its students for their performance. Those are the features of the system I want to consider here. I want to do this because, I will argue, the most frequently discussed reforms ignore major organizational features of our current system, and other possible reforms could do more to deal with the problems we face.

I want to discuss the ways in which the organizational features of the U.S. school system affect the lifetime achievements of the students who move through it. In order to put what I want to say in a more meaningful perspective, however, I will begin by stepping back from the specifics of our school system to make two more general kinds of observations. One of these has to do with the general functions of school systems in industrial societies, and the other has to do with the ways school systems in industrial societies vary and how our system differs from others.

SCHOOLS AND SOCIAL STRATIFICATION

It can be said (Goslin, 1965) that school systems serve three basic functions in modern societies. They transmit the society's culture from one generation to the next, they contribute to the discovery of new knowledge, and they help to allocate members of the new generation to positions in the society. It is that third function that I want to emphasize here.

The school systems in all contemporary societies act as "sorting machines" (Spring, 1976) for the societies. One of their prime responsibilities is to *grade* their students, to sort them into hierarchical categories. School systems do this in two ways. First, they assign grades to the ongoing performances of their students. Students (and their families) are provided with constant feedback about the relative levels of their performances. Second, school systems provide stratified attainment levels, access to which is increasingly restricted to smaller and smaller proportions of an age cohort. There is an inherent association between these two kinds of grading—high grades increase access to higher attainment levels—but the association is complex and varied across societies and levels in the educational system.

In all industrial societies there is also a clear association between levels of educational attainment and adult positions in the stratification system. Although sociologists have more than one way to conceptualize stratification systems (in terms of class, status, or prestige), most of them are based on categories in the division of labor, namely, occupations. Stratification positions defined in all of these ways are systematically associated with levels of educational attainment.

My basic point, then, is that all school systems serve to *stratify* students whose positions in the educational attainment hierarchy are systematically linked with their later positions in the stratified adult society. No school system is *permitted* to produce a uniform set of products. Schools do not, cannot, educate everyone the same. A fundamental part of the "charter" (Meyer, 1977) of all school systems is to prepare young people to live in a stratified society. In fact, an important part of the charter is to *legitimize* the nature of that stratified society. This is a universal feature of all industrial societies. If we lose sight of it, we can engage in hopeless debates and meaningless discussions of possible reforms.

It is not a question, then, of *whether* school systems stratify their students in anticipation of their participation in a stratified adult society. They all do. However, they go about it in highly varied ways, and the differences have significant implications for both the students and the larger society. I will start by looking at some of the different ways of stratifying students so that we can consider more carefully the nature of our own system. I will then discuss some of the implications of doing it *our* way rather than some other way. In particular, I will argue that doing it our way contributes to the problems we are currently concerned about. Finally, I will discuss possible changes that could improve the situation.

DIMENSIONS OF SYSTEM VARIATION

I will focus on four particular dimensions of variation among educational systems so as to highlight the "peculiar" nature of the American system. The four dimensions are: (1) the degree of stratification, (2) the degree of differentiation and standardization, (3) the nature of the interface with the structure of the labor force, and (4) the degree to which "second chances" are possible.

Table 1.   Comparative Rates of Educational Attainment in England, France, Germany, and the United States, Using Two Measurement Criteria[a]

Criteria	England	France	Germany	United States
Completed				
Secondary school	32.2	14.9	41.4	68.7
University-level degree	6.4	4.0	6.6	19.1
Obtained any credentials in				
Secondary school	46.6	29.8	85.6	68.7
Postsecondary education	11.5	7.5	15.6	26.3

[a]See text for explanation of the estimated proportions. Sources: Müller and Karle (1992), U.S. Census (1981).

Degree of Stratification

My earlier use of the term *stratification* referred to the simple fact of a hierarchical arrangement. Here I use the term, as most students of educational systems do, to refer to the rapidity with which the system restricts access to the successively higher levels of attainment. Almost everyone obtains at least an elementary school education in most industrial societies, but only a small proportion of any cohort obtains a degree in higher education. There is, in effect, a progressive sifting out of members of the cohort as they pass through the levels of the system.

This sifting process is found in all industrial societies, but it is done in rather varied ways. The upper part of Table 1 reports what can be called the "survival patterns" (Müller & Karle, 1992) in four societies: England, France, Germany, and the United States. It reports (for the mid-1970s) the proportions of men 30 to 64 years of age who had completed secondary school and who had obtained a university or higher level degree.[1]

It is clear that the U.S. survival rates at both stages were much higher than those in any of the other three countries. However, the other three also differed from one other. A smaller proportion of French than either English or German men "survived" through secondary school. However, more similar proportions of men in those three countries managed to obtain a university degree, so the survival rates between finishing secondary school and obtaining a university degree differed greatly. The proportions obtaining university degrees in all three European countries were far lower than in the United States, however.

[1]The statistics in Table 1 are based on those reported in Müller and Karle (1992) and in U.S. Census (1981). The U.S. data are for 1975 for men between 25 and 64 years of age.

By most measures, these are four highly comparable societies as far as their economies and degrees of social stratification are concerned. Most research on social mobility processes suggests that the amount of intergenerational mobility is about the same in all of them *and* that educational attainment is closely associated with occupational position in all four. It is thus at first rather surprising that there should be variation in their distributions of educational attainment. One reason for this is that the upper part of Table 1 reflects an overly crude method of measuring educational attainment. It is a typical American method, but it presents serious problems when making intersocietal comparisons. We cannot understand these patterns until we consider two other features of the societies' educational systems, differentiation among *kinds* of education and the nature of the interface between educational and labor force structures.

Degree of Differentiation and Standardization

All three European countries recognize more than one kind of secondary and postsecondary credential, and in all of them a division is made between general academic credentials and vocational credentials. Overall, all of them value academic credentials more than vocational credentials, but some vocational credentials are clearly "higher" than some academic credentials. The high-status secondary school academic credentials (Baccalauréat, Abitur, A-level examination) are often offered through separate schools (the lycée, gymnasium, and grammar school). Other secondary school programs provide other, lesser, but still highly regarded credentials.[2] Because of these differences, it is difficult to make direct comparisons among these four systems with respect to educational attainment.[3] It

---

[2]The introduction of comprehensive schools in England reduced the sharp distinction between grammar and secondary modern schools, but there continued to be stratification among secondary schools, some comprehensives not providing programs of study directed toward university admission (Kerckhoff, Fogelman, Crook, & Reeder, 1995).

[3]International comparisons of educational attainment may use different rules of classification and thereby arrive at quite different comparative statistics than I present here. For instance, "The Condition of Education, 1993" (U.S. Department of Education, 1993) makes these countries look much more alike than the upper part of Table 1 does evidently because they count some of the lesser attainment levels in England, France, and Germany as comparable to high school graduation in the United States. In contrast, the OECD (1989) attempt to compare them chooses to classify all vocational credentials together, whatever their level, and essentially sets them aside. Since, by the OECD count, vocational credentials account for 60% of the German credentials and 31% of those in the United Kingdom, their analysis makes the three European countries appear to be even more different than they do here.

is especially difficult because the different types of secondary school credentials provide access to different kinds of postsecondary institutions and programs and to the various sets of credentials they offer.

The important point here, however, is that the educational systems of the other three countries provide for nationally recognized credentials that do not correspond in any direct way with levels of educational attainment recognized in this country. Whereas our official statistics and other classifications of individual educational attainments generally recognize only high school graduation and a college diploma, England, France, and Germany all recognize other credentials at intermediate levels. It is possible to obtain those intermediate credentials without "completing" secondary school or entering university.

For instance, access to university-level programs in England in the 1970s normally required the student to have passed two or more A-level examinations in secondary school. The nationally recognized A-level examinations were normally taken during the sixth form of secondary school (usually at age 18). Yet, pupils with much lower credentials (even those with no secondary school credentials) had access to other postsecondary institutions (e.g., colleges of further education) from which they could obtain valuable postsecondary schooling and nationally recognized credentials. In American terminology, it was not necessary to "complete" (or "graduate from") secondary school in order to enter a postsecondary institution and obtain nationally recognized credentials. They might have been "lesser" credentials, because they were often "vocational" rather than "academic" credentials, but they were very valuable in providing access to desirable employment opportunities.

Those additional credentials are included in the statistics reported in the lower part of Table 1. This leads to a very different picture of the four countries, especially in the pattern of secondary school credentials. Whereas there is no change in the proportions who obtained secondary school credentials in the United States, since we only recognize the high school diploma, there is a sharp increase in the proportions obtaining secondary school credentials in all of the other countries. The change is especially dramatic for Germany. In fact, more Germans than Americans obtained some nationally recognized credentials in secondary school.

Making societal comparisons at the postsecondary level is much more difficult. Because of the deemphasis in the United States on postsecondary credentials other than a college degree, there are no national data on postsecondary credentials, especially for the full adult population and for a period as early as the mid-1970s. The only postsecondary credential besides a college degree that currently receives any recognition in U.S. educational attainment statistics is the Associate degree, but data on Asso-

ciate degrees are not available for the mid-1970s.[4] Census data for that
period report educational attainment in terms of years in high school and
college completed. To estimate the proportion obtaining an Associate
degree for the lower part of Table 1, I used one-half the proportion
reported by the Census as having from 1 to 3 years of college (but not a
college degree). If anything, this probably produces an overestimate, but
it is a useful basis for the present discussion.

The proportion obtaining some kind of postsecondary credential is
still highest in the United States, and that would be true even if the
estimate of Associate degree recipients were ignored. However, there are
huge increases in the proportions in all three European countries who
obtained some kind of postsecondary credential, compared with the proportions who obtained a university degree. Again, the increase is greatest
for Germany. It is smallest for France, where the survival rate remains
the lowest of all four countries at both measurement points.

One reason for the difference in the kinds of credentials awarded in
the United States and these other countries is the decentralized nature of
the U.S. educational system. We strongly emphasize the local nature
of education and resist any attempt to "impose" standardization. That
resistance will preclude the full adoption of national achievement standards or a national curriculum; adoption of either will undoubtedly be
wholly voluntary and thus far from universal. It also means that even
the limited set of credentials we recognize have quite varied meanings
and are based on criteria that can differ widely from one school or district
to another.

Ironically, it is not until American students reach the critical transition
point between high school and college that there exists any nationally
recognized system of achievement assessment—the use of the Scholastic
Aptitude Test to evaluate students' "suitability" for higher education.
And, it is not until students have taken part in some postsecondary
professional programs (e.g., engineering, medicine, law) that sets of nationally recognized criteria of occupational adequacy come into play.
Although the U.S. survival rate is exceptionally high at both the secondary
and postsecondary levels, our educational system lacks both the amount
of differentiation and the degree of standardization of educational credentials found in all of these other countries.

[4]Even at the present time, national data on vocational postsecondary credentials are unavailable except from sample surveys such as *High School and Beyond*. Those data are limited
to single age cohorts, however, and they combine highly varied kinds of credentials in
ways that make it extremely difficult to assess their importance. The fundamental problem
is not record-keeping, however, so much as it is the lack of nationally recognized postsecondary credentials other than the purely academic ones.

Interface with the Labor Force

The more varied credentials offered by European educational systems generally have some direct relationship to kinds of occupations, but, of the three European countries, this is most true in Germany and least true in France. The United States would be ranked below all three of them in this respect, however.

An insightful analysis of the education–occupation linkage in Germany and France by Maurice, Sellier, and Silvestre (1986) refers to the difference between those two educational systems' "capacity to structure" the flow of individuals into the labor force. Germany has a more specialized set of secondary and postsecondary educational credentials that are clearly linked with particular kinds of occupations. The widespread use of apprenticeships, together with specialized school programs, provide young Germans with a highly diverse set of certified marketable skills. In contrast, the credentials in the French educational system are more generalized and less directly occupationally relevant.

As Maurice *et al.* point out, this has three important implications in France, when contrasted with Germany. First, the youth labor market is much more "open" in that the more general French educational credentials are less helpful in matching school leavers with jobs. Second, employers must essentially gamble that the youths they hire can be trained to do the jobs that need to be done. That gamble does not always pay off, of course, so there is much more job changing in the early work careers of young Frenchmen than in those of young Germans. Third, since the relevant training for work in France is largely on-the-job, its nature is determined by employers, and that leads to training that is more firm-specific and less transferable to another employer than is the case in Germany. Career advancement is thus much more dependent on within-firm promotions and on seniority in France than it is in Germany. In all of these respects, the situation in England seems to be somewhere between France and Germany.

This description of the French case should sound rather familiar. The American case is quite similar, and it is much more like the French than it is like either the German or the English case. Young Americans leave secondary school (as either graduates or dropouts) with few, if any, specific certified marketable skills. Our credentialing system is even more general than the French, in fact. Whereas some secondary school vocational credentials are generally recognized in France, this is not the case here. And our technical school and community college credentials are seldom easily transferable from one part of the country to another. Even

U.S. college graduates tend to have very general educational credentials, except for the relatively small proportion who obtain specialized training in such fields as engineering, education, or nursing. Most specialized, occupationally focused programs that abide by some nationally recognized standards in the United States are found in graduate and professional schools.

Second Chances

To my knowledge, there has been no systematic study of the four countries with respect to the frequency with which individuals who lose out at one point in the educational system have a chance to recover from that loss and move on toward higher levels of educational attainment. Rosenbaum's (1986) discussion of the "tournament model" of career attainment suggests that those who lose out at one level do not have a second chance. My own research in Great Britain makes me doubt the universal applicability of that model.

The system of further education in Great Britain provides a second chance even to individuals who have utterly "failed" in the regular secondary school system. The British system offers a variety of secondary school examinations in a wide array of topics, generally at ages 16 and 18, and young Britons' secondary school credentials are based on students' passing those examinations. As in other societies, success at that level opens opportunities for additional education after secondary school. Yet, at least in the 1970s it was clearly possible for someone who had passed no secondary school examinations to obtain valuable, and sometimes quite high-level, credentials after leaving school (Kerckhoff, 1993). The further education system provided a second chance for at least some young Britons. It provided the basis for what might be viewed as a "losers' bracket" or a "double elimination tournament."

It is my impression that neither the French nor the German educational system offers quite the degree of opportunity to those who have "failed" at a lower level as does the British. It is apparent, however, that the U.S. system does not offer such an opportunity. Many Americans take courses at technical institutes and community colleges, of course, but those courses seldom lead to credentials that are generally recognized and honored either by employers or by our national methods of recording educational attainment. In that respect, the courses tend to be about as limited in their utility as firm-based training courses are both here and in France.

Putting the U.S. Educational System in Comparative Perspective

When viewed in this comparative context, our educational system has an unusual set of characteristics. It is less stratified than the European systems I have considered. Much larger proportions of our population complete secondary school and many more obtain a university-level degree. On average, then, Americans are in school longer (and are thus sometimes viewed as "better educated") than the Europeans. Yet, the kinds of credentials they obtain through that more extended educational experience are much more restricted than in Europe. Not only do we recognize fewer kinds of credentials, it is not until university graduation or later that the credentials we award meet a set of national standards or have any very direct linkage with locations in the labor force. Those who do not go to college obtain their job skills through unstandardized on-the-job training or part-time technical courses. In all of these respects, our system is more dissimilar to the German than to either the French or British system, but there are striking differences between our system and all of the other three.

Our system also differs from at least the British in more explicitly following a "tournament model" of attainment. This seems to be taken for granted by most American analysts (Mare, 1981; Hout, Raftery, & Bell, 1993). Failure at a lower level closes access to higher levels. That is less true in Great Britain, largely because the British differentiate among kinds of educational institutions and recognize a wide variety of educational credentials. The British system provides "an alternative route" (Raffe, 1979) to formally recognized educational attainment not available in this country.

EDUCATIONAL CAREERS WITHIN THE U.S. SYSTEM

These special characteristics of the U.S. educational system have significant implications for the educational careers and later stratification locations of American students. Some believe that our system is significantly "better" than the others just *because* it is less structured and provides an extended period during which students can "find themselves" and shape their own destinies before they are classified into levels and kinds of attainment. This is one of the implications many have drawn from Turner's (1960) well-known distinction between "contest" and "sponsored" mobility processes, using the United States and England as examples of those two different ways of organizing schools.

However, I submit that quite the opposite is the case. The effect of our system is to extend the period during which hierarchical distinctions among students are made according to a single dimension of achievement. Then, after that long period, a sharp bifurcation of the distribution is made with few viable options being provided for the lower half of the distribution. I see that as an unnecessarily brutal kind of differentiation that does not adequately serve the needs of either the students or the larger society. In order to present that argument effectively, though, I will need to review some of our knowledge about the processes by which our students become stratified as they move through our educational system.

One of the problems with Turner's differentiation between sponsored and contest systems of mobility was that it essentially ignored the nonacademic "alternative route" that is generally found in societies in which sponsorship is significant in the mainline academic route. Those who are not sponsored through the levels of the academic system do not necessarily fall by the wayside in those societies. There are usually other avenues through which they can obtain nationally recognized credentials that provide them with access to valuable adult positions.

That is not true in the United States. One of the reasons we are so concerned about "dropouts" is that we offer young secondary school students nothing other than the all-purpose high school diploma. One either wins or loses in the secondary school "contest." There is neither a consolation prize nor a losers' bracket to move into. And, one of the reasons we are so concerned to encourage secondary school students to go to college is that the high school diploma has very little direct relevance to the world of work, to becoming a functioning adult in this industrial society. A high school diploma is perhaps *necessary* in order even to be considered by a potential employer, but it is not *sufficient* to qualify one for anything in particular. Increasingly, the same can be said about a college diploma—that it is necessary but not sufficient—and we have witnessed an increased demand for professional and graduate school courses that *do* have direct occupational relevance.

Americans may be "more highly educated" than the English, French, or Germans, but we emphasize *general* education, and we avoid the serious development of "vocational education" as if it were beneath our high academic standards. The European educational systems appear to us to be overly elitist, designed (intentionally or otherwise) to separate sheep from goats and to ensure that the children of higher-status parents have an advantage over those from working-class families.

Yet, many studies have shown that there is no more social mobility in the United States than in these other societies, so it is hard to defend the idea that different kinds of educational systems produce different degrees of societal "openness" (although 25 years ago I was convinced that that was so). Educational reforms all over the world, many explicitly aimed at creating more "open" systems, have generally failed to accomplish that goal (Shavit & Blossfeld, 1993). It is also sobering to recognize that international comparative studies show that students in our less structured and less stratified educational system perform at lower levels than those from the more stratified, differentiated, and standardized European systems (Suter, 1989).

Why should this be so? I suggest that at least one reason is that our educational system *is* organized as a contest, a kind of tournament in which one is either a winner or a loser. There are those who "make it" and those who do not, those who obtain the all-important high school diploma or college degree and those who fail to do so. The problem is not that there are *levels* of attainment. That is true of all educational systems. Rather, the peculiar features of our system that I have just outlined point to other reasons many of our students do not perform up to their potential.

First, the few levels of attainment that receive any kind of recognition by the society come only after many years of preparatory work. There are no way stations or intervening goals for students to strive for on their way to the big prizes—or to turn to when they realize they are not likely to win those big prizes. Second, the levels of attainment are generic, unspecialized. It is not possible for a student to be certified as superior in one area of learning even if less than wholly adequate in another.

Third, the available levels of attainment are not in any direct way linked to later adult goals. It is not clear what their *value* is. Students are told that their lives will be better if they do well in school, but this is a very abstract idea that cannot generate either focused motivation or understanding of the connections involved. Finally, the system is not very good at providing students a second chance if they "fail" somewhere along the way. There are GED programs, of course, and community colleges offer postsecondary courses for those who do not go to a "real" college. But the GED is simply a chance to get back to where one should have been (not a chance to move ahead), and community colleges provide only very circumscribed chances since there is no national system of noncollege credentials.

Besides the high school diploma and the college degree, nothing else *counts*. I stress those two divisions so much because I will argue further that their significance in young people's lives makes some of the other features of the U.S. educational sorting process even more important than they might otherwise be. Anything that increases or decreases the prospects of some students "surviving" at either of those major division points is even more important than in other systems just because there are only *two* divisions, because they come so *late* in the educational career, and because they are based on such *generalized* criteria.

I want to look at two features of our system that both contribute to the problems that are receiving so much attention recently and that reduce the value of the most widely discussed reforms that are being proposed. The two features are the use of internal sorting mechanisms in the schools and the decentralization of organizational control.

SORTING MECHANISMS AND PERFORMANCE DISPERSION

A common practice in U.S. (as well as other countries') schools is to separate students by "ability," either by putting them in different classrooms or in groups within classrooms.[5] The usual justification for this practice is that it provides students of all ability levels with more "appropriate" educational experiences, better suited to their special needs. Evidence is mounting, however, that the actual groupings deviate significantly from the prescribed pattern and that the effect of the practice is quite different from what is intended. It is not possible to present a full review of that evidence here, but it is important to recognize its basic characteristics.

One pattern of findings in these studies is especially important for my purposes. A frequently observed effect of ability grouping is to increase the dispersion of student performances. Students in high-ability groups tend to outperform comparable students who are either ungrouped or located in lower-level groups; students in low-ability groups tend to perform less well than comparable students who are either ungrouped or located in higher-level groups. The very fact of being located in a high or low group leads to an increase or decrease in student performance. Such an effect is found from first grade (Pallas, Entwisle, Alexander, & Stluka, 1994) to high school (Gamoran & Mare, 1989).[6]

---

[5] For purposes of this discussion, I will ignore an additional kind of separation, into separate schools. Although some U.S. schools are so defined (special curricula, high-performance or magnet schools), the practice is more common in other countries (e.g., the Hauptschule, Mittelschule, and Gymnasium in Germany).

[6] Several reasons for this dispersion effect have been suggested. One is that the curricular offerings and teaching practices differ in the different groups. A second is that the social significance of group placement is recognized by students and that influences their motivation and level of academic expectation and effort. A third is that significant others (parents and teachers especially) respond to the students' placements by adjusting their treatment of them, their expectations then indirectly influencing the students. These three explanations are certainly not mutually exclusive, but the clearest evidence to date tends to support the first. That is, schools offer different kinds of materials and use different teaching techniques with groups defined as being at different ability levels (Gamoran, 1986; Pallas *et al.*, 1994).

These studies demonstrate the ways in which the internal organiza-tion of schools can significantly affect the achievement levels of students. Most studies focus on a very limited period in students' school experi-ences, but the research suggests a further hypothesis, namely, that ability grouping has a *cumulative* impact on student achievement across the full period of schooling. One suggestion of a cumulative effect comes from the observation that students' group placements tend to remain constant across time, even when their performance levels would justify their move-ment into a higher or lower group (Entwisle & Hayduk, 1988; Hallinan, 1991). If each experience of group placement has a dispersing effect, and if there is persistent placement, the dispersion should become increasingly great as students pass through the educational system. That is, some students would be increasingly advantaged by their successive place-ments in high groups and others would be increasingly disadvantaged by their successive placements in low groups.

It is difficult to demonstrate such a cumulative effect for the United States because we do not have sufficiently long-term data on a cohort of students. Such data do exist in Great Britain, however, and I have been able to test the cumulative effect hypothesis with those data. I will not go into detail about that research (Kerckhoff, 1993), but it is based on the educational experiences of a cohort of children born in 1958 and followed until they were 23 years old in 1981. Information is available on their ability group placements in elementary and secondary school, the kind of postsecondary courses they took, and the kinds of educational certification they obtained.

Figure 1 reports results of an analysis of those British data. A word of explanation is in order. I first used everyone's position in a hierarchy of test achievement at age 7 to define a common starting point. I then estimated the average net effect of ability group placement (controlling for background and earlier achievements) during elementary school, sec-ondary school, and postsecondary schooling. The effects are measured in percentiles on measures of achievement (test scores and certificates obtained) at ages 11, 16, and 23.

Figure 1 reports the results of that analysis for the men, separated into categories according to their educational attainment at age 23.[7] The categories of attainment range from 0 (no qualifications) to 15–16 (a uni-versity or higher degree). The intervening categories include both wholly academic and vocational kinds of certification, all nationally recognized.

---

[7]Some of the original 16 categories have been grouped together to form 9 categories because of the small frequencies found in some of the original 16. The results were somewhat different for women, but the general fan-shaped dispersion was similar.

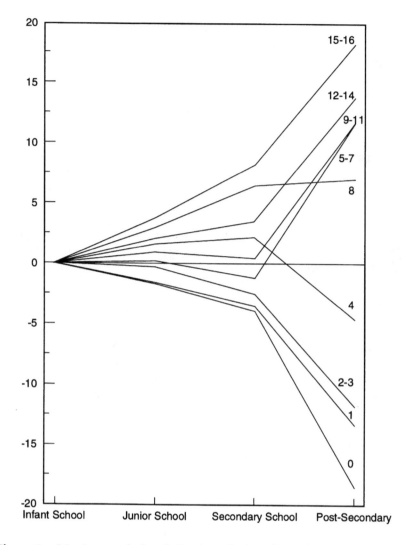

Figure 1. Men's cumulative deflections during their educational careers, by qualifications obtained by age 23. Source: Kerckhoff (1993).

Two features of the figure are worthy of special attention for present purposes. First, although there is clear evidence of a systematic cumulative dispersion of achievements related to ability group placements across all three periods, the amount of additional dispersion increases in each later period, the greatest dispersion occurring during the postsecondary period.

Second, although most of the postsecondary dispersion continued and greatly enlarged the pattern of earlier dispersion—that is, the fan continued to unfold—there are some dramatic deviations from continuity. The combination of those two features is worth emphasizing.

Ignoring the postsecondary period for a moment, it is clear that the effects of ability grouping during elementary and secondary school were cumulative. Those who ended up with the highest-level qualifications at age 23 had experienced successive achievement increments as a result of their placements in ability groups, and those with no qualifications at 23 had experienced successive achievement decrements as a result of their placements. On average, the highest group had gained over 8 percentile points, and the lowest group had lost 4 percentile points by the end of secondary school based simply on their ability group placements.

The analogue of ability groups at the postsecondary level is the type of program from which postsecondary qualifications were obtained: higher education, further education, or training. As one would expect, average gains were greatest from higher education and smallest from training, but gains were obtained from all three sources.

The most consistent cumulative positive effect across all three stages in the educational career is found at the two highest qualification levels. The most common sequence there was for those in high-ability groups in elementary and secondary school to obtain a degree through higher education. Those in high-ability groups during elementary and secondary school had much greater access to higher education. The most consistent cumulative negative effect across all three stages is found at the three lowest qualification levels. The most common sequence there was for those in low-ability groups in elementary and secondary school either to fail to obtain any qualifications or to obtain only the lowest-level qualifications. By age 23, the highest-achieving men had gained about 18 percentile points and the lowest-achieving men had lost about 18 percentile points due specifically to their locations in the structure of the educational system.

Thus, for the top two and the bottom three categories, there is a clear pattern of continuity across all three career stages; some students were successively advantaged and others were successively disadvantaged. Although a great deal of the advantage and disadvantage occurred after they left secondary school, the pattern of gains and losses was well established during elementary and secondary school, and there was a systematic association between those gains and losses and the postsecondary gains and losses. These are the kinds of careers one would expect in an educational system that is stratified so that access to later opportunities is contingent on "success" in earlier stages and in which grouping by ability deflects achievements up and down.

The middle categories are much less orderly, however. The lines for categories 4, 5–7, 8, and 9–11 actually cross each other during the postsecondary period. Some students who were being favored by ability grouping during elementary and secondary school dropped back and some who had neither an advantage nor a disadvantage through secondary school moved sharply ahead.

Those trajectories reflect the features of the British system I emphasized earlier. Categories 4 and 8 represent levels of examinations students usually passed in secondary school: O-levels (category 4) and A-levels (category 8). Those students had some advantages from ability group placements during elementary and secondary school, but since they did nothing further after secondary school, they lost out to some others who obtained postsecondary qualifications. Those who passed O-levels but did no more actually fell back in the hierarchy while those who passed A-levels (a relatively high-level qualification) were passed up by others who obtained significant postsecondary qualifications.

The trajectories for categories 5–7 and 9–11 are even more striking. These are students who were neither advantaged nor disadvantaged by their ability group placements in elementary and secondary school but who obtained rather high-level qualifications after secondary school. Most of those qualifications were obtained through further education, what Americans would call part-time vocational education outside higher education. Even the 9–11 qualifications are not generally obtained through higher education. They are relatively high-level technical and midrange professional qualifications that are superior to most obtainable in secondary school, but they are at a lower level than a university degree.[8]

There are thus two features of Figure 1 that reflect the characteristics of the British educational system. One is two sets of diverging deflections, one set moving up and the other down, because of the cumulative effects of ability grouping. The other is a number of less orderly trajectories involving shifts of direction in the postsecondary period, largely because

---

[8]It is important not to interpret the vertical scale in Figure 1 as an attainment scale. It is a *deflection* scale, a measure of the average number of percentile levels categories of individuals moved as a result of their locations in ability groups or postsecondary programs. The numbers associated with the nine trajectory lines index the early adult educational attainment levels. It is notable that, although category 8 (one or more A-level examination passes) is a higher level of attainment than category 5–7 (Royal Society of Arts and City and Guilds craft certificates), those who obtained the latter *gained* more after secondary school than did those who obtained the former.

of the "second chance" nature of the postsecondary institution of further education.

We do not have adequate data to conduct a parallel analysis for the United States, but I would hypothesize that if we did the results would both resemble and differ significantly from those reported in Figure 1. They would be similar in showing a progressive dispersion of achievements as a function of ability grouping during elementary and secondary school. However, I would also expect the U.S. pattern to differ from Figure 1 in that we would find many fewer crossing lines. There would be a much more consistent pattern of continuing divergence through the postsecondary period, because our system does not provide as systematically as the British system does for a "second chance" through postsecondary programs leading to nationally recognized credentials.

I want to comment on what I see as the implications of these observations for patterns of student achievement in the United States. But before doing that, I need to discuss the other major feature of our system I alluded to before, its decentralized form of organization. I will then discuss the implications of the two features together.

DECENTRALIZATION AND DISPERSION

The decentralized control of education in the United States leads to a great deal of variation among schools. It is generally the case, in fact, that educational systems with centralized control tend to offer much more uniform curricula and much less varied teaching patterns than do systems with localized control (Stevenson & Baker, 1991). Other kinds of variation in our schools have also been shown to affect student opportunities and achievements. For instance, earlier I reviewed the U.S. research findings related to ability grouping as if they showed a uniform effect of the practice on student achievement, but that is only partially true. There is a generally observed pattern of dispersion of the kind I have alluded to, but there is also increasing evidence that both the nature of the practice and its effects vary a great deal.

There seem to be many reasons for variation in the nature of the groups that are formed. Schools of different sizes, with different organizational and scheduling constraints end up with different kinds of grouping systems (Hallinan, 1991). In addition, schools vary in the principles they follow in assigning students to groups (Gamoran, 1992); some more than others rigorously match placement to ability. They vary in the extent to which student (or parent) choice is permitted. They differ in the degree of inclusiveness of the definitions of level (e.g., how high is high when a school chooses students for the high group?). And they differ in the scope of the classification (whether it is subject-specific or covers all course work).[9] As a result, two students with the same set of personal characteristics could end up in very different group locations depending on the school they attend. These kinds of variation are all associated with patterns of student achievement. The patterns differ in both the overall level of student achievement (i.e., a school's productivity) and the variation in student achievement (i.e., the amount of inequality).

Recent research has also focused on the effects of many other kinds of variations among schools besides their internal organization. One of the more potentially important dimensions of variation for present purposes is the degree of "client power" schools are faced with (Bidwell & Quiroz, 1991). Client power refers to the influence students' families have on the inner workings of the school. One, but not necessarily the most important, kind of family influence would be on the ability group to which one's child is assigned. Other instances when parents' influence could matter would include interceding to help a student who has disciplinary or other kinds of problems in school, obtaining assistance with academic difficulties, or seeking help in making contacts with postsecondary institutions.

More important than the possible effects of interceding by individual parents, however, is the general power of clients to influence school policies—whether or not to *have* ability groups or "gifted student" programs, whether to establish magnet schools, whether to invest in vocational education programs, whether to teach phonics or some version of "new math," whether to invest in interscholastic sports programs, and so on.

Why is variation in client power significant for my purposes? First, it is another instance of the extreme variability of American schools and the difficulty we have in making general statements about them or in suggesting any policy innovations. Almost any policies we might propose would impact these highly varied schools in very different ways. Second, it suggests how the very openness of our system makes it especially subject to influences that are less significant elsewhere and that reflect something other than universalistic educational values.

Examples of the effects of varied client power are not hard to find. Careful ethnographic studies of school–family relations (e.g., Lareau, 1989) document the highly varied access to and influence on school processes parents have, and they make it clear how access and influence vary

[9]The British refer to this distinction as "setting" (subject-specific) versus "streaming" (all subjects).

by social class. Parent influence occurs at many critical points in students' educational careers that have long-term effects on the students' attainments. For instance, the mathematics courses students take in middle school act as filters for higher-level courses which, in turn, improve students' access to higher education. Parents who are knowledgeable about the educational system and who are able to influence the kinds of middle school courses their children take can thus significantly facilitate their later educational attainment (Useem, 1992).

Of course, schools vary in their openness to client power. The size of the school, the socioeconomic composition of the community, and the educational philosophy of the administration all seem to influence both the organization of the curriculum and the potential effectiveness of parental influence on students' school experiences (Bidwell & Quiroz, 1991; Smith, 1992; Useem, 1991). The variation of client power within our system means that some students are helped more than others by these influences.[10]

The degree of client power at all levels is generally much greater in the United States than in most other countries. To the extent that is true, our schools are less autonomous institutions. They are less able to define and carry out an educational program based on educational expertise free of "outside influences."

Both the ethnographic studies and the studies of the effects of ability grouping show consistent effects of students' socioeconomic status on their outcomes. The ability group studies show that socioeconomic status affects student group placements, and the ethnographic studies show that middle-class parents have more influence on school processes and their children's school experiences than lower-status parents do. The study of the cumulative effects of ability grouping in British schools from which Figure 1 comes also showed cumulative effects of family socioeconomic status.

Figure 2 reports the pattern of ability group effects for the men in that study when the men were classified by their father's occupational

[10]The importance of client power is most easily appreciated when we think of public elementary and secondary schools. It is also an important factor in other parts of the system, however. Many private schools are heavily dependent on a community base of support. If parents disagree with school policies, they can always move their children to a public school. Only very well-established elite private schools or those with some other strong institutional (usually religious) support can maintain a very high degree of autonomy in decision-making. The same is true at the postsecondary level. Public technical institutes, community colleges, four-year colleges and universities need broad-based public support to function effectively. Client power is experienced by them through both direct public demands and the actions of state legislatures.

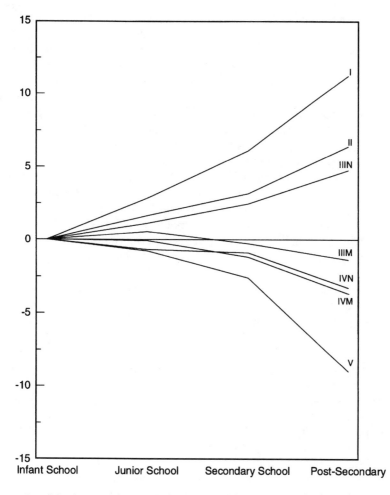

Figure 2. Men's cumulative deflections during their educational careers, by the social class of their father's occupation at age 7. Source: Kerckhoff (1993).

class when they were 7 years old.[11] There is a consistent fan-shaped pattern of dispersions in which males from higher-class families move upwards and those from lower-class families move downwards through the three stages of the educational career. Not only is there a perfect ordering of the deflections by class, there is also a clear division between the top three and the bottom four classes, essentially a middle class versus working class division. By age 23, those from class I families had moved up 11 percentile points and those from class V families had moved down 9 percentile points due to their locations in the structure of the schools.

There is every reason to expect that a similar cumulative divergence by class would be found in all industrial societies. Although we are unable at this time to test it, I should think a defensible hypothesis would be that the amount of that divergence would be even greater in the United States than in Great Britain. That hypothesis is based on the extended period during which ability grouping is experienced in American schools and the greater influence American parents have on their children's school experiences.

There is another kind of "external" influence on students' attainments that is highlighted by examination of the decentralization of control and the associated lack of standardization in our educational system. This is the influence of employers after students leave school. We tend to view the school–work relationship as linking two quite separate institutional arrangements, one that prepares young people for adulthood and the other that provides the avenue for individual adult achievement based on that preparation. But, as we have seen, except at the highest levels of educational attainment, American students generally leave school without any specific certification for particular *kinds* of employment. The transition from school to work is thus a rather chaotic one. There is very "loose coupling" between school and employment.

This is a critical part of the difference between this country and most European countries, the sharpest contrast being between the United States and Germany. There is a weaker association between educational attainment and early job level in the United States than in Germany (Allmen-

---

[11]Figure 1 reports what can be called a "retrospective" pattern of divergence since it organizes the analysis around the levels of educational qualifications the men had attained by age 23. In contrast, Figure 2 presents a "prospective" analysis since it organizes the analysis around the occupational class of the fathers at the initial point in the analysis, age 7. The occupational classes reported in Figure 2 are: I, professionals and high-level managers and administrators; II, semiprofessionals, lower-level managers, and technicians; IIIN, clerks and other lower-level nonmanual workers; IIIM, skilled manual workers and foremen; IVN, semiskilled nonmanual, mainly service workers; IVM, semiskilled manual workers; V, unskilled workers.

dinger, 1989), which leads to more job shifting in the early labor force experience of American workers. American workers' specific job skills are more often dependent on training received on or through the job rather than from regular educational institutions. The kinds of skill employers teach tend to be firm-specific, however, and they tie the workers to particular employers rather than being generally valuable.[12] Training provided by an educational institution must be more generally applicable whereas employer-provided training can be more narrowly defined in firm-specific terms.[13] There is no reason for an employer to be concerned about the general skill level of a worker, only the skills required in that particular firm.[14]

Except for preparation and certification for high-status professional positions, the U.S. educational system remains uninvolved in its students' preparation and certification for the world of work. Not only do our secondary schools not provide direct preparation for the world of work in the courses offered and the certification provided, they also do not usually provide much assistance to students in the transition from school to work. Again, there is more assistance at the higher levels. Colleges, and especially graduate and professional schools, help with job placement, and there are continuing linkages between those schools and potential employers. At the secondary school level, however, about the only generally well-established placement mechanisms are those that help channel the more successful students into higher education. The rest are usually left to fend for themselves in their negotiations with potential employers.

[12]The very different relationship between schools and employers in the United States and Japan is instructive here. In both societies, work-related skills are heavily dependent on training provided through employment. However, employers in Japan recruit their workers from the schools and generally accept those the schools recommend. Thus, the schools are much more directly involved in their students' entry into the labor force in Japan than in the United States. Although job-based training in Japan is probably as firm-specific as in the United States, Japanese firms have deeper commitments to their workers, providing them with long-term employment opportunities. Thus, whether work skills are transferable from one employer to another is less important in Japan (Rosenbaum, Kariya, Settersten, & Maier, 1990).

[13]Raffe (1988) differentiates between the kinds of schooling obtained in "in-service" and "preemployment" training markets. In the former the employer is the buyer, and the schooling functions more like training, while in the latter the student is the buyer, and it functions more like education. The importance of this distinction is reflected in the British use of the terms "further *education*" and "on-the-job *training*."

[14]This rather narrow employer self-interest is one reason why some analysts are skeptical about the merits of involving corporations in the conduct of public education (Spring, 1986). But another reason for skepticism is that there does not exist a set of widely recognized credentials in the United States that *could* be awarded to workers on the basis of training provided by employers.

A DIFFERENT LOOK AT SYSTEM REFORM

I have emphasized several important characteristics of the U.S. school system as it differs from many others. (1) It is less stratified than most other systems; more students stay in school longer than elsewhere. (2) It provides a less differentiated set of credentials than other systems. There are essentially only two levels of credentials (high school and college diplomas), and there are very few qualitative distinctions made at either level. (3) The system is highly decentralized, and, as a result, there is a low degree of standardization of either the schools' offerings at any given stage or the meaningfulness of the credentials they award. (4) Schools in the system are less autonomous than in most other industrial societies; they must contend with relatively high levels of client power. (5) Finally, because of the low levels of credential differentiation and standardization, our educational institutions have a relatively low capacity to structure the distribution of young people into the labor force. That, in turn, means that labor force institutions have a relatively greater capacity to do so.

These features of our educational system have important implications for the achievement patterns of young Americans. The restricted set of credentials available puts a heavy premium on "making it" at each of those levels because each one is an either–or kind of division. Because of that, any factors that operate to increase or decrease the probability of obtaining either of those two kinds of credentials have potentially far-reaching effects on students' adult lives. I have referred to two kinds of influences that have the effect of increasing achievement differences among American students and that vary by socioeconomic status. These are the *internal* mechanisms of grouping students by ability and the *external* influences school processes are exposed to. Finally, the limited number of credentials and their lack of occupational relevance introduces into the labor market several large, relatively undifferentiated categories of potential workers whose final training and sorting into jobs is heavily dependent on corporate America, but that training and sorting seldom leaves workers with any nationally recognized transferable credentials.

Many of the criticisms of our educational system and the proposals for reform based on them are flawed because they fail to recognize the great significance of these organizational features of our system. There is a persistent effort to keep students in secondary school, but the incentive for them to stay there is essentially negative. If they do not stay, they are told, they will have nothing to show for years of what Bidwell and Friedkin (1988) accurately refer to as "punishment." For a large proportion of our students, therefore, "making it" becomes a matter of "sticking it out." It is not too surprising, then, that even many who want to graduate are not highly motivated to learn very much.

Throughout 12 years, the sorting process functions to classify students on a single hierarchical scale and to prepare for the day when that hierarchical distribution will be divided into three major segments: dropouts, those who will only be high school graduates, and the college-bound. The positions of most students in that tripartite division are apparent long before 12th grade. Although almost all schools can tell the relative position of all of their students on a much more refined set of stratified categories, those refined divisions have almost no relevance to the students' futures—except, possibly, to help determine *which* college *some* of them will attend.

Although about 85% of our youth graduate from high school, only about half of our youth even *enter* college and only about half of *them* get a college degree. Those simple statistics tell us a great deal about the problems with our system, if we consider them carefully. If practically all of our students get a high school diploma, the diploma is not a very distinctive or useful educational credential. But, if the only other credential available that has any social significance is a college degree, very few of our students obtain a very meaningful educational certification. To the extent we define a college degree as the only important educational credential, three-fourths of our students are defined as "failures." Our system sends most of them off into the adult world with an all-purpose—and thus purposeless—credential called a high school diploma. Together, our system's decentralization and low levels of differentiation and standardization of credentials lead to a student output that is highly varied but which is not identified as such. Employers are left to sort through this undifferentiated mass to find suitable employees.

We seem to glory in the abstract nature of American education and shy away from any suggestion that it ought to be "practical" or "useful." Yet, it is obvious that our students are only temporarily students, and they will soon be living in an adult world in which occupation is all-important. We are so committed to the two critical divisions created by a high school diploma and a college degree that we cannot seem to see that neither of those attainments has much relevance to one's adult experience except as they are used as very crude signals of merit (Rosenbaum, 1986)—and only the college degree has any value for that purpose. We devote an inordinate amount of our time and energy to help our students "get through" one or the other of those doorways, but we then leave them pretty much on their own to find their way into adulthood. Because college graduates are at least statistically special, they have a distinct advantage, but there is no adequate basis for differentiating among the other three-fourths of our system's products.

It would be unrealistic to propose a wholesale revamping of our system, but I think some possible changes could be very helpful. We hear a great deal these days about instituting national standards for student achievement as well as a national curriculum. I think such proposals miss the mark. Within our current system, instituting national standards will mean having general tests of achievement in broad areas of knowledge such as English, mathematics, and so on. It will also mean classifying students according to their position on some linear scale of adequacy in those areas of knowledge. It almost certainly will *not* mean classifying students according to configurations of skills that have any direct relationship to the labor force. Whatever the basis of the proposed standards (National Academy of Education, 1992), they are unlikely to be any more useful to either students or employers than grade records are now. Studies of students' entry into the labor force indicate that grades are seldom used now because employers do not know how to interpret them in making choices among applicants (Rosenbaum, 1986). Neither grades nor scores on national achievement tests constitute a substitute for occupationally relevant credentials.

The corporate complaint about the adequacy of the educational level of the labor force reflects a fundamental gap in institutional integration in our society. It suggests that the schools have the responsibility to provide adequately educated students to do the society's work, but employers have no responsibility either to help define what constitutes "adequacy" or to help increase the likelihood that students will be "adequate." It also ignores the very important fact that our current economy does not hold out many attractive employment opportunities for those who will not attend college or university. There is a genuine "chicken-or-egg" problem here, of course, but upgrading the "employability" of high school graduates will be exceedingly difficult and have little economic impact unless there are challenging and rewarding jobs available to those who do well (Ray & Mickelson, 1993).

Educators tend to view the gap in an equally one-sided way. In effect, we tell the rest of the society that we "educate" our students, but it is someone else's job to figure out what the dimensions of occupationally relevant variation are and which of our students are high and low on those dimensions. We do very little to provide guidance to either students or employers regarding the "fit" between schooling and adult employment. All of the other societies I have discussed have a closer integration between educational and work organizations than ours does, although the nature of that integration varies greatly.

It should be possible to bridge that gap in our system, and doing so could help to improve the system's effectiveness. It should be possible to define a set of educational criteria for workers who carry out various types of tasks. It is done elsewhere; it ought to be possible here. It should further be possible to design a set of tests that would help both potential workers and their potential employers decide who is likely to do well on particular kinds of jobs. Those are the kinds of tests on which most of the British qualifications referred to in Figure 1 are based. Finally, it should be possible to establish a national certification process that would provide people who pass these tests credentials that would be nationally recognized as much as a high school diploma or a college degree, credentials they could carry with them from job to job.

We are beginning to explore this possibility, as I will discuss below, but we have a long way to go, and getting there will require considerable effort and the cooperation of groups that have not always viewed themselves as partners. It will improve the possibility of such cooperation if we can recognize the advantages of the resulting nationally recognized set of credentials. There are two very important fundamental advantages. First, it would make the sorting of students into the labor force a much more orderly and less costly process. Students would have a clearer idea about what they are qualified to do, and employers would have a better idea about which students would be most likely to be appropriate candidates for which jobs. Second, and even more important from an educator's perspective, it would provide a tangible set of goals that educators could hold out as both attainable and worth attaining and toward which students could be motivated to strive. School could be a more meaningful experience for more of our students.

QUESTIONS AND ANSWERS

A number of questions might be raised about this innovation. For instance, would it tend to transform many of our high schools into trade schools? Not necessarily in any negative sense. If some kinds of academic knowledge and skills are needed in jobs entered by non-college-bound high school students, and there is every reason to believe there are, they could form the basis of the occupationally relevant tests.[15] We somehow

---

[15]It is conceivable that profiles of scores on the proposed national standardized achievement tests could be used to define desirable qualities of applicants for some kinds of jobs. The very general nature of such achievement tests in broad subject areas would limit their usefulness in most cases, however.

manage to accept national standards for licensing lawyers and physicians without demeaning law schools and medical schools with the term "trade school." There must be many other categories of occupations for which some general criteria of adequacy could be agreed upon.

Would this mean that the high schools would be forced to transform their curricula in order to "teach to the tests"? I should think that many schools might well use the new credentials as a basis for organizing their curricula and advising students about what courses to take if they wished to qualify for one or another credential. That would be most likely to happen in schools with few college-bound students. However, that would not necessarily mean teaching anything different from what we now teach. But, even if it did, would that necessarily be bad? Is it better for students to have a potpourri of courses taken in a "shopping-mall high school" or to have an integrated set of courses that provide the basis for marketable skills on which to support an adult life?

Even without formal specialized secondary school credentials, there is some evidence that a set of vocational high school courses taken in a focused area of specialization improves students' placements in the labor force.[16] The impact on labor force outcomes is much greater when vocational courses are taken in postsecondary institutions, but that seems to be because they are more likely to lead to an identifiable certificate or license. Even though the credentials awarded by those postsecondary institutions are seldom recognized nationally, they still have a significant impact on stability of employment and earnings levels. If the credentials were recognized nationally, their impact would undoubtedly be even greater.

Wouldn't it be easier and less disruptive of secondary education for such credentials to be awarded only *after* high school? Perhaps, although many other societies make them part of their secondary school programs. And, unless the linkage between secondary and postsecondary institutions is made more salient to non-college-bound high school students than it is now, the problem of the poorly motivated noncollege students would remain.

The so-called "tech-prep" programs that link secondary school vocational programs with postsecondary vocational programs are attempts to increase the meaningfulness of secondary school for the non-college-bound students by showing them how high school courses can provide

---

[16]This discussion is based on materials reviewed in "National Assessment of Vocational Education: Interim Report to Congress" (U.S. Department of Education, 1994). Some of the findings come from analyses done specifically for that report, but some of them come from earlier studies reviewed in the report.

the foundation for important occupationally relevant postsecondary courses. But tech-prep programs are currently not very well developed, and they are highly varied in their substance. A concerted effort to develop such programs in a coordinated way that linked them up with a set of nationally recognized credentials would contribute greatly to the kind of development I am advocating.

If such programs were strengthened, even if the credentials were based entirely on postsecondary courses in community colleges and technical institutes, they would have two very positive effects on the labor force preparation of noncollege students. First, they would broaden the range of available job locations beyond local labor markets and clarify the credential–job linkage nationally. Second, the existence of such credentials at the postsecondary level would provide secondary schools with clearer alternative guidelines for their noncollege students and a way of conceptualizing the curricula, even if no changes in the curricula were made. Students who are not college-bound could be provided with a set of goals and a number of curricular alternatives that could move them toward postsecondary courses that provide valuable occupational access.

Although our data are far from adequate, it appears that about half of the non-college-bound high school graduates take some kind of postsecondary courses (Lewis, Hearn, & Zilbert, 1993). However, those courses are not currently systematically linked either to secondary school courses or to occupational placements. They could be, and if they were, many high school dropouts and drifters might find high school a more interesting place to be.

Perhaps the most basic question to raise is how it would be possible to institute such an innovation. Clearly, it would have to be done on a national scale if the credentials are to be fully transportable. It is equally clear that the definition of such credentials and the construction of the appropriate tests would require cooperation between educators and the corporate world. Such cooperation could be encouraged and facilitated by the joint efforts of the Departments of Education and Labor. Those two departments are working more cooperatively in the current administration than in previous ones, and a number of their proposals focus on strengthening the occupational preparation of noncollege students.

There are already some signs that such a joint venture might be possible. There are numerous experiments throughout the country that link high school programs with internships or apprenticeships in local industries and businesses. In some cases, school systems have established high schools with special curricular concentrations. Oakland, California, has a dozen "academies" that specialize in such areas as health, computer science, business, and engineering and that provide work experience through the cooperation of companies in the area. Some major corporations, such as the Siemens's Stromberg-Carlson plant in Lake Mary, Florida, have established rigorous apprenticeship programs that require high performance in school as well as successful on-the-job training.

At the federal level, the 1990 Carl D. Perkins Act was designed to strengthen the skills of students in vocational education at both the secondary and postsecondary levels. It calls for states to develop statewide standards, to integrate academic and vocational curricula, to facilitate work experience programs, and to promote the tech-prep programs that link high schools with community colleges and technical institutes. Most recently, the 1994 Goals 2000 and School-to-Work Opportunities Acts provide federal funds to develop career majors and make direct work experience possible. Given our federal form ·of government, however, these initiatives at the national level can only provide financial encouragement for the development of programs at the state and local level. Their success is completely dependent on the degree and nature of the local response, and the response to date has been both limited in degree and highly varied in form.

The most critical part of the Goals 2000 and School-to-Work Opportunities Acts is the proposal to establish a national system of occupational standards and a set of credentials that certify students' occupationally relevant skills. The Acts call for establishing a National Skill Standards Board that will identify broad occupational clusters and create a system of standards, assessments, and certification for the skills needed in each area. The Board is to have broad representation from business, industry, and labor. This is the most critical part of the legislation because, unless the Board is sufficiently prestigious and influential to have its standards, assessments, and credentials widely adopted across the country, the fragmented nature of nonacademic programs and credentials will continue. And that will mean the continued scarcity of attainable and useful goals for the majority of American students.

What the Acts propose is in some ways similar to the call for national achievement standards, but it is different in two important ways. First, they call for a set of achievement standards that are directly linked to kinds of labor force requirements, not just to general achievement areas such as mathematics or science or reading. Second, they propose that students who successfully meet those standards will not just be given a score but will be awarded a nationally recognized credential that will directly affect their job prospects. These are essential ingredients in any attempt to increase the labor force relevance of educational programs.

SUMMARY AND CONCLUSION

I have used a comparison of the educational systems of England, Germany, France, and the United States in order to highlight the distinctive characteristics of our system. In particular, our system is different from the others in the following ways: Students stay in school longer in the United States. Our system is much more decentralized. There is a lower level of standardization of the educational programs and less uniformity of the meaning of the credentials awarded. Our schools are less autonomous, more subject to influence by their "clients." Our system offers a less differentiated set of credentials, especially at the secondary school level. There is a lower degree of direct occupational relevance of the credentials it does offer.

These distinctive characteristics generate educational processes that are widely subject to family and community influences. Since school "grading" produces a single hierarchical ordering of students according to general academic criteria, such influences increase the variance in student academic performance. But, because of the limited kinds of educational credentials awarded, the system ultimately produces a sharp division in that hierarchical ordering between the college-bound and other high school students. There is an unhealthy concentration of attention on the minority who will obtain college degrees to the detriment of the large majority who do not. The lack of significant credentials other than the high school diploma and the college degree deprives most students of very meaningful educational goals with apparent direct relevance to their later adult lives.

I have argued that establishing a set of occupationally relevant credentials, based on the cooperative efforts of government agencies, educators, and corporate and labor representatives, would constitute a major improvement in our educational system. This would not require centralization of school control. Decentralization is one of the most well-established features of our school system; any attempt to change it is certain to meet with strenuous resistance. Establishing a set of work-related credentials would not require any change in that aspect of our system. States, districts, and individual schools could relate to the proposed credentials in the same highly varied ways they now relate to preparing students for the global division between the high school-only students and the college-bound.

A set of noncollege credentials would have a very different feedback effect on what happens in high school than would standardizing broad achievement tests or the curriculum. The credentials would provide a set of tangible, obtainable goals for the non-college-bound as well as a means of integrating noncollege postsecondary coursework and jobs with secondary school curricula. In contrast, national curricula and achievement standards would provide a means by which we can accomplish in a more rigorous and uniform fashion what we are now doing somewhat haphazardly—sorting students into progressively more divergent performance levels in anticipation of a major bifurcation of the distribution at the end of high school.

A set of nationally recognized noncollege credentials would also provide "second chance" opportunities for students with a broad range of achievement levels (from high school dropouts to college dropouts). Those second chance opportunities could come either during high school or afterwards. A refinement of the sorting process through a national curriculum and national achievement standards cannot do more than give those students a clearer indication that they are not "making it." Most students who would not meet the proposed standards already know where they stand.

This is not to argue against national curricula or achievement standards but rather to argue that they will not resolve the problem faced by more than half of our students who finish school with no meaningful certification of accomplishment. Scores on standard achievement tests will do no more to motivate students or to point them toward suitable kinds of employment than high school grades do now (Rosenbaum, 1986).

The availability of a set of occupationally relevant credentials would provide the basis for two significant improvements in the situation I have described. First, it would provide a larger proportion of our students with a set of tangible, meaningful, and attainable educational goals. It would give more students a reason to put forth the effort to do their best in school, not just to get good grades, but to learn what is necessary to obtain a useful credential and be a more productive adult. Second, it would reduce the chaos in the early matching of individuals to jobs and provide a known foundation on which later training, in or outside the labor force, could build. That would not only help those entering the labor force, it would reduce the costs to employers. Those reduced costs, in fact, should be an incentive for employers to help to develop such a system of certification in the first place.

Whatever the reaction to this particular proposal, I would hope that examining our educational system in comparative perspective would help us consider alternative approaches. The kind of societal comparison I have made is a narrowly restricted one. It is wholly concerned with how the system is organized. It is not concerned with the substance of what is taught, how well it is taught, how consistently it is taught, or how accurately records are kept of what is learned. All of those are important issues, but they are not the only important ones.

Organizational changes do not have to be utopian to be significant. The present suggestion is that we establish a more differentiated set of nationally recognized educational credentials, especially ones that have occupational relevance, at the secondary and/or postsecondary school level. To do that, we need to enlist the participation of educators, the federal government, employers, and organized labor. It should be possible to establish such a set of credentials, and I suggest that it would have a positive effect on both student achievement and the effectiveness of workers in the labor force. It would help our educational system more effectively fulfill its charter as the "sorting machine" for the society.

REFERENCES

Allmendinger, J. (1989). *Career mobility dynamics—A comparative analysis of the United States, Norway, and West Germany.* Berlin: Max-Planck-Institute für Bildungsforschung.

Bidwell, C. E., & Friedkin, N. E. (1988). The sociology of education. In N. Smelser (Ed.), *The handbook of sociology* (pp. 449–471). Beverly Hills, CA: Sage.

Bidwell, C. E., & Quiroz, P. (1991). Organizational control in the high school workplace: A theoretical argument. *Journal of Research on Adolescence, 1,* 211–229.

Entwisle, D. R., & Hayduk, L. A. (1988). Lasting effects of elementary school. *Sociology of Education, 61,* 185–198.

Gamoran, A. (1986). Instructional and institutional effects of ability grouping. *Sociology of Education, 59,* 147–159.

Gamoran, A. (1992). The variable effects of high school tracking. *American Sociological Review, 57,* 812–828.

Gamoran, A., & Mare, R. D. (1989). Secondary school tracking and educational inequality: Compensation, reinforcement, or neutrality? *American Journal of Sociology, 94,* 1146–1183.

Goslin, D. A. (1965). *The school in contemporary society.* Atlanta: Scott, Foresman.

Hallinan, M. T. (1991). School differences in tracking structures and track assignments. *Journal of Research on Adolescence, 1,* 251–275.

Hout, M., Raftery, A. E., & Bell, E. O. (1993). Making the grade: Educational stratification in the United States, 1925–1989. In Y. Shavit & H.-P. Blossfeld (Eds.), *Persistent inequality: Changing educational attainment in thirteen countries* (pp. 25–74). Boulder, CO: Westview.

Kerckhoff, A. C. (1993). *Diverging pathways: Social structure and career deflections.* London: Cambridge University Press.

Kerckhoff, A. C., Fogelman, K., Crook, D., & Reeder, D. (1995). *Going comprehensive in England and Wales: A study of uneven change.* Newbury Park, England: Woburn Press.

Lareau, A. (1989). *Home advantage: Social class and parental intervention in elementary education.* New York: Falmer.

Lewis, D. R., Hearn, J. C., & Zilbert, E. E. (1993). Efficiency and equity effects of vocationally focused postsecondary education. *Sociology of Education, 66,* 188–205.

Mare, R. D. (1981). Change and stability in educational stratification. *American Sociological Review, 46,* 72–87.

Maurice, M., Sellier, F., & Silvestre, J.-J. (1986). *The social foundations of industrial power: A comparison of France and Germany.* Cambridge, MA: MIT Press.

Meyer, J. W. (1977). The effects of education as an institution. *American Journal of Sociology, 83,* 55–77.

Müller, W., & Karle, W. (1992). Social selection in educational systems in Europe. *European Sociological Review, 8,* 233–254.

National Academy of Education. (1992). *Setting performance standards for student achievement: A report of the National Academy of Education panel on the evaluation of the NAEP trial state assessment.* Stanford, CA: National Academy of Education.

OECD. (1989). Educational attainment in the labour force. Chapter 2 of *Employment outlook,* a report of the Education Committee of the Working Party on Employment. Paris: Organization for Economic Co-Operation & Development.

Pallas, A. M., Entwisle, D. R., Alexander, K. L., & Stluka, M. F. (1994). Ability group effects: Instructional, social or institutional? *Sociology of Education, 67,* 27–45.

Raffe, D. (1979). The "alternative route" reconsidered: Part-time further education and social mobility in England and Wales. *Sociology, 13,* 47–73.

Raffe, D. (1988). Modules and the strategy of institutional versatility: The first two years of the 16-plus action plan in Scotland. In D. Raffe (Ed.), *Education and the youth labour market: Schooling and scheming* (pp. 162–195). New York: Falmer.

Ravitch, D. (1992). *Developing national standards in education: The federal role.* Paper presented at the annual meeting of the American Sociological Association, Pittsburgh, PA.

Ray, C. A., & Mickelson, R. A. (1993). Restructuring students for restructured work: The economy, school reform, and non-college-bound youth. *Sociology of Education, 66,* 1–20.

Rosenbaum, J. E. (1986). Institutional career structures and the social construction of ability. In J. G. Richardson (Ed.), *Handbook of theory and research for the sociology of education* (pp. 139–171). New York: Greenwood.

Rosenbaum, J. E., Kariya, T., Settersten, R., & Maier, T. (1990). Market and network theories of the transition from high school to work: Their application to industrialized societies. *Annual Review of Sociology, 16,* 263–299.

Shavit, Y., & Blossfeld, H.-P. (Eds.). (1993). *Persistent inequality: Changing educational attainment in thirteen countries.* Boulder, CO: Westview.

Smith, J. B. (1992). *The decision to take algebra in 8th grade: The dual roles played by parents and schools in matching students to mathematics courses.* Paper presented at the annual meeting of the American Educational Research Association, San Francisco.

Spring, J. (1976). *The sorting machine: National educational policy since 1945.* New York: David McKay.

Spring, J. (1986). Business and the schools: The new partnerships. In K. M. Borman & J. Reisman (Eds.), *Becoming a worker* (pp. 244–259). Norwood, NJ: Ablex.

Stevenson, D. L., & Baker, D. P. (1991). State control of the curriculum and classroom instruction. *Sociology of Education, 64,* 1–10.

Suter, L. E. (1989). *An examination of country differences in mathematics achievement: A synthesis of research results from the IEA second international mathematics study.* Washington, DC: National Center for Education Statistics.

Turner, R. H. (1960). Sponsored and contest mobility and the school system. *American Sociological Review, 25,* 855–867.

U.S. Census. (1981). *Population profile of the United States: 1980.* Series P-20, No. 363. Washington, DC: U.S. Government Printing Office.

U.S. Department of Education. (1983). *A nation at risk: The imperative for educational reform.* Washington, DC: U.S. Government Printing Office.

U.S. Department of Education. (1993). *The condition of education, 1993.* Washington, DC: U.S. Government Printing Office.

U.S. Department of Education. (1994). *National assessment of vocational education: Interim report to Congress.* Washington, DC: U.S. Government Printing Office.

Useem, E. L. (1991). Student selection into course sequences in mathematics: The impact of parental involvement and school policies. *Journal of Research on Adolescence, 1,* 231–250.

Useem, E. L. (1992). Middle schools and math groups: Parents' involvement in children's placement. *Sociology of Education, 65,* 263–279.

11

Creating Linkages in the High School-to-Work Transition
Vocational Teachers' Networks

James E. Rosenbaum and Stephanie Alter Jones

INTRODUCTION

A classic problem in the study of organizations is that of inducing members to work toward organizational goals. In theory, organizations pursue clearly delineated aims. Such clarity of purpose leads them to pose formal requirements for meeting their goals, to mobilize resources devoted to the goals, and to identify rules and duties to direct individuals in the processes of implementation (Parsons, 1956).

However, organizational goals are not always clear. Ambiguities may arise because of changing conditions, shifts in clients, or new initiatives of key actors (Thompson & McEwen, 1958). Ambiguities also arise when official goals do not fit the organizational climate, when members encounter different interpretations of their duties, or when organizational duties, incentives, and goals do not match.

What happens when formal goals and duties do not fully correspond to organizational norms? When norms suggest general aims that are not advanced by specified duties, what actions do members take? In particular, this chapter asks: What actions do teachers take when they encounter situations in which their goals and duties are underspecified? Do they improvise to pursue larger organizational aims?

James E. Rosenbaum and Stephanie Alter Jones   Center for Urban Affairs and Policy Research, Northwestern University, Evanston, Illinois 60208.

Restructuring Schools: Promising Practices and Policies, edited by Maureen T. Hallinan. Plenum Press, New York, 1995.

Ambiguity in the Teachers' Role

Teachers face organizational ambiguity in preparing students for work after high school graduation. No formal practices or procedures tell teachers or students what career options exist, the criteria for making choices, or the steps leading from school to work. High schools rarely offer a survey of job options for their graduates. Teachers may have only incidental information on possible jobs (and those may not be jobs with career potential). Furthermore, teachers have little information about employers' hiring requirements. With no institutional mechanism for conveying information about employers to teachers, teachers may lack the knowledge that would enable them to prepare youth for work and to recommend them to employers. Moreover, with no formal role for high schools in the work-entry process, vocational teachers may be uncertain about the goals of vocational training. Indeed, research reveals that vocational preparation seems to have mixed benefits for youth entering the job market. While job access is affected by educational credentials (Althauser & Kalleberg, 1981; Karabel, 1972; Thurow, 1975), it is not consistently affected by vocational training (Kaufman, 1967; Rosenbaum, 1976; Grasso & Shea, 1979; Hotchkiss, Kang, & Bishop, 1984).

The lack of formal connections between school and work not only poses problems for teachers; it creates problems for students and employers as well. High school graduates have difficulty getting jobs, they experience frequent unemployment, and their jobs commonly offer poor pay, poor job security, and few training or advancement opportunities (Rosenbaum & Kariya, 1989; Borman, 1991). Indeed, many youth enter an entirely different labor market than adults, a "secondary labor market" of unskilled jobs offering little or no advancement potential (Doeringer & Piore, 1971; Osterman, 1988). Few youth gain access to primary labor market jobs (Osterman, 1980; Borman, 1991), and they often see no way to get such jobs. Consequently, work-bound students have difficulty understanding how school benefits them, and research indicates that motivation and behavior problems arise from poor articulation between school behaviors and work attainments (Stinchcombe, 1964; Rosenbaum, 1989; Rosenbaum & Nelson, 1994; Mickelson, 1990). Disorganization in the school–work transition prevents work-bound students from seeing schools' relevance.

Furthermore, although a number of studies have found that employers need information about youths' academic skills and work habits in order to hire good workers (SCANS, 1991; NAS, 1984), many employers nevertheless mistrust the information they get from high schools. Despite their needs, employers often ignore schools' evaluations of students. As a result, high school grades have little relationship to students' subsequent job outcomes, including wages (Meyer & Wise, 1982), entry into primary labor markets (Griffin, 1981), or entry into high-status occupations (Johnson & Bachman, 1973; Rosenbaum & Kariya, 1991). Indeed, although employers report that college grades affect their hiring decisions, they report that high school grades do not (Crain, 1984; Bills, 1988). These findings are especially surprising since employers' complaints about employees' academic skills imply that hiring could be improved if based on grades (CED, 1985), and since research indicates that high school achievement predicts workers' subsequent productivity (Bishop, 1987; Gamoran, 1994).

These circumstances are so pervasive in the United States that they appear unavoidable. Yet these disordered labor market experiences contrast markedly with the work-entry processes in other nations. In Japan, employers have direct contacts with high schools, which convey information from teachers to employers and help match graduating seniors with appropriate jobs (Kariya & Rosenbaum, 1987; Rosenbaum & Kariya, 1989). In Germany, a public employment agency passes information from schools to apprenticeship programs to facilitate the placement of students based on their school performance (Hamilton, 1990). Such institutionalized processes of preparation and transition allow Japanese and German teachers to help students experience an orderly work-entry process into jobs with good pay, benefits, and advancement opportunities.

Furthermore, American teachers do not typically have difficulty helping college-bound students prepare for transition. Because the college application process is defined by specific practices that provide students with clear steps to follow, teachers do not face ambiguity in preparing students for college entry. The orderliness of the college application system enables teachers to provide useful information and advice on the time lines to follow, the range of choices, and the requirements that define realistic options for individual students. Many secondary schools have built up extensive resources, including alumni networks, historical data on students, and college literature, which both teachers and students can use. By virtue of their familiarity with the application processes and the available resources for college-bound students, teachers can actively take part in counseling, socializing, and evaluating students for an appropriate college path after high school. As a result, teachers' college preparation duties closely correspond to organizational norms.

Although schools do not specify what teachers can or should do to help work-bound students, organizational norms dictate that teachers should help all students, assisting both work-bound and college-bound students equally. However, American society offers no explicit procedures for high schools to facilitate students' transition into the work force, and teachers receive virtually no guidance as to the role they might play in aiding work entry. Under such circumstances, where organizational norms encourage teachers to help students but organizational rules and duties do not specify what actions to take, teachers must either ignore the larger mandates of school and societal norms or they must improvise to pursue these aims.

Teachers' Response to Underspecified Goals

As our society gradually becomes aware of the difficulties that work-bound youth encounter, reformers have increasingly called for new programs to create order in the high school-to-work transition (W. T. Grant Foundation, 1988). Academic researchers and policymakers have proposed various program alternatives, including apprenticeships, tech-prep, career academies, and mentorship. However, these programs largely ignore the critical middleman role of teachers. Situated between students preparing for the world of work, and employers searching for appropriate graduates, teachers are in a unique position to provide information, contacts, and guidance to both groups. Nevertheless, given the conflict between norms and duties regarding school assistance, teachers receive little encouragement or direction for helping students.

Despite both the lack of order and the lack of teacher guidance at the institutional level, it is possible that teachers' informal actions may create some order at the individual level. Although their schools' lack of attention to job counseling, recommendation writing, or job placement may discourage teachers from providing work-entry assistance, teachers nevertheless see themselves as helping professionals (Lortie, 1975). With a large body of recent literature indicating that work-bound youth need help getting jobs (Hamilton, 1990; W. T. Grant Foundation, 1988; Stern *et al.*, 1992; Witte & Kalleberg, 1994) and that employers need help getting good workers (NAS, 1984; SCANS, 1991), many teachers may feel called to step in. In response to requests from individual students or employers, some teachers may improvise, taking informal initiatives to assist both groups. Moreover, in the absence of a system for helping students enter the labor force, teachers' informal efforts may introduce order and direction into the work-entry process. While such individual activities may go unnoticed generally, this invisible assistance may establish the basis for an informal system: teachers' initiatives may be filling the gap left by schools, employers, and society.

Such informal assistance, if it occurs, would have considerable theoretical and policy importance. While sociologists have shown how personal networks introduce social structure into individuals' jobs searches (Granovetter, 1973), institutional actors' networks have the potential to create new labor market structures for anyone who passes through the institution.

Teachers and other institutional actors may form connections that could introduce systematic features to unstructured labor markets (Rosenbaum, Kariya, Settersten, & Maier, 1990). Specifically, we examine whether teachers take informal initiatives, and if so, whether they create an organized set of networks that define students' job options, posing clear criteria and clear procedures for labor market entry. Such networks, operating within the school, will have some of the benefits of informal networks, but they may be more widely available to students. This could have particular importance for low-income and minority youth who less often have personal or family contacts. Thus, in those places where teachers act as "middlemen"—passing information about employers' requirements to students and information about students' qualifications to employers—new social structures might emerge.

It is easy to overlook the teacher's role in aiding youths' work entry because it gets little formal recognition. Despite calls for research on how teacher–employer contacts can influence students' job placements, we have little research on teachers' involvement facilitating students' transitions to work (Wirt, Muraskin, Goodwin, & Meyer, 1989). While teachers cannot be held accountable for activities that lie beyond their formal responsibilities, it is important to understand the extent to which teachers engage in informal activities. Even improvised and incomplete help from teachers may influence the actions of students and employers who lack information about and connections with one another. Moreover, school reforms that encourage teachers' initiatives and make them more systematic and effective will likely experience greater success than those that do not recognize teachers' key roles. The present study examines the range of teachers' helping activities and the likelihood that some of those activities might form the basis for a more structured and orderly path from high school to work.

This chapter describes the informal roles that teachers play in the school-to-work transition and the various tasks they undertake to assist students with the work-entry process. We describe teachers' conceptions of their responsibilities toward students and employers and whether they experience any informal pressures to provide such help. We further examine the actions and contacts that teachers actually initiate and their assessments of the types of help necessary to facilitate movement from school to work. To the extent that patterns of informal help arise, they have the potential to create invisible structures that guide students' work-entry process. Finally, we investigate teachers' reports of the social and institutional constraints that prevent them from doing more, and we suggest reform practices that would enable more teachers to assist youth in their transitions to work.

THE RESEARCH

Methods

This chapter draws from detailed face-to-face interviews with teachers in a variety of vocational areas at four high schools in the Chicago metropolitan area. The 26 respondents come from two racially mixed city high schools and from two largely white suburban schools, one in a working-class suburb and one in a middle-class suburb. One school has a vocationally focused curriculum, while the other three are comprehensive schools offering vocational programs of varying depth.

We focus on vocational teachers because they serve a larger portion of the students who will enter the work force directly after high school and thus have the opportunity to provide work-bound youth with information about and exposure to labor market standards, practices, and points of entry. Furthermore, instructors in vocational areas are likely to have contacts with employers through their industry experiences or advisory connections. Therefore, such teachers provide a source of insight into the possibilities of school involvement with students' transitions, and their views can help us understand the present role of teachers in the transition process and in influencing students' work entry.

In early 1993, teachers participated in one-hour structured interviews at their schools. We asked for the teachers' own perceptions of their job descriptions, the role of their vocational programs, their observations about work-bound vocational students, the nature of teacher relationships with local employers in their industry areas, and their influence on student plans and job entry. Counselors, administrators, and students were also interviewed in the project schools, and additional school outcome data were obtained to provide checks on the teachers' reports.

Although our small, qualitative sample allows us to make only tentative generalizations about the larger teacher population, our data provide rich descriptive indicators of teachers' perceptions and behaviors. This study explores types of teacher activity and contacts that have neither been prescribed by schools and society nor examined by previous research. These findings could have conceptual importance, showing how teachers respond to the needs of work-bound students and their potential employers. Thus, despite their uncertain generalizability, these findings have the potential to introduce new insights that may guide theory, policy, and future research.

Because of disjunctures between the worlds of school and work, employers, teachers, and students have a number of needs that neither schools nor workplaces adequately meet. Employers need information about youths' academic skills and work habits in order to hire good workers, but they do not trust the information schools have to offer. Teachers need information about employers' requirements in order to prepare youth for work and to recommend them to employers, but they do not have facilities for getting such information. Students need to know that school tasks and evaluations are relevant to meeting their future needs, but they do not get the message that school is relevant. In light of these three disjunctures, linkages designed to communicate reliable information among these groups have the potential to benefit them all. As we review teachers' accounts of their practices in helping youth prepare for work entry, we consider the extent to which they address these various needs. We examine the following questions:

1. How do vocational teachers view their responsibilities for helping work-bound students get post-high school jobs? What incentives or disincentives do they encounter?

2. How do vocational teachers characterize the help work-bound students need?

3. How do vocational teachers respond to the needs of students and employers?

4. How are vocational teachers influenced by constraints?

Given the recent policy debate around ideas for facilitating the high school-to-work transition, it is valuable to examine teachers' roles in shaping the futures of work-bound students. Given strong normative pressures and weak task specification, teachers would have to improvise informal actions and contacts in order to influence students' job placements. By eliciting teachers' views of their interactions with students and employers, we can begin to understand the nature of vocational teachers' roles, and we can propose policy alternatives in order to help teachers better serve the needs of work-bound students.

FINDINGS

Teachers' Views of Their Responsibilities and Students' Needs

In order to understand teachers' behaviors, we first sought to understand their views of both the schools' goals and their job responsibilities for helping graduates enter work. Across our sample, teachers clearly agree. Virtually every teacher reports that helping students gain employment after high school is not part of their job. It is neither a responsibility of theirs, nor of the schools more generally. Indeed, even cooperative education teachers and work coordinators who facilitate and evaluate students' participation in part-time jobs assert that helping students arrange post-high school jobs does not fall into their professional domain. One city coop teacher explains: "It's our purpose to give them job experience, not to place them in a full-time job after graduation."

Moreover, nearly every teacher reports that there are no incentives to encourage them to assist students in getting jobs after high school. None of the high schools rewarded such activities, and indeed, none provided any time or relief from other job duties for such help. In response to our query about incentives, teachers replied: "just that you like doing it." It's "your own conscience, that's all."

Despite the lack of formal expectations for teacher help toward workbound students, vocational teachers feel that their students need help entering the labor market. Contrary to the economic model that portrays workers seeking jobs in rational, orderly ways, these teachers see their students as lacking many characteristics essential to the operation of such a rational process. They note that students lack future orientation; they are not used to practical, applied knowledge; and because of their immaturity and inexperience, students hold unrealistic expectations about the job world with regard to job requirements, market conditions, work environments, and pay scales.

Indeed, while vocational teachers face no formal organizational pressures to help students get jobs, they do face informal pressures from students. Most vocational teachers report that students ask them for assistance. Over three-quarters (76%) of our respondents reported that seniors regularly approached them for help, and another 10% observed that students regularly went to the coop teachers for help. The extent of student desire for assistance is evident in a number of teachers' stories:

A suburban business education teacher with a cooperative work program reports that, "From the students who are in my class, I would say 90% of the students would ask me for help in finding a job after graduation. Sometimes kids who aren't in my classes come in and ask me to help them find a job .... There are always five or six who come back after they have graduated and ask me for a job."

An urban coop teacher who doesn't even teach senior students notes that, "About 10% of all the seniors ... a lot who aren't in my program, ask me about jobs."

An industrial woods shop teacher in a middle-class suburb states that, "Probably between 60 and 70 (students) have asked me in this year alone."

Even in higher-income suburban areas where it is commonly assumed that students have relatives, friends, or neighbors who can help them get jobs, teachers see many students needing help in the school–work transition. As a result, many teachers feel a personal responsibility to do more than what their job requires them to do.

Teachers' Help and Contacts

Our analyses indicate that teachers conceive of their help responsibilities in varying ways. On the one hand, they recognize that helping students get jobs after high school lies outside the scope of their responsibilities, and they receive no incentive or recognition for helping. On the other hand, they see that many students need guidance and assistance in order to enter and remain in the labor force successfully. These teachers face a choice between simply doing their jobs and extending their duties to include helping students gain entry to the work world. Since neither jobs nor their personal training specify what they should do, teachers take a number of different approaches.

The teachers in our sample exhibit varying levels of relationship to employers that range from exceptionally strong to quite weak, yet they all express interest in helping young people make the transition to the labor market. As a result, they all participate in activities that in some way introduce their students to the employment opportunities before them. In response to the needs of students and employers, teachers offer what they can: in some cases information, in others, connections that lead to jobs.

Our interview questions elicited responses about numerous types of teacher assistance in such areas as student planning, motivation, teaching strategies, evaluation, counseling, employer contacts, and job recommendations. We analyzed the nature of the help each teacher offers and why they provide the assistance they do. We then coded their responses to capture each different help statement. During an hour-long interview, each of the 26 vocational teachers in our sample noted between 8 and 34 different statements of help activity related to students' transition needs.

Befitting their position as "middlemen" situated between students and employers, teachers provide assistance through relationships with both groups. In response to the needs of students and employers, teachers provide four kinds of help: information, exposure, matching, and warranty. Within each of these types of assistance, teachers attend to student needs in various ways.

In providing the first type of help, informational help, teachers use their knowledge about employers and work to give students information necessary for understanding the adult world. Some teachers provide only generalized information about employers and their practices. These teachers apply textbook, media, or common knowledge to the preparation of students for the world beyond the classroom. This approach stresses school success as the means to labor market success, and it appeals to students' self-esteem needs and desires to be considered independent adults. A work program instructor in the inner city notes that, "I encourage them. Tell them that what they learn in all of their classes will help them after high school."

Other teachers present more specific information: simple skill and performance standards, the practical realities of working conditions and pay scales, and the procedures of finding, keeping, and advancing in jobs. Still other teachers use simulation, job anticipation, and relevant job preparation activities to focus students' ambitions around realistic goals and to equip students with specific skills that correspond to the needs of particular employers. However, without actual employer contacts, teachers can bring only their own experiences to this instruction. A suburban business teacher makes this clear: "I would really ... find out what the kid wants and give them suggestions on where to look [in searching for jobs] . . . I don't personally have any contacts." A city instructor comments, "I would instruct the student on the dos and don'ts of getting a job. You know, to dress conservatively, neatly. . . ." Others note that, "We talk about entry-level all the time—you can't go in at the top . . . . You have to work your way to the top." Nevertheless, with this type of help, teachers do not focus students on specific job areas or clear time frames, thus these helping activities fit within conventional expectations of the teacher's mission.

With the second type of help, exposure to the work world, teachers bring work-related experiences into the classroom and bring students out to workplace situations in order to inform them about general job characteristics and work behavior expectations. Field trips, guest speakers, coop jobs, and simulations motivate students to prepare for the "real world." This type of help requires that teachers establish at least minimal contact with employers.

Some teachers provide exposure to selected types of employers, preparing students to understand the practices of employers in their vocational area. One teacher describes how she accommodates employers' needs: "I change [my textbook selections] based on what's happening with the economy, what's happening in the news, what [local] employers would like to talk about—would like me to talk about." Another remarks, "I add on or take out material depending on what I learn during the summer about employer and industry needs." However, no relationship is required with exposure help. Employers serve just as contacts or as abstract information sources, while teachers rely mainly on their classroom pedagogy to inform and assist students.

With the third type of assistance, matching students with employers, teachers use ongoing relationships with employers to match their students with particular jobs that lead to careers in their vocational areas. Teachers draw from their knowledge of both students' and employers' skills, needs, and personalities in order to match students with the employers most likely to hire them. These teachers inform students about the demands of jobs with particular employers and the requirements for advancement in these jobs. They engage in extra efforts to build and maintain long-term relationships with employers. A business education teacher in a middle-class suburb explains: "I have a lot of contacts with employers, and I use the same ones year after year. I think one of the reasons why the program is so successful is because I have such strong links to employers."

Many of these teachers provide students with routes to specific, primary labor market jobs through their personal contacts with specific employers. One city shop teacher describes his method of preparing students for specific employer needs: "If I met an employer who told me we need a person to work on this and use this piece of machinery, I would go out of my way to take one or two students aside and say, 'If you can learn this, you've got a job.' And I go out of my way to actually teach them this." Teachers involved in matching express confidence that they can get employers to consider their students for primary labor market jobs.

Finally, the fourth type of help, warranty, is an elaboration of this basic matching idea, in which teachers provide dependable signals of students' quality in connecting their students to specific employers. Teachers engage in additional efforts to maintain relationships with employers, to promise them dependable standards, and to incorporate these standards in their curriculum and student evaluations. Warranty linkages therefore put teachers in a pivotal role in defining the job world for students and in nominating students for jobs.

Teachers who offer warranty help also report a high rate of successful placements. As a result of his trusted relationships with employers, the coordinator for the industrial cooperative education program in a middle-class suburban school can state, "If I recommend a kid, 98% of the time they will get the job." A teacher who works with marketing students remarks similarly, "A lot of times they'll go on my judgment," or if his contacts aren't hiring just then, "I'll say, 'but if you do need somebody, give me a call and I'll find a person who I think would be a good person to do what you're looking for.'" At the inner-city vocational school, one instructor claims that "I haven't recommended a kid yet who hasn't gotten the job .... if they want the job, they can have it ... if I recommend them," and his fellow machine shop teacher echoes the belief: "Employers stay with the teacher." Warranty teachers stake their claims on their quality standards, knowing that good experiences help to maintain their relationships with employers. As the heating and air conditioning instructor at the urban vocational high school confides, "If you send them good people who will be good employees, they will come back to you."

Teachers involved in both matching and warranty activities can be characterized as participating in "career linkages," for they effectively make students' classroom performance the first step on a career track into the work world, a "quasiapprenticeship" for specific adult jobs. These teachers show students that the education and training they receive in the vocational classroom is relevant to real jobs, and their performance affects the kind of job they will get. They involve themselves actively in such practices as job prospecting, matching particular students with particular employers, building long-term relationships between the school and the local business community, and creating school programs to aid the job search/job placement processes. Teachers who create career linkages take initiatives that go beyond their customary job responsibilities.

The Incidence of Different Types of Help Activities

Naturally some teachers help more actively and more often than others. Moreover, some teachers more easily connect with the work world by virtue of their positions as teachers in cooperative education programs, or because of continuing activity in their industry area, professional association, or union. Nevertheless, we find that each teacher reports helping students in multiple ways across the categories of our typology.

All teachers reported giving informational types of help designed to familiarize students with the work world, and all reported participating in exposure-level activities requiring at least casual interaction with employers. Moreover, almost all (24/26) have at one time or another attempted to build more enduring relationships with employers in fields relevant to their vocational programs, and all but 6 teachers could report recent specific employer contacts. Many of these contacts are only used to provide exposure activities such as class presentations or field trips, yet even these hold potential for development into more active, long-term relationships. Thus, it appears that teachers are neither averse to the prospect of connecting with employers, nor too isolated and overburdened to give attention to employer relationships as a way to serve their students' needs. Indeed, a few of our sample teachers reflected that they might have personal contacts that could help their graduates; however, they had not considered exercising them.

Nevertheless, we find that matching help is much less frequent than exposure. While all of our respondent teachers have had at least one contact with employers in their vocational area, and all but two indicate a familiar or ongoing relationship with employers they could potentially use as contacts, only about half of our 26 vocational respondents actually engage in matching students with employers ($n = 13$). Nevertheless, it is striking that so many teachers know employers well enough to address their labor needs. A suburban marketing coop teacher conveys this point when he says of employers, "What they'll do is call back and ask me, 'What do you think of this person? Can you tell me?' . . . If I've had a student for a long time, it's real simple to tell them . . . ." Such teachers also note that it is easy for them to direct students to jobs where their skills and personalities will fit employers' needs, and employers often value these referrals. Moreover, several of these matching teachers go even further. A group of eight vocational teachers participate in activities of both matching and warranty. These instructors report that they build enduring relationships with specific employers based on familiarity, trust, high standards, and clear signals of student quality. With regard to students, they offer authoritative knowledge of the job market, connections to employers who trust their recommendation, and in some cases, they even promise jobs. The sheet metal instructor from a vocational high school claims that "five or six students out of every class of ten get a job through me. Whoever wants one, gets one." This teacher finds jobs for his students through systematic reliance on employers who trust him, and because they trust him, his contacts hire young people into good-paying jobs with advancement potential. As the instructor asserts, "Ninety percent of the students I send turn out wonderful," adding with a break in his voice, "I feel in my heart that if I can't get them a job, I didn't do my job."

Because of the familiarity and history in their employer relationships, these teachers can provide clear information about students tailored to a specific employer's needs. They can advise students about the most appropriate job settings based on knowledge of personalities and advancement opportunities as well as starting pay. These vocational teachers say that they recommend the best students for the best jobs. They tell other students "that there are jobs, but you're not going to get the best job, because you haven't performed"; they tell employers "exactly what they're getting"; and they refuse to recommend students of inadequate quality, even if this means that they must refrain from recommending any student at all. Thus, for these teachers, their role as "middlemen" requires not only that they get good students into good jobs, but that they also provide their employer contacts with good workers. Their emphasis on quality in these relationships assures this. By matching appropriate students with employers and by promising a certain level of student quality, these teachers gain the trust of employers and the ability to influence employers' hiring decisions.

Do Constraints Prevent Teachers from Giving Linkage Help?

Why isn't linkage help more common? Teachers report many constraints that hinder this kind of help. Indeed, both individual and institutional barriers limit their active involvement in linkage activities. Every one of our respondents encountered difficulties assisting students' transitions from school to work, noting between 4 and 28 barriers to offering help. These vocational teachers noted constraints in three main areas: difficulties with students, difficulties with employers, and problems embedded in the institutional context of the school.

First, many teachers stress student problems: immaturity, lack of motivation, lack of future orientation, weak skills, and unrealistic ambitions. Second, many teachers stress employers' mistrust: they observe that employers don't approach teachers, don't ask for references from teachers, and don't pay attention to the school's signals of quality (grades). Third, and most common, many teachers note problems related to the institutional context of the school.

Given the structural arrangements of their schools, teachers note that assisting students with jobs after high school is (1) not one of their job duties; (2) not an activity they have time for; (3) not an activity the school supports; and (4) not an activity that their current resource and incentive structure encourages. Furthermore, teachers indicate that because of the drawbacks of students, and the lack of interest of employers, whatever help they do give cannot accomplish much. These excuses seem plausible.

They are consistent with the results of previous research on schools and the labor market, and most teachers voice similar concerns. Indeed, the linkage teachers mention the same problems as others who do not help as much.

However, teachers differ markedly in their response to these constraints. While these problems with students, employers, and the school prevent many teachers from performing linkage activities, some teachers do not let these constraints prevent them from establishing links and helping students get jobs. A construction shop instructor in a vocational high school declares, "You have to be a salesperson and try to sell them [employers] on what we're doing and how it fits in with what they're doing." But, his sheet metal colleague insists, "Any teacher could do it if that teacher wanted to make the effort." These teachers reject the intractability of the constraints they face, and they are able to overcome employers' mistrust of school evaluations, initiate relationships with employers who can give students skill-relevant jobs, and improve students' motivation and planning.

Because of its complexity, linkage requires a number of different activities to make it effective. Linkage requires teachers to address employers—making and maintaining contact with them, and discovering their needs and hiring criteria. Linkage also requires teachers to address students—showing them how they must develop their vocational, academic, and work skills to become better workers. Finally, linkage requires teachers to provide a bridge between these groups, designing curricula and teaching methods to incorporate employers' needs, and evaluating students according to these criteria. Therefore, in order for linkage to occur, teachers must both convey information to employers about how well particular students fit their needs, and make their student evaluations trustworthy and easily understood.

Constraints do exist, and they are likely to make linkage activities harder. But constraints do not prevent some teachers from initiating and maintaining very strong linkages with employers. These teachers mention constraints, but they do not consider them an excuse to prevent linkage activities.

Furthermore, despite the constraints that mitigate against teachers' developing linkages, maintaining relationships with specific employers, and training students to fit with employers' needs, nearly all teachers engage in activities that form the building blocks of linkage. Since even the most infrequently helping vocational teachers have contacts, provide exposure, and desire to aid students in their school-to-work transitions, we find clear evidence that more teachers are able to provide career linkage assistance than currently do so. If schools provided encouragement and incentives for such behavior, it is likely we'd see more of it.

Do Career Linkages Compromise Students' Academic Learning?

Critics have raised legitimate concerns about specialization in vocational education and its potential restriction of students' career options. This critique requires reexamination since great expansion of higher education opportunities has led many vocational students to attend college (Wirt et al., 1989; Rosenbaum, 1995). However, the charge that vocational programs teach only narrow, job-specific skills presents a challenge to our linkage model. Career linkage help is clearly oriented to specific jobs, so critics may worry that it discourages academic skill attainment.

In fact, we find the opposite. Our findings suggest that career linkages are usually used to encourage students to work harder in academic areas. We find that six of the eight teachers who engage in matching and warranty activities (career linkage) also stress the importance of doing well in academic subjects. Moreover, teachers report that their linkage activities encourage an academic emphasis, and their linkages make this academic emphasis more convincing to students. On their own, students cannot easily see that employers need academic skills, since entry jobs generally do not require such skills. However, teachers who have strong linkages with employers know employers' long-term needs, and they make their students aware of these needs in order to prepare them appropriately for those jobs.

Although ordinary teachers without linkages give students generalized advice about the value of academic skills, linked teachers can give specific evidence of employers' demands for those skills. Students are less likely to dismiss the suggestions of a teacher who knows that a particular local employer only promotes students with good math and writing skills. Moreover, linked teachers do not just exhort students to learn reading, math, science, or writing skills; they tell students that those skills will influence which of them get strong teacher recommendations and, consequently, who gets hired.

Thus, while vocational education is often seen as stressing manual skills, teachers who have linkages with employers also stress academic skills. They offer specific incentives for doing well in academic classes, explain how specific academic skills are used in particular jobs, and monitor students' academic achievement. These findings suggest that even the most focused vocational teachers can use their vocational emphasis as a means of showing students the relevance of academic skills and motivating students to perform better in academic courses.

CONCLUSION

Discussion

The United States offers a poorly organized system of labor market entry to work-bound high school graduates. Nonetheless, our sample teachers are nearly unanimous in saying that work-entry assistance is neither their responsibility nor that of the school, and no incentives encourage them to assist students. However, they also are unanimous in saying that students need help. How, then, do teachers respond?

While our sample is small, nonrandom, and of uncertain generalizability, there is no reason to believe that the phenomena discovered here are not present to some degree elsewhere. Qualitatively, it is striking that all of the teachers in this sample take actions to overcome the difficulties youth face in entering employment, and many take actions neither prescribed nor encouraged by schools or society. Sociologists and economists studying the school–work transition have not recognized these activities and contacts. Yet even this small fraction of teachers represents an important and largely unexplored phenomenon. Moreover, our results provide a possible explanation for a puzzling finding in the literature. Research indicates that vocational education only improves students' earnings if they get skill-relevant jobs (Grasso & Shea, 1979; Wirt et al., 1989), but these studies do not indicate what determines whether students get skill-relevant jobs.

Despite the lack of a system, teachers make many kinds of efforts to aid students' work entry. We have identified four types of help: information, exposure, matching, and warranty. It is noteworthy that, in the latter two, teachers' informal networks facilitate information transmission and matching processes similar to the more formal network procedures of other nations like Germany (apprenticeships) and Japan (school linkages). Apparently, many teachers see the need for such activities and provide them on their own.

Nearly all teachers have some contacts with employers, but teachers use them differently. Some rely only on information about employers to prepare their students for work; some exercise their employer connections at some level. Teachers who have only weak or casual contacts can use them to provide students with exposure to the work world through class presentations, field trips, or other activities that involve employer participation. Such assistance enables students to learn about the work world, but exposure does not typically offer them access to jobs.

Teachers who have contacts with members of their trade organizations or with specific employers in their industry have knowledge of specific skill and personality requirements and can prepare students to fit those requirements. This matching allows teachers to rely on their employer contacts to help shape classroom content and process, to motivate students, and to establish informational connections with employers who sometimes hire students for jobs. They can tell students whether a particular skill or work habit, such as punctuality or testing the quality of one's work, is required by certain employers, and they can tell their employer contacts whether a student meets the requisite skill, work habit, and performance standards for a job opening. Typically, these teachers can tell employers when they have a good job candidate. Matching allows teachers to provide information about employers to students and about students to employers. As a result, matching becomes more than an instructional procedure; it creates a pathway for information between students and employers and thus a potential career pathway.

Teachers who promise warranty can establish relationships that go one step further. Having turned their contacts into long-term, trusting relationships with employers, warranty teachers can provide dependable information that causes employers to defer to their judgment when considering their recommended students for good jobs. Teachers must extend themselves to offer warranties; they must be willing to "go out on a limb," and to "put my reputation at stake." More than one of the teachers offering warranty assistance states, "You must build credibility among the employers . . . or else they won't call you again and then you'll hurt the next kid down the line who would have qualified." This concern for the relationship is important, for it signifies the care teachers put into their evaluations and explains employers' willingness to trust them.

As noted earlier, most high school graduates face a labor market that provides no clear paths into primary labor market jobs. Students do not see anything they can do in high school to improve their job opportunities, and as they approach graduation, they do not see any steps they can take to gain access to good jobs, unless they have family contacts. In contrast, teachers who engage in matching and warranty create a "career linkage" pathway for their students, preparing them for skilled jobs and putting them into contention for such jobs. In their classes, they evaluate students according to standards trusted by their employer connections. Thus, their recommendations markedly increase students' chances of getting hired. In such cases, teachers' informal networks not only alter students' motivation in class; they create a social structure providing dependable routes into primary labor market jobs. In effect, working in these teachers' classes is akin to taking the first step on a career ladder leading to responsible, "adult" jobs. These classes are tantamount to "quasiapprenticeships."

If outsiders performed these matching and warranty actions, they might seem simply to mimic the workings of an employment service that makes work-entry more orderly by imposing criteria and procedures. The fact that teachers perform these matching and warranty activities and engage in "career linkage," despite the obvious constraints and the lack of encouragement or incentives, is significant, for they bring procedures and criteria into the school. This lends order to the school–work transition by institutionalizing its activities, making them comparable to the tasks of those involved in facilitating school–college transitions.

Two cautions must be noted in interpreting these findings, however. First, these accounts of teacher practices come from the teachers themselves. Nevertheless, we obtained some supportive evidence from other sources. A survey of 651 seniors in our sample schools found that many students believed their teachers could get them jobs after high school (Rosenbaum & Nelson, 1994). Additionally, in a survey of 51 employers from the areas surrounding the study schools, several employers confirmed that some of these vocational teachers had established connections that provided a valuable source of good workers for their job openings (Rosenbaum & Binder, 1994).

Moreover, the 13 teachers who reported involvement in matching activities, and the 8 involved in both matching and warranty provided a convincing degree of qualitative detail about their employer contacts and their requirements for recommending students. Given the unanimous belief that matching activities are neither a duty nor a valued activity in schools, there appears to be little reason for teachers to fabricate these detailed stories, so we find these teachers' reports believable. Nevertheless, further research is needed to verify the frequency of various types of teacher assistance with work-bound students and to identify the outcomes of students aided by these processes.

Second, one must consider the potential effects of teacher linkages on hiring discrimination. Teachers' influence opens up new opportunities for jobs, but also new opportunities for bias. While teacher self-reports are inadequate for assessing whether they discriminate, it is noteworthy that teachers report that minorities and women do well in their classes and are recommended for and successful in getting good jobs.

Of course, even if teachers show some bias, they are likely to exhibit less bias than employers since they know students better. Prejudice is probably more likely when employers review hundreds of job applications or consider applicants in 15-minute interviews, than when teachers evaluate the work of their students over one or more semesters of daily interaction. However, since teachers' self-reports do not represent the best method of assessing discrimination, and since we presently lack objective data for such assessments, we cannot reach dependable conclusions on this issue.

Regardless of the bias that may affect the work entry of particular groups of female and minority youth, all youth must overcome widespread employer discrimination against recent high school graduates. Regardless of class, race, or gender, youth rarely get primary labor market jobs (Osterman, 1980). Even trade apprenticeships, an important route to skilled manual jobs in this country, avoid taking recent high school graduates, and youth apprenticeship programs dedicated to this age group enroll only about 1% of the population of traditional apprenticeship programs (GAO, 1991). If teachers can provide orderly access to primary labor market jobs for their students, significant improvement in job opportunities for all youth might result.

Policy Implications

Currently, there is much interest in starting apprenticeship programs modeled on the German system. While we agree that this effort merits attention, we must stress that it requires a high level of financing, commitment, and know-how from employers. While German employers have developed this commitment and know-how over more than 500 years, American apprenticeships have a much shorter history and serve fewer than 5000 youth nationwide (GAO, 1991). It is not apparent that American employers or schools can easily implement apprenticeships on a widespread basis. Most new programs are very expensive and can serve fewer than 100 youth.

On the other hand, our findings suggest that vocational teachers can create a quasiapprenticeship experience in the classroom that provides skills, work habits, and evaluations that lead to appropriate jobs. They can prepare students for their next step into entry-level work, as well as for higher-level positions, as do professional schools which prepare students for advancement as well as for entry jobs.

Obviously one cannot make policy based on extraordinary individuals, and the most active teachers may be just that. However, one of the obvious features of these teachers, their acceptance of responsibility for helping students get adult jobs, does not require anything more extraordinary than a different job perspective. Teachers see the need, and they provide many types of assistance to students and employers on their own time and initiative. Thus, it seems likely that some school practices and attitudes could encourage them to help more. Schools interested in strengthening the school-to-work transition should consider the following:

1. High schools must make employment assistance part of the school's job. They must give teachers the message that it is important to spend time helping students get jobs, just as they spend time writing college recommendations and advising students about college choices.

2. High schools must provide time in the teacher's paid workday to do this. Obviously, this presents new costs that will raise some controversy given limited school budgets. Yet the incremental costs are vastly smaller than the costs required to create entirely new training and apprenticeship programs and the bureaucracies necessary to administer them.

3. High schools must provide some incentives for teachers to do this. Most colleges hire job placement staff to cultivate contacts with employers and place students in jobs (Kariya & Rosenbaum, 1994). High school teaching and counseling staffs could be structured to serve both college placement and job placement needs equally.

4. Teachers must build personal relationships of trust with employers, determine their needs, and design curricula and student evaluations that reflect those needs, in order to match students and employers and provide dependable evaluations for the employers who will hire their graduates.

Much of this process for facilitating students' transitions to work is familiar to vocational teachers. They attempt to help things along in many ways. Only the last part, matching students and employers and providing dependable evaluations for both, is new, but it radically transforms all of the rest. In conveying dependable evaluations to familiar employers, vocational teachers give all of their other activities a clear purpose and make an impact on students' future job possibilities. Students can learn valuable skills in the classroom, their school performances can indicate work capabilities, and vocational teachers can recommend students to potential employers. In the process, students can see that their school experiences are relevant and important for their future, for they see themselves on the first step of the ladder to their future careers.

ACKNOWLEDGMENTS.   This paper is based on research conducted with Amy Binder, Stephanie Jones, Takehiko Kariya, Melinda, Krei, Shazia Miller,

Ginny Mills, Karen Nelson, and Kevin Roy. We thank Maureen Hallinan for helpful suggestions on an earlier draft. We are also indebted to the Spencer Foundation, the Pew Charitable Trusts, and the W. T. Grant Foundation, and Northwestern's Center for Urban Affairs and Policy Research for support of this research. Of course, the ideas presented here do not represent their views.

REFERENCES

Althauser, R. P., & Kalleberg, A. L. (1981). Firms, occupations, and the structure of labor markets: A conceptual analysis. In I. Berg (Ed.), *Sociological perspectives on labor markets*. New York: Academic Press.

Bills, D. (1988). Educational credentials and hiring decisions: What employers look for in entry-level employees. *Research in Social Stratification and Mobility, 7*, 71–97.

Bishop, J. (1987). *Information externalities and the social payoff to academic achievement*. Working Paper #8706. Cornell University Center for Advanced Human Resource Studies.

Borman, K. M. (1991). *The first "real" job: A study of young workers*. Albany: State University of New York Press.

Committee for Economic Development. (1985). *Investing in our children: Business and the public schools*. New York: Author.

Crain, R. (1984). *The quality of American high school graduates: What personnel officers say and do*. Unpublished paper, Johns Hopkins University.

Doeringer, P., & Piore, M. J. (1971). *Internal labor markets and manpower analysis*. Lexington, MA: D. C. Heath.

Gamoran, A. (1994). *The impact of academic course work on labor market outcomes for youth who do not attend college: A research review*. Unpublished draft, National Assessment of Vocational Education.

General Accounting Office. (1991). *Transition from school to work: Linking education and worksite training*. Washington, DC: U.S. Government Printing Office.

Granovetter, M. (1973). *Getting a job*. Cambridge, MA: Harvard University Press.

Grasso, J. T., & Shea, J. R. (1979). *Vocational education and training: Impact on youth*. Berkeley: The Carnegie Council on Policy Studies in Higher Education.

Griffin, J. L. (1981). Determinants of early labor market entry and attainment: A study of labor market segmentation. *Sociology of Education, 54*, 206–221.

Hamilton, S. F. (1990). *Apprenticeship for adulthood*. New York: Free Press.

Hotchkiss, L., Kang, S., & Bishop, J. (1984). *High school preparation for employment*. Columbus, OH: National Center for Research in Vocational Education.

Johnson, J., & Bachman, J. (1973). *The transition from high school to work*. Ann Arbor: Institute for Social Research, University of Michigan.

Karabel, J. (1972). Community colleges and social stratification. *Harvard Educational Review, 42*, 521–562.

Kariya, T., & Rosenbaum, J. E. (1987). Self-selection in Japanese junior high schools. *Sociology of Education, 60(3),* 168–180.

Kariya, T., & Rosenbaum, J. E. (1995). Institutional linkages between education and work as quasi-labor markets. In *Research in social stratification and mobility,* forthcoming.

Kaufman, J. K. (1967). *The role of the secondary school in the preparation of youth for employment.* University Park: Institute for Research on Human Resources, The Pennsylvania State University.

Lortie, D. C. (1975). *Schoolteacher: A sociological study.* Chicago: University of Chicago Press.

Meyer, R. H., & Wise, D. A. (1982). High school preparation and early labor force experience. In R. B. Freeman & D. A. Wise (Eds.), *The youth labor market problem.* Chicago: University of Chicago Press.

Mickelson, R. A. (1990). The attitude–achievement paradox among black adolescents. *Sociology of Education, 63,* 44–61.

National Academy of Sciences (NAS). (1984). *High schools and the changing workplace: The employers' view.* Washington, DC: National Academic Press.

Osterman, P. (1980). *Getting started: The youth labor market.* Cambridge, MA: MIT Press.

Osterman, P. (1988). *Employment futures.* London: Oxford University Press.

Parsons, T. (1956). Suggestions for a sociological approach to theory of organizations. *Administrative Science Quarterly, 1,* 63–85.

Rosenbaum, J. E. (1976). *Making inequality.* New York: Wiley.

Rosenbaum, J. E. (1989). What if good jobs depended on good grades? *American Educator, 13(4),* 10–43.

Rosenbaum, J. E. (1995). Policy uses of research on the high school-to-work transition. *Sociology of Education,* forthcoming.

Rosenbaum, J. E., & Binder, A. (1994). *Do employers really need more educated youth?* Paper presented at the meeting of the American Sociological Association, Los Angeles.

Rosenbaum, J. E., & Kariya, T. (1989). From high school to work: Market and institutional mechanisms in Japan. *American Journal of Sociology, 94(6),* 1334–1365.

Rosenbaum, J. E., & Kariya, T. (1991). Do school achievements affect the early jobs of high school graduates in the U.S. and Japan? *Sociology of Education, 64,* 78–95.

Rosenbaum, J. E., & Nelson, K. A. (1994). *The influence of perceived articulation on adolescents' school effort.* Paper presented at the meeting of the American Educational Research Association, New Orleans.

Rosenbaum, J. E., Kariya, T., Settersten, R., & Maier, T. (1990). Market and network theories of the transition from high school to work. *Annual Review of Sociology, 16,* 263–299.

Secretary's Commission on Achieving Necessary Skills (SCANS). (1991). *What work requires of schools: A SCANS report for America 2000.* Washington, DC: U.S. Department of Labor.

Stern, D., Raby, J. M., & Dayton, C. (1992). *Career academies*. San Francisco: Jossey Bass.

Stern, D., Stone, J., III, Hopkins, C., McMillion, M., & Crain, R. (1994). *School-based enterprise*. San Francisco: Jossey Bass.

Stinchcombe, A. L. (1964). *Rebellion in a high school*. Chicago: Quadrangle Books.

Thompson, J. D., & McEwen, W. J. (1958). Organizational goals and environment. *American Sociological Review, 23*, 23–31.

Thurow, L. (1975). *Generating inequality*. New York: Basic Books.

W. T. Grant Foundation Commission on Youth and America's Future. (1988). *The forgotten half: Pathways to success for America's youth and young families*. Washington, DC: W. T. Grant Foundation.

Wirt, J. G., Muraskin, L. D., Goodwin, D. A., & Meyer, R. H. (1989). *National assessment of vocational education* (Vol. I).Washington, DC: U.S. Government Printing Office.

Witte, J., & Kalleberg, A. L. (1994). Determinants and consequences of fit between vocational education and employment in Germany. In N. Stacey (Ed.), *School-to-work: What does research say about it?* Washington, DC: U.S. Office of Education.

Index

259